BONDED BY BLOOD

Bernard O'Mahoney is the author of a number of true-crime books, including the bestselling *Essex Boys*, *The Dream Solution* and *Wannabe in my Gang?* He has also written of his experiences in the army and on a tour of duty in Northern Ireland in *Soldier of the Queen* and of his gradual transition from Nazi thug to Nazi opponent in *Hateland*.

BONDED
by BLOOD

MURDER AND INTRIGUE
IN THE ESSEX GANGLANDS

BERNARD
O'MAHONEY

MAINSTREAM
PUBLISHING
EDINBURGH AND LONDON

First published in Great Britain in 2006 by
MAINSTREAM PUBLISHING COMPANY
(EDINBURGH) LTD
7 Albany Street
Edinburgh EH1 3UG

ISBN 9781845961640

Reprinted, 2007

A catalogue record for this book is available
from the British Library

Typeset in Sabon and Badhouse

Printed in Great Britain by
William Clowes, Beccles, Suffolk

I dedicate this book to my beautiful wife, Emma Elizabeth O'Mahoney, who died in my arms on 2 December 2004, just four months after we married, aged twenty-six.

I would like to thank the following people for helping me through the darkest days following my loss: Vinney, Siobhan, Glen, Ebony, Lauren, Adrian, Natalie and Karis, Debra, Michael, Carol, Finn, Lilly, Hughie, Kate, Leah, Molly, my mother Anne, Jacquelyn and Ann Lippett, Gavin and Sue, Andy Byrne, Miss South London, Toene Shadiya, Kassy McGuiness, Chop Lambert, Chemical Earl, Page 7 Fella Leo, Baron, Burdo, Good Game, Good Game Boss Eye, Bouldie, Mally, Marcus, Lee, Mark (duck) Green, Kevin Carvell, Darrel Edwards, Auntie Patricia and Uncle Paul, brother Jerry, Amy, Leanne, Tino, Ken Hassle, Liverpool Lenny, Corrine Payne, Peterborough Bobby, Stevie Dee, Brett, Martin (Whizz Kid) Moore, the Cowley family, Julie Ford, Wes and Zoe (He's not with me, woman), Shane, Whizzer, Taffy, Little Tony, Rachie, Jim Dean senior, Jim junior, Mad Jack, Gary Jones, Emma Bailey and her inseparable other half, Erica Els, Tracie d'Cruz, Solicitor Hugh Cauthery and last but by no means least, Dr Wilson, for the time he gave up to be with me and the care he showed.
    Until we meet again, Emmie xx

www.bernardomahoney.com
www.justiceforleebalkwell.com

Prologue

Today, I intend to put the events of November and December 1995 behind me. I have waited more than a decade for this day, this hour, this moment to arrive.

Teenager Leah Betts died in November 1995 after taking an Ecstasy pill that was supplied by my associates. The following month, three of those associates were murdered in cold blood. Those two terrible events have dominated my life ever since. They have dictated where I live and where I spend my time; divided my friends and torn my family apart.

Leah's father appeared on national television and claimed I was responsible for the death of his teenage daughter. His words hit me hard: very hard, in fact, because I was not given the right to reply to his allegation. The police and others suspected me of executing my three former friends: I feared not only reprisals but that I could end up serving a life sentence for crimes I did not commit.

With the advances in forensic science and the countless overhauls of the judicial system following a spate of miscarriages of justice in the '90s people may scoff at the thought of such a thing happening in this day and age. Unfortunately, it did happen; fortunately, it didn't happen to me. I was not the only suspect in Essex Police's misaligned sights for the murder of my three associates. Two other men, Mick Steele and Jack Whomes, became suspects after their one-time friend, Darren Nicholls, levelled his accusing finger in their direction. Nicholls had been arrested for importing cannabis and offered to give police the names of the killers in return for a reduced sentence for himself.

Ten years after Nicholls's dubious evidence secured their convictions, Steele's and Whomes's cases were referred back to the Court of Appeal. I, along with many others, thought justice would finally be done and they would be freed. After a five-day hearing, their appeals were dismissed. For them, the fight goes on; for me, it's probably over.

That is why I am here today, down the lane where the executions took place. It's not the first time I have visited this ghastly place, but it will be my last. I want closure; I want to clear my mind, exorcise the faces of so many young, dead people that haunt me. The truth will be told one day, but not until the guilty and I have gone to our graves. I am standing on the spot where the three men met their deaths. I can visualise the Range Rover they arrived in making its way down the narrow, uneven, potholed track on the night of 6 December 1995. The snow was falling heavily and had bleached the surrounding fields.

In the driving seat was 26-year-old Craig Rolfe. Earlier that afternoon his partner, Diane Evans, had been busy wrapping Christmas presents when he returned home with their daughter, Georgie. The couple had spent about an hour and a half together before Rolfe announced that he wanted Diane to be ready by seven o'clock because they were going out. Rolfe said he had booked a table for six at the Global Net Café, a restaurant on South Street in Romford. They would be joined by two friends and their girlfriends. Rolfe then dropped Diane off at Lakeside shopping centre so that she could buy a new dress to wear that night. Diane was never to see him again.

Tony Tucker, 38, another of the would-be diners, sat in the front passenger seat of the Range Rover. After dropping

8

off Diane earlier that evening, Rolfe had picked him up from his house. Tucker's partner, Anna Whitehead, recalled that her boyfriend was wearing jeans, a white vest, a North Sails sweater and Caterpillar boots. He was also carrying his Nokia mobile phone. Like Diane, Anna didn't think her partner would be away long because they were due to be in Romford, a 20-minute journey from their Basildon home, later that evening for their meal. Anna was never to see Tucker again.

It was surprising that Tucker and Rolfe had an appetite because earlier that afternoon they had enjoyed a meal at the TGI Friday's restaurant in Lakeside with friends Peter Cuthbert and Pat Tate.

Tate, 37, sat immediately behind Tucker as the Range Rover made its way down the track. Tate had started the day in a foul mood. He had rowed with his ex-girlfriend and the mother of his son, Sarah Saunders. She had asked him for a new car because a Volkswagen Golf Tate had given her a few weeks earlier was proving to be unreliable. On more than one occasion, Sarah and her young son, Jordan, had been forced to walk along busy roads after the vehicle had ground to a halt. Tate, on the other hand, was driving around in a Mercedes that he had acquired after using Sarah's details to get a bank loan. When Sarah finally lost her temper and pointed out this injustice to Tate, he went berserk. Tate, Tucker and Rolfe drove around to Sarah's mum's and 'repossessed' the Volkswagen, then Tate, in a blind rage, threw all of Sarah's possessions into the street. Concerned for her safety, Tucker and Rolfe had physically grabbed Tate and bundled him into their car. It was the last time Sarah was ever to see Tate alive.

By the time Tate had joined Tucker and Rolfe at TGI Friday's his mood had changed dramatically: few can recall ever seeing him so happy. Tate had given the waitress a tip and asked her for a date. They had exchanged phone numbers. Tate promised her he would be in touch. It was a promise that would unwittingly be broken.

The Range Rover lurched from side to side as it made its way slowly down the farm track. The occupants laughed and warned Rolfe to watch where he was going.

At a quarter to seven, Tate's mobile phone rang. It was Sarah. She wanted to apologise for the row they'd had earlier. Tate couldn't have been more polite.

'Oh, don't worry. I am sorry for going mad and everything else,' he said. Before Sarah could reply, he continued, 'Listen, I can't talk at the moment, I'm with people, give me a call tomorrow and we'll sort it all out.'

'OK, goodbye,' said Sarah. The line went dead. Tate had hung up. He would never get the chance to 'sort it all out'.

The 'people' Tate had mentioned to Sarah sat alongside him in the rear of the Range Rover. A co-conspirator lurked nearby, watching and waiting; eager for the prey to fall into the deadly trap that had been set.

The car stopped where I am now standing. In its path stood a locked five-bar gate. A sign facing the car and its occupants read: 'Countryside premium scheme. Farming operations must still take place, so please take special care to avoid injury. The use of guns or any other activity which disturbs people or wildlife are not allowed on this land. Enjoy your visit.' Nobody was going to take any notice of it. The time now was approximately ten to seven. Diane, Anna and Tate's date for the night, Clare, would have been glancing at their watches as they put on their make-up and their finest threads. They would have been thinking that the boys would be home soon to take them out to dinner. This was to be no ordinary meal: they were all going out to celebrate becoming millionaires.

Tucker, Tate and Rolfe had bragged about their 'big deal' for weeks. Their minds mangled with drugs and their common sense blinded by greed, they genuinely believed tonight was the night they were going to become rich. Fucking mugs.

As eight o'clock drew nearer, Tucker, Tate and Rolfe's anxious dinner dates began to call their men. A message left on Tucker's answering machine said, 'Hello, babe, give us a ring and let me know how you're getting on. I'm all ready now. Bye.' The calls were in vain: dinner was going to be ruined and the boys were going to be late – very late.

When the Range Rover had pulled up in front of the locked gate, the man sitting next to Tate in the rear of the car got out, claiming he had a key to open it. The man who had been lying in wait emerged from the bushes with a pump-action shotgun in each hand. The interior light had come on because the Range Rover door was open, thus ensuring those sitting inside the car couldn't see what was going on outside because it was pitch-black.

The man holding the shotgun handed one to his accomplice before leaning through the open rear door of the Range Rover. From less than two feet away, he fired his first shot into Rolfe's neck, leaving a huge open wound. The shotgun barrel was so close to Rolfe's head the explosion caused burns to his neck and the seat headrest. The second shot hit Tucker in the right side of the face near his cheek. Tate, in the back of the car, was then shot in the side of the chest, damaging his liver. Rolfe hadn't suspected a thing: his hands remained on the steering wheel, his foot wedged firmly on the brake pedal. Tucker remained relaxed, sitting in an upright position, his legs crossed, his mobile phone in his hand.

Tate, who had witnessed his friends being slaughtered, began to squeal like a baby, pleading with the assassins to spare his life. In a vain attempt to make himself a smaller target, he tried to crawl into the corner of the car, bending his knees and covering his face. Panic-stricken, he smashed the rear passenger-door window in a hopeless effort to escape.

The gunman coolly reloaded and turned the smoking barrel of his gun away from Tate, then shot Rolfe behind the right ear. The blast exited between his eyes, totally disfiguring him: one eye hung down on his cheek.

Tucker was then shot on the right side of his face again, this time just above the jaw. The blast exited through the left side of his mouth; pieces of his jawbone, teeth and tissue splattered all over the dashboard and windscreen. A third shot slammed into the back of his head, causing his skull to fracture so severely a gaping fourth wound appeared above his right ear. The pathologist later said that Tucker's head had 'exploded'.

Tate was screaming throughout the onslaught, begging for mercy, but he was never going to be shown any. The gunmen had agreed upon a pact whereby each of them would fire shots into the victims' bodies so one could not give evidence against the other should they be arrested.

During the executions, one of the weapons fell apart. One gunman grabbed his accomplice's pump-action shotgun and shouted, 'Give me some cartridges! Give me some cartridges!' When they were given to him, he reloaded, then walked around the car to the window nearest Tate and shot him through the back of the head at point-blank range. Tate received a second shot to the head, but this only caused a superficial wound. When the weapons fell silent, the gun smoke cleared to reveal the carnage. Rolfe, Tucker and Tate lay dead. Flesh, bone and brain tissue were sprayed throughout the car. Blood poured from their wounds. It was a gruesome scene.

Throughout the night, Tucker's loved ones, unaware that he was dead, left messages on his mobile's answering service. One female in tears pleaded, 'For God's sake, Tone, phone me. Speak to you later. Bye.' Another caller said, 'We are worried, ring as soon as you can.'

The following morning farmer Peter Theobald and a

friend, Ken Jiggins, scraped the ice and snow from their Land Rover and set off to feed their pheasants. Driving down Workhouse Lane from the farm, they saw the Range Rover parked in front of the gate. They thought it might belong to poachers. Jiggins got out of the Land Rover and tapped on the passenger-side window because he thought the occupants were asleep. He didn't think the vehicle had been there overnight because there was no ice or snow on the windows, unlike on his vehicle, which had been parked only a few hundred yards away in identical conditions. There was no response, so Jiggins peered inside. He saw the blood-soaked bodies and rang 999 on his friend's mobile phone. The call was logged at 8.05 a.m.

In a state of shock Jiggins explained to the emergency operator, 'We just drove down our farm track to go and feed our pheasants and we came across a Range Rover with three people in it. At first, we thought they were poachers, but when we looked inside we realised they were dead. There is blood all over the motor and all over them.'

Within a short time, the quiet farm track was swarming with police, as the investigation began. Tucker's answering service continued to record appeals from his loved ones to contact them. They would soon realise that reports of three men found dead in a Range Rover appearing in the news bulletins could well be Tucker, Tate and Rolfe.

A female left a message saying, 'Tone, it's only me, time now is five past ten. I still have not heard from you. Could you ring, please, and let us know you are all right because at the moment I think you are dead. They have just said on the television that there are three men dead in a Range Rover. I think it's you.'

All traces of what happened down the lane that night are now gone. The five-bar gate has been replaced and the sign warning walkers about the use of guns on the land has also been removed. A new sign advises the public of a different kind of danger: 'Warning – snakes.' Fortunately, the biggest snakes ever to visit this lane are long gone.

Although there is nothing to see, I felt a need to come here. Walking away from the scene of those grotesque executions, I feel relief tinged with sadness. Relief because the nightmare is over, sadness because every other step I take on my journey back to the main road brings to mind an incident or a face from my dismal past. Disco Dave bowling to the front of the queue outside Raquels nightclub; Larry Johnston, currently serving a life sentence for murder, launching himself at some unfortunate customer he deemed to have upset him; Chris Lombard, a gentle giant, saying for the hundredth time that he was giving up working the door at Raquels because his girlfriend thought it was too rough. Chris is now dead, cut down in a hail of bullets. Kevin Whitaker, murdered by Tucker and Rolfe, his body discarded like rubbish in a roadside ditch. John Marshall, shot dead; Kevin Jones, Andreas Bouzis and Leah Betts, poisoned in their prime by Ecstasy supplied by my associates. I am recalling names as if off a war memorial and then picturing the face of each fallen comrade or foe in my head. The victims, of course, didn't fall in any war, but at times it felt like we were fighting one. It's hard to understand how so many young people connected, directly or indirectly, to such a small circle of friends could end up dead or imprisoned for life.

I'm at the top of the lane now. Cars are driving along the A130, taking commuters to work in Chelmsford and Basildon – normal people going about their everyday business. That's what I want to do: be fucking normal. I'm tempted to turn around and look down the lane for a last time, but I don't. I have to look forward and keep on looking forward if I am ever going to escape my past. I first told this story six years ago in a book called *Essex Boys*. A few of the incidents surrounding the murders remain as

I told them then, but fresh evidence concerning the murder convictions of Whomes and Steele and startling revelations about the victims' tyrannical behaviour have only recently come to light and, until now, have remained untold. I am therefore going to tell this story for the last time and then I am going to try and forget that the terrible events described in this book ever happened.

Chapter 1

Like all parents, Jack and Pam Whomes wanted what was best for their five sons – Terry, Jack, John, William and David – and daughter Jayne. When Pam and Jack had been kids, the East End of London had been a relatively safe place. The fact everybody knew one another within the close-knit community of Canning Town, where they lived, ensured that. But in the 1970s, families began to move out of the East End to new towns, like Basildon in Essex, to be replaced by immigrants. The mood in east London began to change.

Pam and Jack talked about starting a new life elsewhere, but it remained just talk until one afternoon when their eldest son nearly lost his life. Terry, then aged 11, was confronted by an Asian youth on his way home from school on the Barking Road in Canning Town and stabbed in the face. His parents decided enough was enough and moved out to rural Suffolk the very next weekend. Jack Whomes senior set up his own business as a motor mechanic and after two years the family purchased a property with thirteen acres of land in the village of Haughley Green.

The family's arrival was met with resentment by some members of the community: these locals felt their idyllic way of life was being threatened by East End migrants – or East End yobs, as they often referred to them. The parish magazine reported that Haughley Green was being targeted by families moving from London to escape city life. But the

Whomes family soon settled in and eventually people in the village did warm to them. Children would flock to their house because Terry, Jack and John had motorbikes and old cars that they drove around the fields. This interest in cars and motorbikes developed as the Whomes brothers grew older, and they all became extremely good mechanics. Jack, in particular, was very proficient.

In 1990, Suffolk Police arrested Jack and John Whomes in an early-morning raid. The brothers had two cars and a van, which had been stolen and their registrations and engine numbers changed. Jack and John denied any involvement in the thefts, so the police bailed them pending further inquiries. Those further inquiries dragged on for two years until eventually Jack and John were charged with conspiracy to obtain property by deception and handling stolen goods. The brothers stood trial at Ipswich Crown Court.

After three weeks, they were convicted and bailed so that pre-sentence reports could be compiled. In February 1992, they returned to court, where they were both sentenced to 16 months' imprisonment. It was, to say the least, a shock for the brothers, as it was the first time they had been in trouble. At Norwich prison, John and Jack were given the job of working on the servery at meal times, but, after just ten days, they were moved to an open prison called Hollesley Bay in Woodbridge, Suffolk.

In 1887, Hollesley Bay was founded as a colonial college that trained people intending to emigrate. When the Whomes brothers arrived, its purpose was to provide different regimes for adult Category D offenders: life-sentence prisoners at the end of their custodial time and young offenders. It was the largest prison farm within the Prison Service and had a stud of Suffolk Punch horses, which were shown at local, county and national shows. Inmates were pretty much free to roam for up to two miles around the grounds, which included an area of the local beach. It was a prison to which inmates did not mind being sent.

John and Jack were put into a wing called the Cosford Unit. One evening, while queuing for their meal, they got talking to a man who introduced himself as Darren Nicholls.

Nicholls had appeared at Chelmsford Crown Court on a charge of distributing counterfeit currency and was sentenced to three years' imprisonment. Eight months earlier, he had been invited to a meeting with two men he believed were faces from Basildon's criminal fraternity. The two men dropped the names of Basildon hard men and claimed they wanted to get their hands on as much counterfeit money as possible, as they were planning to 'pay' for drugs off a rival gang with it. Nicholls, an impressionable loudmouth, told the men he could supply them with £250,000 worth of counterfeit £10 notes at a cost of £2 each. Nicholls was purchasing the notes for £1.50, so stood to earn £25,000. The deal was struck and the conversation turned towards the drug deal rip-off the two men said they were planning. One of the men asked Nicholls if he was concerned about getting ripped off himself. Nicholls laughed and said, 'Listen, right, I've got a gun at home. If anyone ever tried to rip me off, I'd blow their fucking brains out.'

Nicholls agreed he would meet the men at a hotel at the South Mimms service station on the M25 once he had got the counterfeit notes together. When Nicholls arrived at the hotel a few days later, he was surrounded by armed police and arrested. The two 'Basildon faces' he had done the deal with were undercover police officers.

After a short spell at Chelmsford prison, Nicholls was transferred to Hollesley Bay. Despite the relaxed regime and stress-free environment, he proved to be extremely unpopular with the other inmates. Many of them believed he was informing on them to the prison officers. This conclusion was reached because Nicholls seemed to spend more time trying to win favour with the officers than he did socialising with his fellow prisoners. However, a month after Nicholls began his sentence, his luck changed dramatically. There was a protest by the prisoners over the quality of the food they were being served. They insisted that it be replaced. They shouted, banged tables and refused to move until their demands were met. The prison officers listened to their grievances at first but eventually told the inmates that if they did not comply with their request to leave the canteen, they would have them shipped out to a closed prison where they would lose all of the privileges they enjoyed at Hollesley Bay.

Nicholls and three other inmates were the only ones who refused to budge. Finally, the prison governor went to speak to Nicholls and his fellow protestors. The governor listened, examined the food they were complaining about and agreed he would look into the matter. As none of the four had eaten, he arranged to have fresh ham and cheese rolls prepared for them. When the men sat down together to enjoy their food and their victory over the prison officers, one of them, a large, intense-looking man, leaned towards Nicholls and held out his hand.

'Michael Steele. But you can call me Mick,' he said. From that moment on, Nicholls's life in prison changed dramatically. Steele, who was well respected by the prison staff and other inmates, took Nicholls under his wing.

Steele was serving a nine-year sentence for drug importation. In the early '80s, he had purchased a 33-foot motor cruiser in which he would sail over to Ostend once every two weeks. Upon his arrival, he would purchase a large quantity of tobacco from a shop near the harbour, load it onto his boat and sail back to England. Once the route and technique were tried and tested, Steele switched to smuggling cannabis. It's a fault of human nature, I suppose: whatever we have, we always want more. Mick Steele is no different. He used the profits from his trips to purchase a single-engine Cessna aircraft for £38,000. Soon, he was flying back and forth to the Continent, importing large loads of cannabis into England.

Customs officers had been tipped off about Steele's activities and mounted Operation Water-ski in an effort to catch him. But Steele, a very intelligent man, realised he was under surveillance and decided to outfox Customs officers rather than cease his smuggling operation. With financial restraints on their surveillance team, Customs couldn't afford to follow Steele all of the time. They reasoned that if they just watched his plane, they would catch him red-handed importing drugs. Steele realised what Customs were up to and purchased a second aircraft, which he kept at a different airfield. Steele would drive out of his home and notice the Customs officers following at a discreet distance in his rear-view mirror. If Steele drove in the opposite direction to the airfield where his first plane was kept, Customs would pull over and leave him be. Within just a few hours, Steele could fly to Holland using the second aircraft, pick up the consignment of drugs, unload them and be back home with Customs thinking he had just popped out to do some shopping.

But in May 1989 Steele's luck ran out. He arrived at the Albert pub in Colchester to hand over his latest consignment, which he had transferred from his plane to a white Fiat van. Two Customs officers had followed him but didn't have the back-up to arrest him. Steele noticed them and drove off at speed. In desperation, the Customs officers tried to ram Steele's vehicle, but he managed to avoid them by crossing the central reservation and driving the wrong way down a dual carriageway.

Steele laid low for weeks, but meanwhile his mother

fell ill and the police knew Steele would risk everything to ensure she was OK. They put a surveillance team in the hospital where Mrs Steele was being cared for. When Steele walked onto the ward, one of the officers approached him and asked him who he was.

'I'm Jeff,' Steele replied, 'I'm trying to find my wife.'

For a moment, the policeman hesitated, but Steele looked so composed the officer thought he couldn't possibly be the man they were looking for. 'OK,' the policeman said, 'off you go, it's not you we are looking for.'

'I hope you catch him,' Steele replied, before walking off towards the exit. Just as he was about to step outside, another officer shouted, 'That's Steele, you fucking idiots, grab him!'

At his trial, Steele faced ten charges of smuggling. He pleaded guilty to one – the one he had been arrested for – and not guilty to the other nine. Those that had been accused of assisting Steele with the drug importation said they thought he was smuggling in tobacco. They were all acquitted. As the case unfolded, the jury were shown surveillance pictures which Customs claimed showed Steele and others unloading drugs. Steele pointed out that Customs were wrong. The pictures couldn't have been taken where or when Customs said they had been. In fact, it looked as if several of the pictures had been taken at a later date than Customs had claimed. The evidence against Steele began to crumble, and eventually the prosecution case collapsed.

Steele was cleared of nine charges, but he still had to be sentenced for the one to which he had pleaded guilty. The judge sentenced him to nine years' imprisonment and ordered that the courts seize £120,000 of his money, half of his former marital home, £15,000 from his mother's home, his 33-foot motor cruiser, his £38,000 aircraft and his Toyota Land Cruiser. To Steele, it may have seemed like a harsh sentence: little did he know his association with drug smuggling was going to cost him even more in the future.

The man who was going to use his knowledge of drug smuggling against him was using Steele from the day he met him. Darren Nicholls, boosted by his 'friendship' with Steele, bragged to the Whomes brothers about the clout he had in the prison. He told them if they wanted anything, whether it be alcohol, drugs or bodybuilding steroids, he was the man to see. Nicholls was not the type of person the Whomes brothers wished to be associated with. Jack was vehemently against the use of drugs. Some considered him an oddball because he did not drink or smoke, but it was just the way he was. Despite this, the Whomes brothers did not ignore Nicholls because after a few days they noticed he was constantly on the phone to his wife, crying about not being able to cope with prison life. They realised his boasts about being a big drug dealer in prison were a mask for the fact he was weak and unable to do his time. In short, they felt sorry for him.

Mick Steele's cell was opposite the Whomes brothers' and inevitably they would exchange pleasantries. After a short period of time, Steele learned that Jack, like him, was fascinated by anything mechanical and the pair soon became good friends. John, Jack, Steele and Nicholls began to spend more time together. Steele would often talk about a good friend of his named Pat Tate, whom he had met at Swaleside prison on the Isle of Sheppey in Kent earlier in his sentence. Tate's then girlfriend, Sarah Saunders, used to visit him there and on one occasion recognised a fellow visitor, Jackie Street, in the waiting room. Jackie used to own Longwood riding stables in Basildon where Sarah had once kept her horse. The two got chatting and both were surprised to find their partners, Tate and Steele, had become friends in the prison. After that first meeting, Sarah and Jackie would meet up before each visit and spend an hour or so outside the prison talking to each other. The two couples soon became friends. Eventually, Tate and Steele were moved to HMP Blantyre House, an old country home in Goudhurst, Kent. They shared a cell, and Steele had taught Tate how to use computers.

Steele told the Whomes brothers and Nicholls that Tate had been going through a difficult time and Steele had written to him urging him to apply for a transfer to Hollesley Bay. Tate, he said, had now done this and had been accepted, so he would be joining him there soon.

When Tate arrived, Steele introduced him to John, Jack and Nicholls, and they all began to socialise together. Tate worked as the prison gym orderly and he would supply inmates not only with steroids but also heroin, crack cocaine, speed and cannabis. Nicholls, an unfit, podgy man, was encouraged by Tate to work out and soon he had acquired a steroid-enhanced muscle-bound frame. This new look, combined with the stature of associating with Tate and Steele, gave Nicholls confidence and he began to talk and act like some sort of gangster. Nicholls and Tate became particularly close, training at the gym together and spending time in each other's cells. Tate told Nicholls that he had been in trouble for as long as he could remember. At the age of 12, Tate said, he had found a wallet with more than £300 in it on the roof of a parked car. It turned out that the money was intended for a Christmas party being held by the local police. Tate spent the money on a leather coat, a record player and taxis and restaurants with his friends during trips to Cambridge.

When the police caught up with Tate, he was charged with theft and sent to an approved school. Tate confided in Nicholls that his time there and his childhood in general had been pretty awful. He felt aggrieved about the way he had been treated, and so vowed to dedicate the rest of his life to waging war on the law-abiding members of society.

In December 1988, Tate had robbed a Happy Eater

restaurant in Basildon. He had arrived there off his face after a weekend of non-stop clubbing with Sarah Saunders. After the couple had eaten, Tate got into a dispute with the staff about his bill. To compensate himself, he punched the cashier and snatched £800 from the till. When he was arrested, Tate was found to be in possession of small amounts of cocaine, cannabis and speed which he said were for his personal use.

On 29 December 1988, Billericay magistrates decided that Tate would see in the New Year within the confines of Chelmsford prison. Tate, however, had made other plans. He jumped over the side of the dock and made for the door. Six police officers joined the jailer and jumped onto his back, but he broke free and ran off. One WPC received a black eye and another officer was kicked in the face, as they tried to block Tate's escape. He ploughed his way out of the court to an awaiting motorcycle. Roadblocks, which were immediately set up, failed to trap him. His escape was so speedy, the police couldn't say what type of motorcycle it was, or whether he was alone or had travelled as a passenger.

Several days later, Tate surfaced in Spain. He remained there for a year but made the mistake of crossing over into Gibraltar, where he was arrested by the British authorities and later sent to prison.

Since Hollesley Bay was an open prison, there was no shortage of contraband. Alcohol and drugs, even sex with visiting females, were readily available. Steele, Tate, Nicholls and the Whomes brothers would often have alcohol and Chinese takeaways smuggled in to them and sit up late into the night eating, drinking and having a laugh.

One afternoon, Tate and John Whomes were walking back to the unit after meeting John's brother, Terry, who had dropped off new T-shirts and a couple of bottles of whisky. John had put on the T-shirts and hidden the whisky in his jacket pockets. Tate and John had then given Terry an order for Chinese food, which he was going to deliver later that evening when it got dark. As Tate and John neared the unit, a prison officer came out and asked, 'What have you got on you?'

'We haven't got anything,' Tate and John replied.

The officer said that he had watched them meet somebody, and therefore if they did not come clean, he was going to search them. John took his prison sweater off, then the T-shirts his brother had given to him. 'Here,' he said, throwing them at the officer to catch. 'That's all I was given – T-shirts, which we are allowed to have anyway.'

The officer said that without prior permission nothing was allowed to be handed in, therefore John would be charged. He told Tate and John to follow him before turning and marching off towards the unit.

'You can't nick John for those T-shirts,' Tate said.

'I can, and I'm going to,' replied the officer.

'You don't understand. I'm telling you that you can't and won't nick John for those T-shirts, or I will fucking kill you.'

The officer did not reply, he just continued walking. When John entered the unit, he took his jacket off and gave it and the whisky to another inmate. John and Tate were then called into the office, where Tate began to tell the senior officer what he could and couldn't do regarding John and the T-shirts. 'He's just a young boy,' he said. 'If you nick him for that, it will increase tension on the unit and there will be trouble. Serious fucking trouble.'

The senior officer said that the matter would be considered and they would be informed of any decision in due course. Tate and John left the office and went up to their rooms. Later that night, Terry arrived outside the rear of Cosford Unit with the Chinese meal. Jack leapt over the balcony, ran over to Terry, collected the meal and made his way back to John, Tate, Steele and Nicholls, who were already busy consuming the smuggled bottles of whisky.

The next morning, John was working at the prison stables when two officers arrived and told him that he was being taken to the punishment block. A few minutes after being placed in a cell, John heard shouting and realised Tate was also going to be put in a cell. Unlike John, six officers were escorting Tate because he was being uncooperative, calling them wankers and arseholes. Tate and John spent the night in the punishment block but were able to talk when let out of their cells for meals and showers.

Tate told John that nothing would happen, that they would only be reprimanded. But the following morning they were told they were being sent to HMP Camp Hill on the Isle of Wight. Tate told John that he was going to feign a back injury so they would diagnose him as unfit to travel. He lay on the cell floor, writhed about and screamed in agony while clutching his back. John alerted the prison officers and they called for the prison gym orderly, who was trained in first aid. The orderly entered Tate's cell and, after five minutes, emerged saying that Tate was unfit to travel to Camp Hill. The only prison Tate could be sent to was one with a prison hospital. HMP Highpoint, which they were told was just as relaxed as Hollesley Bay, had a hospital and was just down the road in Newmarket. The following morning Tate and John were handcuffed and taken from Hollesley Bay in a van.

Later, Tate told John that the gym orderly who had been to assess his 'injured' back was a member of staff he had in his pocket. 'Some of the screws I worked with in the gym let me do anything I wanted,' Tate said. 'When the officer came in the cell, I told him I needed him to say I had a bad back. The officer just laughed and said no problem.'

On the way to Highpoint prison, the van transporting Tate and John broke down. A piece of debris on the carriageway caught the brake pipes and tore them off. The driver was forced to pull over and inform the police of the situation. Although Tate and John were handcuffed together, while they waited for assistance the officers agreed to take the cuffs off as it was dangerous for them to sit manacled together in the van on the side of a busy main road. The only safe place to wait was on a grass bank on the other side of the carriageway. Tate and John scrambled to the top and sat in the sunshine eating fruit Tate had brought with him in a bag. When a police car arrived, the officers sat and talked with Tate and John while they waited for a replacement van. Tate kept asking one of the prison officers if he could read his confidential prison file because he was concerned his latest outburst would affect his chances of parole. At first, the officer was reluctant to do so, but then one of the police officers said, 'Go on, let him, he seems an OK lad.'

The file was handed over and Tate spent the rest of his time waiting reading it. When the replacement van arrived, everybody helped transfer Tate's and John's possessions from one vehicle to the other. Tate had ten boxes, John had one. When they arrived at Highpoint prison, Tate was given a trolley on which to put his boxes. He looked at the officer who had brought it to him, said he was unable to bend because of his bad back and walked off towards the reception with John. The officer loaded Tate and John's boxes onto the trolley and pulled it along himself. When they entered the reception area, the officers present looked from John and Tate to the officer transporting their stuff as if to say, 'Who the hell are these two guys?' They were then told all of the boxes would have to be searched before they would be allowed into the prison. Tate replied that that wouldn't be possible.

'What do you mean that won't be possible?' the officer asked.

'If you leave our possessions alone, I won't play up,' Tate said. 'If you touch our possessions, I will.'

The officer looked at Tate then addressed his colleague, the one who had pulled the trolley into reception. 'Take these two and that trolley to unit four.'

Tate and John walked out of reception following the officer pulling the trolley. On the unit, John and Tate were locked up together in the same cell. As soon as they were alone, Tate emptied one of his boxes onto the bed. It appeared to contain cartons of All-Bran, Alpen and other breakfast cereals. Tate cut along the side of one of the boxes and tipped out a handful of muesli. He then shook the carton and a large bar of cannabis resin fell out. Tate opened up several other cartons, which contained heroin, cocaine and steroids; soon there was a large pile of illegal drugs heaped up on the bed. Tate then cut the cannabis into eighths and quarters. The following morning, his 'shop' opened. In no time at all, the prison was flooded with drugs.

After a few days, Tate heard that the north wing was the best one to be on because the inmates there had jobs outside the prison. John and Tate applied to be moved. John waited two months before his request was granted; Tate went the following day.

John was given a job working with disabled people at a centre in Haverhill while Tate was employed on a car-boot sale adjacent to the prison – an ideal job to keep his business running in prison. Friends and associates would visit his stall and leave items full of concealed drugs, and Tate would pass them any money he had earned and wanted spirited out of the prison.

John, who'd never had anything to do with drugs, asked Tate if he would refrain from selling and taking drugs in the cell they shared. John explained that if any drugs were found in the cell, both he and Tate would be charged. To John's surprise, Tate agreed and the drugs were moved to another cell whose occupants were paid 'rent' by Tate for storing them.

Around this time, several inmates were complaining that items such as phone cards, shampoo and postage stamps were going missing from their cells. Tate noticed that a young Asian man was constantly on the telephone, so he assumed that he was guilty of stealing the phone cards at least. Rather than confront the man, Tate barricaded the wing doors to prevent prison officers entering and called a meeting with all 69 inmates on the wing. It was agreed that Tate and John would search all of the cells while the other inmates waited together. If any of the stolen items were found in any of the cells, they would know who was responsible.

Despite a rigorous search nothing was found, so everyone returned to work. The search may not have yielded results, but it certainly caused one inmate to fear for his safety. A group of inmates was approached and told that the Asian man was responsible. The inmates were also told where he stashed his hoard of stolen goods. An outbuilding was searched and the goods found. The group then went in search of the Asian man. They found him on the second floor of the wing and attacked him. As the battered and bloodied man was being kicked and punched, Tate arrived on the scene.

'Stand back, stand back!' he shouted. 'That's not the way to fucking do someone.' Tate then walked into his cell. When he came back out, he was holding a large tomato sauce bottle, which he smashed against the wall. He bent over the Asian man, grabbed him by the throat, then rammed the broken sauce bottle into his face before twisting it left and right numerous times. Some of the men present said they felt sick, but Tate was not finished yet. Tate picked the man up, walked two or three steps, then threw him over the landing rail. Fortunately for the man, he was out cold. Two floors below, there was a sickening thud as his body hit the concrete floor. Tate hit the prison officers' alarm bell with his elbow and said to the horrified inmates, 'That's how you fucking do someone. Clean this mess up, quick.'

He then walked into his cell, leaving the men to mop up the blood, while on the ground floor officers gave the badly injured man first aid. The Asian man lived, but he was moved to another prison for his own safety. Nobody was ever charged in relation to the incident.

One afternoon, Tate went into his cell and said to John, 'You're not going to believe this. Someone I had in my pocket at another prison has just started work here. I'm out of here to an easier prison. I can get him to do anything for £500.' John doubted Tate, but by the end of the week, Tate's transfer request had been granted and he had been moved to HMP Spring Hill, an open prison near Aylesbury in Buckinghamshire.

Chapter 2

In 1986, I was about to embark on a path that would lead to my involvement with the Whomes brothers, Mick Steele, Darren Nicholls and, more significantly, Pat Tate.

Forget what you read in the tabloids about cushy prison life – regardless of some of the so-called 'perks' bestowed upon inmates, it's a complete shit-house experience. On 8 July 1986, I'd just finished serving six months of a twelve-month sentence in one of Her Majesty's dustbins. I was in a pub in Codsall, Staffordshire, having a heated discussion with a friend about people who'd been slagging me off to my girlfriend's parents. A man kept interrupting, and in the end I'd had enough so I whacked him over the head with a bottle. It was no big deal, but the police have never had a sense of humour where I have been concerned.

Prison didn't agree with me at all. It was a tortuous cycle of petty rules, petty screws and countless wannabe movie-star gangsters. I was more than happy to be striding towards the gate that stood between me and freedom that summer's morning. Two years had passed since I had been at liberty in England. After the bottling incident, I'd gone on the run to South Africa – I'd previously been locked up for wounding, so it was odds-on that I would be sentenced to another term of imprisonment if I attended court. I didn't fancy it, so I fled. When I eventually made my way back to England, I was arrested at Dover ferry port.

That was now history. I was thinking all the philosophical shit you have to think when you come out of an institution: a fresh start, a new beginning, no more trouble. Futile crap, I know, but essential to raise your expectations and give yourself some sort of hope for the future.

On the train journey south, I sat in silence, staring out of the window considering my prospects. I had met my girlfriend Debra in Johannesburg while she was there working as a rep for a British hairdressing company. Debra had later returned home and as parole is not an option for prisoners with no fixed abode, she had agreed to let me use her address in Basildon to secure mine. Debra and I were just good friends in South Africa: a romantic relationship hadn't developed. Our first embrace was in the police cells in Dover where she'd come to meet me as I re-entered the country.

As a result of my lifelong reluctance to conform, I had ended up in six different prisons during the six months I had served. First was Shrewsbury, then Birmingham; after that, I went to Ranby in Nottinghamshire. From there I went to Lincoln, back to Birmingham and finally to Stafford.

I hadn't been at Ranby long when they put me in solitary confinement for allegedly trying to escape. It was, of course, nonsense. I'd merely gone for a stroll in an out-of-bounds area. But the screws wouldn't listen. They refused to let me shatter their fantasy. They'd foiled an escape attempt – and nothing could be allowed to detract from their achievement. Not even the truth.

This was my first experience of solitary. My new apartment suite had been fitted out to minimalist standards. The bedroom consisted of a slab of concrete; the bathroom a plastic bucket. I was permitted the following possessions – although not all at the same time: the prison clothes I stood up in (minus shoes) and bedding (pillow, sheet and cover). At night, in order to get the bedding, I had to hand over my clothes. I had nothing to write with or read, not even the Bible, and certainly no telly or radio. You'd have provided more home comforts for a dog. A small, high window made of thick frosted glass ensured I could barely distinguish night from day.

The cell had obviously been designed to destroy any traces of humanity remaining in its occupant. My only human contact – and I'm probably stretching the definition here – came from twisted screws. Mercifully, this never lasted more than a few minutes each day. I came to understand how silence could sometimes be described as deafening. The dirty beige walls seemed to close in on me. Hearing the jangle of keys would make my heart jump. I'd hope the screws were coming to let me out. And they knew it. One screw used to put his keys in my door, take them out again and laugh. Another told me that long-term prisoners could apply for ownership of their cells under the Conservative government's Right to Buy scheme. I didn't want them to think they could get to me. When I heard them coming, I'd sit cross-legged on the floor with my back to the door. I wouldn't even turn round at meal times, when they'd slide a tray of slop across the floor towards me. It really used to annoy a few of them. 'You think you're fucking clever, don't you, O'Mahoney?' one used to say. 'I bet that when the other kids wanted to play cowboys and Indians at your school, you insisted on being a fucking Mexican!' Eventually, they moved me to HMP Lincoln, where I returned to normal prison life. Debra had been very loyal, visiting me in every prison I kept getting sent to. Despite all the hurdles, we got on well.

My first sight of Basildon new town was Laindon station and the Alcatraz Estate. It got its insalubrious name because of the warren of alleyways and building-block flats that it was comprised of. The plan was to ring Debra from the station and she would pick me up in her car. But because she only lived five minutes away from the station, I thought I'd surprise her. However, even though I had her address, it was almost impossible to navigate the estate. It took me almost an hour before I at last saw Debra again. Unfortunately, an hour was exactly the time I was allowed in the town before I had to report to my probation officer. I might have done my time in prison, but the authorities still weren't going to let me be rid of their rules.

I've had several probation officers in my life, so I know the pointless ritual. Sit down, smile, 'How are you?'

'Fine.'

'How are you feeling?'

'Fine.'

'Do you regret the crime?'

'Every moment of every day.'

'Do you think you'll be in trouble again?'

'Who, me? Never!'

'Congratulations, Mr O'Mahoney, you've just won your freedom. See you again next month. Goodbye.'

Probation, in my humble opinion, is about as much use as tits on a bull.

Coming out of prison is a shock to the system. Employers tend to shun you and socially you are deemed to be dubious and unacceptable. Despite all of these problems, Debra and I did eventually settle down to what most would consider a normal life. Debra had her own hairdressing business and I used to commute to London every day, where I worked as a heavy goods vehicle driver.

The estate we lived on was really rough. Parties would go on all night, making sleep impossible. I would leave the house for work at quarter to five in the morning and return at seven in the evening. More often than not, I'd fall asleep on the train on the way home and end up in Southend, having missed my stop. One of our female neighbours would hold a party whenever she found a new boyfriend

– so I could rely on her disturbing my sleep at least three times a week. The bark of her dog would accompany the pounding music. Revellers would urinate, fornicate, vomit and argue on the stairs outside my front door.

One night, I reached the end of my short tether. Around two in the morning, the sound of a screaming row tore me out of my sleep. I put on a pair of boxer shorts and opened the front door. My neighbour and her latest boyfriend stood in the stairwell exchanging unpleasantries. I walked the few paces over to them and said to the boyfriend, 'I'm not having a debate about it, mate. I get up in two hours. Fuck off or I'll kill you.' He just grinned at me moronically. The alcohol fumes from both of them could have put me over the drink-driving limit.

I'd had enough. Bang. I chinned him. He flew backwards down the stairs. His girlfriend started screaming. I told her to shut up, closed my door and went back to bed. A short time later, someone started banging loudly on my front door. I got up again and thought, 'If it's the boyfriend, he's going over the balcony.' I opened the door to a stern-faced policeman. Several other officers stood in the background with dogs. I could see my neighbour and her boyfriend, the latter bleeding from facial wounds. As soon as he saw me, he shouted, 'That's the cunt! Arrest him!' The officer said he wanted to question me about an alleged assault and threats to kill.

'For fuck's sake, mate,' I said. 'Unlike most of the scum around here, I work for a living. I'm up in less than two hours. How can I not react when these people are pissing, puking, fucking and fighting on my doorstep all night?'

The policeman looked at me in my boxers, then looked at the drunken boyfriend – who'd now begun to scream obscenities – and told me to go to bed. My neighbour found herself a new boyfriend.

The partying continued, so in the end I broke into her flat

one day when she was out and smashed her stereo to bits, stamped on all her tapes and tried to hurl her snarling dog over the balcony. The hound sensed my hostile intentions, however, and scampered around the flat, bared its teeth whenever I got near and stayed just out of my grasp. I was making too much noise and to avoid being caught I abandoned my mission. The dog lived to bark another day, but my neighbour became quieter.

In June 1987, Debra and I had our first child. I named him after a good friend of mine, an armed robber named Vinney Bingham from Huyton in Liverpool. Our son Vinney brought us a lot of happiness. Our pretty uneventful lives suddenly had meaning. Vinney was our world, a labour of love rather than an unwanted chore, which was what most of the kids on our war-torn estate appeared to be. Two years later, we had a daughter whom we named Karis. We adored her equally.

The strain of travelling to London every day and working long hours with two small children in the house began to tell. When I got home, all I wanted to do was sleep but with screaming neighbours and kids that became impossible. I decided to seek out additional income locally. Through a friend, I was told about a job that was going as a nightclub doorman at a place called Raquels in Basildon town centre. I spoke to the manager and he arranged for me to meet the head doorman. A large, muscular man shook my hand and introduced himself.

'Dave Venables,' he said. 'I hear you want work.'

Venables looked me over, asked a few questions and then told me I could start the following weekend. The wages, he said, were £40 per night, cash in hand.

I remained at the club for a short while talking to him about things in general. Venables told me I was entering the Basildon nightclub security scene at a time of change following a spate of retirements, deaths and public disorder.

A bouncer named McCabe, who was once all-powerful, had recently died in a road accident and the infamous West Ham United football hooligans, known as the Inter City Firm, had smashed, slashed and stabbed the hardcore of Basildon's doormen at a rave that had been held in the town. Madness had reigned that night, Venables told me. The ICF had come prepared with coshes, hammers, 'squirt', tear gas and knives. The unwitting doormen had nothing to defend themselves with other than their muscle-bound bravado and reputations. They soon lost them both. The ICF rampaged through the hall, hacking, slashing and stamping on the retreating bouncers, whose crime it was to have had one of the ICF members ejected over a trivial remark.

Being a good doorman isn't about going to the gym and throwing around your steroid-bloated frame, it is about diplomacy and trying to understand the psyche of the psychos you encounter. The Basildon bouncers were now learning this valuable lesson. Those who escaped the lecture in the main hall were captured on the car park and given the most brutal of tutorials. They were beaten and their flesh ripped open with Stanley knives; one blood-soaked bouncer was thrown into a lake. It was a miracle nobody died. Many of those who avoided hospital 'retired' immediately from the security industry.

Things had changed. Lager louts with bad attitudes had been replaced by smartly dressed, drug-fuelled, knife-wielding villains. Commuting to Essex from the East End of London, these villains wanted to flood the county with the 'love drug' Ecstasy. Disco rather than rave, bouncer versus firm member, pints instead of pills – they were all on a collision course and, without realising it, I was stepping into the epicentre. I thanked Venables for helping me out and told him that I would be at the club the following weekend.

That Friday, I drove into town looking for what had

resembled a trendy bar during daylight – at night it looked like some sort of night shelter for down-and-outs and the clinically insane. Dodgy-looking geezers and even more dodgy-looking girls hung around outside the bar entrance. Like moths, they seemed drawn to the blue neon light that announced, or warned, you were about to enter The Piano Bar, an annexe of Raquels. I later learned these former customers were barred from entering for a variety of unpleasant offences, but they still turned up every night and huddled beneath the light to spit abuse at customers entering the bar and attack those who objected to the insults.

It's bad enough at the best of times being surrounded by drunks, but when you're a doorman the experience is even more unpleasant, so on my first night I was pleased to learn that I was going to work in Raquels itself, the nightclub next door. Only later did I find that it was here that the real heavy drinkers washed up when the pubs closed and here that most of the trouble occurred.

Venables introduced me to my fellow doormen. Most of them were there, like me, just for a bit of extra cash. They didn't seem like a proper firm to me. I wasn't exactly confident in their ability to sort out any trouble if it came, but I kept my mouth shut, my head down and started work.

It didn't take long for me to realise that things were not running the way they should be at Raquels. Local hooligans would cause trouble in the club and the next night the doormen would let them back in to cause more. The men on the door thought that if they barred one of these troublemakers, they could end up being assaulted on the street or, even worse, they'd come round to their house. I was of the opinion that if they wanted trouble, they could fucking have it. And if they came into the club and started anything, they would be barred regardless of who they were. Simple as that.

One Saturday night, I was working on the door at Raquels with a man named Larry Johnston. He was one of the few doormen I felt safe working with. If a fight broke out, I knew instinctively that Larry would be alongside me in the thick of it. The problem with Larry was he always had to go the extra mile. When the fight was over, he couldn't resist one last spiteful kick, or stamping on one of the bruised and bloodied bodies that lay motionless on the floor. I was convinced that one day Larry's over-enthusiasm for the job would result in somebody's death.

On that particular evening, a group of men who had left the club minutes earlier approached the door and asked to be let back in. The club was due to close and so I told them that wouldn't be possible. The men were very drunk and became abusive. I wasn't particularly bothered because if you work on the door, you endure that kind of nonsense all the time. You have to accept it goes with the territory. I stood watching them in silence. People were standing around listening to the men giving us abuse and it wasn't doing much for the team's image, so I thought the best thing to do would be to go inside and close the door for a while. I was hoping they would grow tired of their game and walk away.

As soon as we went inside, the men, obviously getting braver because of our lack of response, started kicking and banging on the door. Larry smiled, pushed the door open and we both ran outside. The men began to run. Neither Larry nor myself were built for jogging around Basildon town centre, so we stopped and stood in the road. The fleeing men, who had been desperate for a fight moments earlier, also stopped running and stood facing us several yards away. They started shouting, calling us 'wankers', and chanting, 'Kill the fucking bouncers! Kill the fucking bouncers!'

Rather surprisingly – or unsurprisingly in Basildon – they

were joined by several other men from a nearby burger-bar queue. This group, who had no grievance with us whatsoever, began to hurl pallets and the iron bars that were used to make up the market stalls adjacent to the club. Bottles, stones and anything else the men could lay their hands on rained down on us. It was pretty pointless standing there waiting for their aim to improve, so Larry and I went back into the club and closed the doors.

Whenever a fight broke out in the club, either bar staff, the DJ or those in the reception area activated an alarm. A light on the DJ's console would tell him which alarm button had been struck, so he could then announce over the PA system 'Door to reception, please' or 'Door' to wherever. Nine times out of ten, it was 'Door to the dance floor' because a jealous boyfriend was attacking somebody who dared to look at his girlfriend. When we walked into the foyer, the siren was blaring, the blue light on the ceiling was flashing and all the other doormen had arrived from upstairs.

There were eight of us in total. Everyone armed themselves, some with pickaxe handles and washing-up bottles filled with industrial ammonia – family size, of course. Others chose smaller weapons, such as knuckle-dusters or coshes, which were easier to conceal should the police turn up. I had a sheath knife I always carried and an Irish hurling stick, which is a bit like a hockey stick but with a broader striking area.

When everybody was ready, we opened the door and ran back into the street. One of the men ran towards us with an iron bar, screaming hysterically. I swung the hurling stick, bringing it crashing down across the top of his head. He lay on the floor where he fell, bleeding but motionless. Larry ran over and kicked the man in the head and body several times. This spiteful act incited the crowd and they ran at us. Within minutes, the street had turned into a battleground strewn with debris and bodies. The baying mob was now about 100 strong, its number having been swelled by passers-by, people turning out of a nearby club and those queuing for taxis.

Unbeknown to me at the time, there were actually three separate groups fighting. The men who asked to re-enter the club wanted to do so in order to fight another group of men who had assaulted one of their friends earlier. When the alleged assailants had walked out of the club at closing time and into the disturbance in the street, the group to whom we had originally refused entry had attacked them. The third group was made up of the homeward-bound revellers, who had joined in for the hell of it.

We didn't know who was who, and so we resorted to hitting everybody that appeared to be involved in the fighting. Within a few minutes, the police arrived on the scene but rather than restore order their presence seemed to make matters worse. The crowd backed off at first but then re-grouped and started throwing missiles again.

Nobody could see much point in standing in the street being used for target practice, so, along with the police, we retreated into the club foyer to await reinforcements. As we did so, two officers stumbled on a wooden pallet that had been thrown into the middle of the road and the crowd charged. Soon they were surrounded, being kicked and struck with weapons. Their colleagues inside the foyer asked us to help them, so we all went outside and managed to retrieve the two officers from the crowd. It wasn't long before police reinforcements arrived, their blue flashing lights and wailing sirens creating panic among the crowd, which dispersed in all directions.

'You'd better lose that,' one of the officers said. I still had the blood-stained hurling stick in my hand. I wasn't surprised he had chosen to advise me rather than arrest me, because it had been an extremely dangerous situation we had faced together; the officers who had fallen could easily have died.

On the Monday, the local newspaper published a story about the incident headlined 'Policeman Injured as Youths Fight'. It read:

> A policeman was taken to hospital after a disturbance outside a nightclub in Basildon. Acting Inspector Ian Frazer was injured when youths turned on police as they tried to break up a string of fights in the town square near Raquels disco. Scuffles broke out among 100 people at 2.15 a.m. yesterday and back-up police crews were called from Basildon, Billericay, Wickford, Southend and Grays. Mr Frazer was treated in Basildon hospital for cuts and bruises but not held overnight. A man charged with assault is due before magistrates today.

It was not an exceptionally violent incident for Raquels. The lunatics who got drunk out of their tiny minds in there thought nothing of stabbing, cutting, glassing or even shooting those who displeased them. I can recall one unfortunate man who was out on his stag night being pushed into a fire exit where he was repeatedly slashed with a Stanley knife. His crime? He had unwittingly shown a local idiot 'disrespect' by accidentally bumping into him. The would-be groom needed 160 stitches – a lesson in 'respect' he will undoubtedly never forget.

I could never understand why Venables allowed these people to take liberties with him – he was certainly no fool. But he didn't want any confrontation when the going got rough. Hardly the attitude of a doorman.

Venables offered me an additional night's work at an Essex venue called Epping Forest Country Club. It was there that I first met David Done. He was an obsessive bodybuilder from Romford. We got on very well and soon after we met he came to work at Raquels. He did his job well at first, but after a few weeks he started arriving late or leaving early, relying on our friendship to ensure no questions were asked, or if they were that I would make excuses for him. Larry took exception to the favours being bestowed upon Done and began making comments about him being a 'part-time doorman on a full-time doorman's pay'. The atmosphere between the two became quite hostile. One evening as Done prepared to leave early, Larry asked if he would give him a lift home. Done said he couldn't, as he was going the opposite way, so Larry kicked the door panel of his car. Done jumped out and started shouting. Larry responded by pulling out a knife. I couldn't believe how quickly the situation was escalating. I asked Larry to put the knife away, but he told me to fuck off and keep out of it. I see very little or no point in holding talks with deranged men wielding knives, so I took out my bottle of industrial ammonia and squirted him in the face with it. Larry was temporarily blinded and then permanently sacked. David Done remained. I was annoyed we had fallen out because I liked Larry, but what choice did I have? I couldn't stand by and watch a friend kill another friend.

Epping country club started playing rave and house music on Sunday nights and it was soon 'the place' to be seen in Essex. Crowds queued for hours to get in and extra staff were taken on to meet the demand, thus Done and I were asked to work there. Doormen, drug dealers and all the 'club people' who had worked Friday and Saturday used to go there because it was their only weekend night off. It was not long before I got to know many people on the London club circuit. I became friendly with one man in particular.

Tony Tucker was an absolutely huge man in his mid-30s. He was an up-and-coming face in the Essex underworld, running a very well-organised and well-respected door firm that supplied security at clubs in Essex, Suffolk and

London. Tucker had worked as a carpenter before starting up his security business. He was a very abrupt and rude man to those whom he deemed to be below him – and that was most people. If people he didn't know tried to strike up a conversation with him, Tucker would glare at them as if they were mad or stupid. One evening while working at a club in Wandsworth, south London, Tucker confronted a group of black doormen. They were meant to be working with him but had congregated on a stairwell that led to the fire exit. Never unsure of himself, Tucker began shouting abuse at them, calling them useless and lazy. One of the guys objected to this and pulled out a CS gas canister and sprayed him with it in the face. The group then pounced on Tucker and beat him senseless before leaving via the fire exit.

The following night, Tucker came to Epping seeking help from everybody he knew; he was ranting and raving that he wanted revenge. He asked me to accompany him and I suppose that was the nod that started our close friendship. Despite working with his assailants and knowing they were from Brixton, Tucker never did find the men who had beaten him up. At the time, some said he wasn't too keen on looking for them just in case he *did* find them. Despite his reputation, many close to Tucker considered him to be no more than a bully and a coward.

David Done's obsession with bodybuilding had resulted in him having a serious problem with steroids. His addiction to these performance-enhancing drugs meant he was always short of money. He even resorted to being a pizza delivery boy to help finance his drug craving. He refused to listen to reason and his addiction began to affect his judgement. One Monday morning, Done rang me up and told me that he had been sacked from Epping country club for allegedly selling drugs. I knew this was false: Done had nothing to do with drug dealing. I told him that if he was sacked, then all of the door staff should walk out in support of him. I said I would pick him up and we would go and see Joe, the head doorman, to see if we could get to the bottom of it. When we arrived, I asked Joe who had told him Done was dealing. He said the club had received an anonymous telephone call. I got quite annoyed and reasoned that if the person who alleged Done was a dealer didn't do it openly and with some form of corroboration, then they shouldn't be believed. Eventually, Joe relented and Done got his job back

That evening, I received a phone call from Venables, who said the management at Epping wanted me to be sacked instead of Done. No reason had been given. What particularly annoyed me was that now I had been sacked, Done refused to stand by me. He said that he needed the money – the fact I'd lost my job was unfortunate but there was nothing he could do. I was livid and my friendship with Done became at best strained.

Done worked at the Ministry of Sound occasionally and, in an effort to patch up our friendship, he got me a job there to replace the nights I had lost at Epping. The Ministry door team were a powerful firm: nearly every man could have 'a row'. Done was a good friend of Carlton Leach's, who had once been the head doorman at the Ministry of Sound, but Leach had recently been sacked and his door team removed from the club. Two brothers from south London, Tony and Peter Simms, had taken over and there was immediate conflict between Leach and the Simms brothers. I asked Done if Leach minded us working for Tony and Peter because I felt our loyalty lay with Leach – he was, after all, Done's friend. Done said they had discussed it and Leach was fine with us continuing to work there.

A few days later, I learned that Done had lied to me. When he had approached Leach, he had been told that it would be appreciated if he didn't work for Tony and Peter Simms. When Done had explained that he needed the money, Leach

47

told him he would pay his wages not to work there. Done decided he would take money from both the Simms brothers and Leach. I told Done I wanted nothing more to do with his deception, so we ended up falling out once more.

I was still seeing a fair bit of Tony Tucker. He asked me what the problem was between Done and me, so I told him. Tucker, who was also a good friend of Leach's, was incensed; he said he was going to go down to the Ministry to stab Done. I told Tucker Done was not worth it. Instead of attacking Done, Tucker simply told Leach that Done had been taking money from him and the Simms brothers. When confronted, Done denied it and slagged me off, claiming that I was a liar and had been trying to cause trouble. Done and I fell out for the last time. We never spoke again.

One night while working at the Ministry of Sound, I hit a man in the face with a lead cosh. He had been threatening another doorman and me because we had refused him entry since he was drunk. We had politely asked him to go away several times but our good-natured requests had fallen on deaf ears. Eventually, we told the man 'Fuck off – or else.' His response was to step forward with a raised fist.

Smack! The sound of the lead cosh making contact with the man's jaw and cheekbone echoed all around us. I knew something had broken in his face, I knew I had hurt him. He fell motionless to the ground and another doorman advised me to disappear. The following day, Peter Simms rang and said the man had suffered a broken jaw and a fractured eye socket. 'Management would prefer it if you didn't return,' he said. Peter and his brother Tony are decent men and had been good to me. I didn't want to repay them with grief, so I said I understood.

Back in Basildon, Raquels continued to be a cauldron of trouble, which would simmer and then boil over every night. Trouble came not only from the customers but also increasingly from those I worked with. Venables knew I

48

had the serious hump with the way he ran security. A good friend of his, Dave Godding, and a man named Joe had been involved in a fracas in The Piano Bar and Joe had hit a man and dislocated his arm. Godding wanted me to call an ambulance. I refused, because if you do that, the police will arrive too. Godding went behind my back and dialled 999. Then he had the nerve to tell me he was going to ring Venables and complain about me. I went berserk. I shouted at him, telling him in no uncertain terms what I thought of Venables. Godding got very nervous and left the club. The next day, the manager, Ralph Paris, asked me to come in and see him in his office. Ralph told me Venables had resigned that morning because he said he didn't think he could work with me any longer. I didn't have a problem with that.

Before I'd arrived at the club, people had taken liberties all the time. I decided to use excessive violence to combat violence, and by doing so I had reduced the amount of trouble. People were thinking twice about starting anything in the club. It's easy to say with hindsight now but I should have realised that excess would eventually be met with excess.

Chapter 3

The Raquels door team was still made up of local men and they were still afraid of the local louts who had earned their reputations in the playground and were intent on taking them to their graves. The only way I was going to regain control of the club was if I brought in people from elsewhere who wouldn't be scared of taking them on. But for now, the local doormen were all I had and I would have to make do.

I was nervous about my position, but controlling the door of a nightclub is all about front. I couldn't show my fear or walk away after criticising Venables: I was going to have to stand my ground.

The legacy of the last door firm was over and I was determined not to make the same mistakes as my former boss. More and more people began to get seriously hurt; knives and other weapons were regularly used. On the surface, revellers were beginning to see a decrease in violence but behind the scenes those who wished to cause trouble were paying dearly.

In one incident, a local man came to the front door and became abusive because I insisted that he be searched before he entered the club. He went away and returned with a rounders bat. Maurice Golding, a doorman from Bristol who worked for me, was hit across the head and the man ran away. We all chased him and the manager followed, trying to reason with me to calm down. We caught the man 500 yards away from Raquels outside the local bingo hall. The doorman who caught him began to hit him, but I told him to stop. I kneeled on the man's chest and cut him twice with a sheath knife: once on the face, once on his upper thigh. The manager was outraged. I posed the question: if he had chased Maurice with the bat and Maurice had fallen over, what would he have done with the rounders bat? It was only right that he got a bit of his own medicine.

Another night, a man from Leeds was refused entry because he was drunk. He produced a knife and began waving it and shouting obscenities. I told him to put the knife down, but he kept shouting, 'Do you want some? Do you want some?'

'It's up to you which way this goes,' I said. 'Put the knife down.'

He refused. He was slashed and left with a deep, open wound to the left-hand side of this face. Again, I justified this by asking what would have happened if I had walked towards him without a knife and he was still brandishing his? I've always said the aggressor dictates the way things go. If they put their hands up, I'll put my hands up. If they pull out a weapon, I'll pull out a weapon. It's entirely their choice. Violence is a messy business.

One Sunday evening I arranged to go to Epping country club with three drug dealers: Steve Curtis, Nathan Kaye and David Thomkins. I had met them in the Ministry of Sound. They told me that they were from the Bristol area. I had agreed to introduce them to Tony Tucker because he was trying to recruit new drug dealers for his clubs.

I'll always remember introducing Steve, Nathan and Dave to Tucker. He asked me if they had any drugs with them. I asked them and they said they could sort Tucker out but they would want £40 from him. Tucker looked at me, looked at them, then started to laugh. 'Tell them to hand over what I asked for or I'll take the fucking lot.' This was typical of Tucker. He wasn't in the habit of paying for things, particularly drugs.

I decided that I would discuss a deal of my own I had in mind with Tucker concerning doormen for Raquels. I explained to Tucker about the trouble I was having and said I needed the backup of a strong firm. I told him that if he went into partnership with me, I would run the door and he could reap whatever benefits there were to be had from providing invoices and any other 'commodities' – drugs, protection, debts and so on. I would not bother him with the day-to-day running of the club. The only time I would call on him was if I had a severe problem and needed backup. In return, trouble or no trouble, he would make money each week from the club. Tucker nodded in agreement and we shook hands.

On 4 September 1993, Tucker and I began working together at Raquels. The agreement brought new faces onto the scene in Basildon. Men who worked for him and were looking for a change would come and work with me. One evening, I got a call from a doorman who said his mate, Gavin, was looking for work. Apparently Gavin had been sacked from a club in Ilford after sending a customer to hospital. The doorman said he'd already spoken to Tucker on Gavin's behalf but had been told there was no work. This struck me as odd because I'd already mentioned to Tucker that I needed an extra doorman. I suspected he had another reason for saying no.

The politics of the door is worthy of academic study. The microcosm is a catty little world built on bubbling jealousies, stifled resentments and long-borne grudges. One week someone was in favour, the next he was a grass, a bottler or a wanker. People won't speak to each other for years for quite petty reasons. Perhaps someone sweated on their towel in the gym, or tipped over their nail varnish.

Many bodybuilders are better manicured than Jordan and Jodie Marsh put together; if you could calculate which groups spend the most on sunbeds, leg-waxing and hairdos, you'd find it a toss-up between call girls and bodybuilders. I hated all that doorman politics. I like to take people as I find them, not as they're 'generally known'.

I rang Tucker and asked him about employing Gavin. He said he didn't really like the guy, although he couldn't, or wouldn't, give a reason. In the end, he said, 'It's up to you, Bernie. If you need someone, then take him on.' So I rang back my contact and told him to send Gavin along.

When I got out of my car at Raquels that Friday evening, I noticed an Asian-looking bodybuilder locking up his car. I was always very vigilant when entering and leaving the club. I felt that was the point at which a doorman was most vulnerable to attack from people seeking revenge. The Asian man walked towards me and asked, 'Are you Bernie?' After eyeing him up with caution, I said I was. He stuck out his hand and said, 'All right, mate. I'm Gavin.'

During the evening, I asked Gavin why certain people seemed so set against him working at Raquels. He explained that Tucker had once turned up at a club where he was working and hadn't wanted to queue, pay or show any sort of respect to the doormen. That would have been typical of Tucker. He'd walk to the front of any nightclub queue and when asked for money he would look at the door staff with utter contempt. Tucker had ended up being bashed. He'd lost a bit of face – an unforgivable outrage in the world of the door. As a result, he didn't want to give work to anyone who'd been part of that door firm.

I liked Gavin from that first conversation. Quiet and uncomplicated, he meant what he said and said what he meant. His catchphrase with leery customers was, 'What's your problem, mate?' Then he'd usually try reasoning with them. If they continued to be aggressive or violent, he had no hesitation in creating new customers for the NHS. He didn't care for reputations – and could certainly fight. In fact, he turned out to be one of the best doormen I ever employed. In a short time, he became the man I relied on most when war broke out. Away from Raquels, he became my best friend.

One evening, two skinheads with tattoos on their heads and necks came to The Piano Bar. They arrived with four non-skinhead friends. I could see them looking at Gavin, then making remarks and laughing. They started doing the same to me. One of them stood behind me, aping me. I turned round and grabbed him by the throat, pushing him backwards as I did so. He fell back and hit his head on the corner of a small glass pillar, which shattered – as did his tattooed head. Gavin heard the sound of breaking glass and ran from the other side of the bar with a bottle in his hand. He told me later he thought I'd been attacked with a glass. He saw my 'attacker' on the floor but couldn't see the gash at the back of his head. Gavin whacked his bottle a few times over the skin's already-skewered skull. Then we both pulled him up and dragged him to the doors. His mates seemed too stunned to do anything. We threw him into one of the glass doors, which also smashed, cutting his upper arm. He was still struggling a bit, so we beat him before throwing him down the stairs. His mates meekly followed him, only shouting abuse when they'd got safely outside.

About half an hour later, customers near the exit doors began screaming and shouting, 'Fire! Fire!' Gavin and I ran to the stairwell and saw flames leaping up from the bar entrance. I told the manager and staff to deal with the fire, then Gavin and I ran out through the flames into the street. We found the skin with the sore head standing there with a red petrol can in his hand. Perhaps the earlier beating had slowed his reflexes because, although he looked surprised to see us, he didn't run immediately, a significant mistake on his part.

I ran across to him, my Irish hurling stick in my hand.

He dropped the petrol can. 'It wasn't me. It wasn't me,' he pleaded. He turned to run, but I hit him across the back with the hurling stick. He fell to the ground. Gavin began kicking him in the head with his steel boots. The skinhead begged us not to beat him any more. Gavin stamped on his head and I hit him so hard across the back with the hurling stick it broke. He lay there unconscious.

We picked up the petrol can and doused him with the remaining fuel. The other skinhead, who'd run a short distance away, began screaming, 'Please don't burn him! Please don't burn him!' We told him to come to us, as we weren't going to do anything. He wasn't stupid; he stayed where he was. We gave him the impression we were about to light the fire. The skinhead became hysterical. In the end, we threw down the petrol can and walked back to the club.

A week later, the skinhead who'd run away came to the club's front door, pissed out of his head, asking for 'that fucking Paki'. Gavin and I dashed downstairs to the dissatisfied customer.

'What's your problem, mate?' said Gavin.

'You, you Paki cunt,' said the skinhead. 'You're going to get this.' He took out an axe from the inside of his jacket, but before he could use it, I'd squirted him in the face with ammonia and Gavin had slashed him across the head with a blade. We threw him outside amid a flurry of kicks and punches, then slammed the door shut. The skinhead lay howling outside in the gutter. Eventually, he got up and skulked off. We received regular death threats and warnings on the grapevine, but the skinheads never came back.

Not all of the customers were violent villains. Many were just amusing freaks. One character I grew to like was an awesomely thin creature in his late teens. Around six foot and with lizard-like features, he'd gulp and stutter violently when he tried to talk. We named him Disco Dave. On Mondays, we used to hold an under-18s night, which attracted 300 potential and actual juvenile delinquents from the local estates. We wouldn't sell them alcohol, but that didn't make any difference: they'd just get pissed beforehand. Like their sociopathic parents, these kids would then indulge in brawls, beatings and drunken gropes.

One night, we got called to a disturbance on the dance floor. As I approached, I noticed a heap of around ten writhing, spitting kids. They appeared to be attacking someone who lay on the floor beneath them. We dragged the kids off one by one to find a bleeding man at the bottom. This was my first meeting with Disco Dave. Apparently, he'd taken off his shirt to expose his gruesomely underdeveloped body. A group of youths objected. Disco told them to fuck off and they'd steamed him.

I cleaned him up and suggested he go home and instead come to the adult nights, as it was now a few years since he'd been under 18. He said he didn't have enough money to attend the adult nights or to get home. I agreed to give him a lift when the club closed. He waited for me patiently. Every time I tried talking to him he became engulfed in violent gulping and stuttering. In the end, I decided silence was the best policy. I told him to sit in the back of my car to prevent idle chat.

On the way to his house, I was stopped by the police. This wasn't unusual: they were always on my case. When I saw the flashing blue light, I told Disco to let me do the talking because I wanted to get home at a reasonable hour. The policeman walked up to the driver's door and asked me the usual questions. I said, 'I've been to work and I'm going home, and – before you ask – he's fuck-all to do with me. I'm just giving him a lift home.'

The officer then asked Disco for his details. Disco was so nervous that he gulped, stuttered, spat and blinked for so long that in the end the policeman said, 'It's all right, mate. Forget it. Off you go.'

I suppose I adopted Disco Dave as a sort of club mascot. I knew he had no money, so I used to let him in free. I could see this made him feel important. One day, I told him that in the future he should ignore the long queues, march straight to the front, walk past the door staff, cashier and those searching and, if *anybody* said *anything*, he had to say, 'My name's Disco Dave. I don't pay. And I don't give a fuck.' Nothing more. Nothing less.

One evening, the company directors and other VIPs visited the club. They were all standing around the reception area when Disco walked in wearing trainers. One of the directors looked at Disco, then looked at me, and stood waiting for me to say something. I just shrugged. The director decided to intervene. He said to Disco, 'I'm afraid you can't come in wearing trainers, sir.'

Disco looked straight at him, gulped and, with the pride and arrogance of a bullfighter, stuttered out the words 'My name's Disco Dave. I don't pay. And I don't give a fuck.' He then marched past the director and all the door staff and disappeared upstairs.

'Who on earth is that?' the director said.

'Don't ask,' I replied. 'He's a fucking nightmare.'

When we went upstairs later, Disco was dancing on a raised podium with his shirt off, looking like a complete fool. Indirectly, he'd helped us rebuff the charge that we'd become too violent to customers. Indeed, the director thought we ought to impose our authority a bit more firmly. He hadn't liked our completely hands-off approach to a stuttering, skeletal representative of the undead who'd pushed his way into the club without paying.

Since our partnership began, I had seen a lot more of Tony Tucker socially. He invited me and all the other doormen from Raquels to his birthday party at the Prince of Wales pub in South Ockendon. He also asked me to take Steve, Nathan and Thomkins along from Bristol, so that there would be a supply of drugs for him and his guests. Tucker was in a very good mood. The party was a real success. Doormen from everywhere were there. Most were out of their faces on cocaine, Special K or Ecstasy, or a cocktail of all three and more.

In the early hours of the morning, I was sitting on the floor of an upstairs room with Steve, Nathan and Debra. A man in his early 20s pushed open a door, which struck me. I looked at him, waiting for him to apologise, but he just smirked and asked me what the matter was.

'You've just knocked the fucking door into me,' I said.

'Well, you're a doorman, aren't you?' he replied.

It was a stupid thing to say because it was obviously intended to cause trouble. I got up and walked towards him. He walked out to the kitchen and I followed him. Friends of Tucker's followed us, but before the fight could start, we were separated. It was only later I learned he was Craig Rolfe, Tucker's closest friend. I discovered that Rolfe was possessive of his friendship. I told him that, out of respect for Tucker, he shouldn't cause trouble at his birthday party. Rolfe seemed all right afterwards, but he still had an attitude. When I was explaining to Tucker a few days later what had gone on, he told me why Rolfe had this chip on his shoulder. On Christmas Eve 1968, a man was found dead in a van that was parked in a lay-by at the side of the A13 between Stanford le Hope and Vange in Basildon. The dead man had been found slumped in the seat of a grey Austin van. His name was Brian Rolfe, a market trader from Basildon. At the post-mortem later that day, the cause of death was determined as a fractured skull.

In less than 24 hours, the case had been solved. On Boxing Day, a 19-year-old motor fitter, John Kennedy from Basildon, was charged with the murder together with 23-year-old Lorraine Rolfe, the wife of the murdered man.

A few weeks earlier, the couple had run away together

to start a new life in Birmingham, but Lorraine discovered she was expecting her husband's child and opted to return to him rather than live with the jobless Kennedy. The affair continued, however, and Kennedy became increasingly frustrated at Lorraine's refusal to end her marriage.

He decided he had had enough. He broke into the couple's Linford Drive home, crept up to the main bedroom and as Brian lay asleep next to his wife, smashed his skull to pieces with three blows from a ten-pin bowling skittle that weighed nearly four pounds. Brian's skull was crushed like an eggshell.

When Lorraine Rolfe was charged, it is reported she replied, 'I never touched him, honest, on my baby's life.'

Lorraine was at that time the mother of three children and was expecting a fourth – Craig. When the case came to trial at Maidstone in March 1969, the prosecution alleged that Lorraine and Kennedy murdered Brian Rolfe and tried to fake a roadside robbery. Both pleaded not guilty to the murder charges. Kennedy was found guilty of murder and jailed for life. He was also given a concurrent sentence of seven years for breaking and entering the Rolfe family home and stealing £597. During this episode, Lorraine gave birth to Craig in Holloway Prison. Not surprising, then, that he had a chip on his shoulder, or that he'd chosen a life of crime.

By the age of 16, Rolfe had grown into a classic juvenile delinquent: at odds with everything that society had to offer and accumulating several minor criminal convictions along the way. He worked for a short time as a tyre fitter and then as a plasterer, but the only trade in which he ever excelled himself was drugs. Whatever was on offer, Rolfe would sample or sell it.

Rolfe met Diane Evans after her family had moved to the Basildon area. The couple started seeing each other on a casual basis when Diane was 18. The relationship went from strength to strength and shortly after Diane's 19th birthday the couple moved into Rolfe's mother's home. Keen to impress his attractive girlfriend, Rolfe stepped up his drug-dealing operation in nightclubs around Essex to fund a better lifestyle for them both. The relationship was turbulent, to say the least, but regardless of how much the couple fought and argued they remained hopelessly devoted to each other.

Rolfe was far from intelligent, but it didn't take him long to realise that selling pills to nightclub revellers was never going to make him rich. If you wanted to make serious money, the quickest but most dangerous way was to order large amounts from suppliers and simply not pay them. Stupid or fearless, I'm not sure which, but Rolfe became very proficient at it.

Rolfe and Diane's daughter, Georgie, was born in the autumn of 1990. A few weeks later, Rolfe made a drugs sale which would dictate the path the rest of his life was to follow. A man turned up at Rolfe's home, having been told by friends that he had good quality cocaine for sale. As is the norm, a small test sample was given to the man to try. 'This is fucking good gear,' he said. 'Where did you get it?'

Rolfe, high on his own supply, replied, 'Fuck knows, I ripped off some idiot for it in Southend.'

The pair fell about laughing and spent the day snorting the rest of the cocaine together. The man was Tony Tucker – Rolfe had found his kindred spirit.

Rolfe and I never really did see eye to eye after our first meeting. Our views clashed on most things. However my association with Tucker was business, Rolfe's was personal, so like and dislike didn't really come into it. Rolfe had a fairly serious cocaine problem and hanging around with Tucker helped because there was a constant supply at a discount price, if not for free.

Merging with anyone in business is always potentially

hazardous, but particularly so if you're involved in our line of work. When I had taken over Raquels from Venables I had, in the eyes of those concerned, become top of that particular heap. However, when I merged with Tucker, who ran a much larger door firm, I was seen as the new boy in his organisation. Long-standing members of his firm resented me. They felt threatened by a newcomer who had a degree of clout. The fact that I was also introducing people like Steve, Nathan and Thomkins to the mix caused further resentment. Tucker's doormen had their own people who they were earning from. I didn't know they had dealers and thought I was being helpful.

Shortly after Tucker's birthday party, Steve and Thomkins began working at Club UK in Wandsworth, where Tucker ran the security. (Their position had been discussed at Tucker's birthday party.) For the exclusive right to sell drugs in there, they paid Tucker £1,000 per weekend. On average, their return for Friday and Saturday nights was £12,000.

On Christmas Eve 1993, the firm celebrated in style. My brother, Michael, and his wife, Carol, came to a party we were attending in the West End. It was held at one of the most exclusive clubs in the UK at the time. There were long queues of people outside, which we ignored as a matter of course. These events where the firm got together were extraordinary. Because of our connections with door teams, nobody paid to get in anywhere, or for drinks or drugs. In some places, huge bags of cocaine, Special K and Ecstasy were made available to the firm and their associates.

When you looked around the dark room, you were surrounded by 40 or more friends, all 'faces'. The music was so loud it lifted you; you were all one – we had total control. Those in the firm created an atmosphere that demanded respect from other villains. Straight people hardly noticed. On the surface, everyone was friendly, but there was this feeling of power and evil. Tucker felt it, too. Often he would look across a club and smile knowingly. Looking back, we revelled in the atmosphere we created wherever we went. We were living like kings but behaving like animals.

It was a memorable Christmas for me. After the party, we went back to Steve and Nathan's flat in Denmark Court in Surrey Quays, an exclusive development in the south London Docklands. Strewn across the floor, spilling out of a carrier bag, lay more than £20,000, the proceeds of that weekend's drug dealing. They earned so much money, they didn't know how to spend it or where to put it. Unfortunately for Steve and Nathan, it was to be their last lucrative Christmas: their drug-dealing operation was about to come to an abrupt halt.

In March 1994, 20-year-old Kevin Jones collapsed and died in Club UK after taking Ecstasy he had purchased there. It didn't take long before the names of Steve, Nathan and Thomkins were given to police as possible suppliers of the drug that killed Kevin. Instead of raiding their homes and arresting them, the police mounted a surveillance operation in the hope that they could arrest and convict those at the top end of the drug chain. On 6 May 1994, the police pounced and found 1,500 Ecstasy pills in a car parked beneath Steve and Nathan's flat. The car was not registered to either man. Police checks revealed it had, in fact, been reported stolen in Bristol some weeks earlier.

At the same time as the police swooped in London, Dave Thomkins was arrested at his home in Bath. Steve and Nathan were placed under arrest and refused bail, while Thomkins was interviewed and granted bail pending further inquiries. Nathan's girlfriend, an Asian princess named Yasmin, and Steve's girlfriend, a stunning Swede named Ulrika, were also arrested. They told me later that they had refused to answer police questions and so had been granted bail pending further inquiries.

As soon as Dave Thomkins was released, he rang and told me what had happened. I said I would organise a solicitor for Steven and Nathan and that we should meet up for their appearance at Tower Bridge Magistrates' Court. Yasmin and Ulrika also attended the hearing. Steve and Nathan were granted bail on the condition they give a £20,000 surety. They were told they would have to remain in custody until it was paid.

When I told Tucker about the arrests, he began shouting and screaming. He was worried that Steve and Nathan were going to grass on him for taking rent. I told him that there was absolutely no chance of that. Thomkins and I met Yasmin the following day and she gave us £20,000 in cash. We took the money to Leman Street police station in the City, pushed it over the counter and asked for our friends to be released. The officer at the desk was gobsmacked. He didn't know how to proceed, so Thomkins and I were kept waiting for hours while inquiries were made.

We were taken into a room and asked where the money had come from. We told the police a family friend had lent it to us. In the end, the officer said they were going to refuse it. Bail would be granted only if it could be shown that the money had been in an account prior to Steve and Nathan's arrest. After making several frantic phone calls, we found someone who was able to do the necessary and the following morning Steve and Nathan were released on bail.

It was becoming increasingly clear to me that people in the drug trade were operating on borrowed time. To be successful, a drug dealer has to make it known to as many people as possible that they have gear for sale: it's no good them standing in a nightclub with 500 Ecstasy pills in their pockets and keeping the fact to themselves. The more people you tell, the more pills you sell: the trade-off is that the chances of being arrested rise dramatically.

Chapter 4

Back at Raquels a new manager named Mark Combes had taken over
and an agreement was soon reached that the way forward
was to have rave nights. This new music culture that was
sweeping across the country was going to replace the three
hours of chart music and five slow dances at the end of each
night, interrupted at regular intervals by morons trying
to fuck or fight each other, which had been the format at
Raquels for years. There was no place for violence on the
rave scene – all the kids were into the fashionable 'peace
and happiness' thing. To the revellers, Raquels was now
trouble-free. Most of the violence was behind the scenes or
away from the premises.

When word got round about the proposed change
at Raquels, Mark Combes was soon approached by a
promotions team from Southend who were very professional
and very successful. They were, at the time, hiring out a
club in the Southend area that didn't hold enough people to
fulfil the demand they had created. The promotions team
was looking for larger premises. A deal was struck and a
date was set for them to begin.

The following day a man named Mark Murray came
into Raquels and asked to speak to me. He told me that
he sold most of the gear in the clubs around the Basildon
and Southend area and had heard that the promotions team
from Southend was coming into Raquels. He asked me if

we could come to a financial agreement that would allow him to sell drugs exclusively in the club.

I rang Tucker and he asked me to tell Murray that he could have his deal. The 'rent' for operating in the club would depend on the amount of drugs he sold per night. If the club became busy because of the rave nights, then the deal would be adjusted accordingly, making the sale of drugs more lucrative for all involved. For now, both parties agreed to see how things went. It was going to be the door staff's job to ensure there was no trouble from other dealers and also that an early warning of any police presence would be given.

On Friday, 25 July 1994, Raquels opened its doors for the first house and garage night promoted by the team from Southend. It was absolutely packed because this type of event was rare in a violent town like Basildon, where peroxide blondes, cheap drinks and drunken nights were the norm. We kept all those types out and for those not involved in the politics it really was an enjoyable night.

There was no trouble among the customers and the atmosphere in there was fantastic. It's hard to describe. You could feel the music, it was so loud. It was hard to see anything because of the darkness and smoke, but already there was a feeling of unity among the revellers. With the crowds and the house music came a demand for Ecstasy. Raquels was hit by an avalanche of drugs. Local men were quickly recruited by Mark Murray and dealers were everywhere in the club. The demand was being met.

I had now recruited what I considered to be an ideal door. I had doormen who were not bullies. They were friendly and could mix with the people who were entering the club and were not seen as intimidating. Yet if someone wanted trouble, they would get it – and they would regret it. None of the men were from the Basildon area; they came from south and east London, so they weren't impressed by the local men's reputations. They took people how they found them and dealt with them accordingly. Without exception, everybody accepted it.

On the face of it, the police now had a peaceful club. They could divert their attentions elsewhere. The occasional victim was of our own kind and so of little concern to them. Previously, we had endured twice-weekly visits from the constabulary, but we rarely saw them now. We had a club full to capacity with peaceful people. The customers were getting what they wanted and the firm got what it wanted. The lunatics had taken over the asylum.

Another lunatic was making himself at home in rather different surroundings. Pat Tate had secured his favourite gym-orderly job upon his arrival at HMP Spring Hill and had managed to talk officers into letting him train at a local gym. There, Tate met several local girls whom he invited back to the prison. At first, they thought he was joking, but Tate assured them he always meant what he said. Soon Tate and his female entourage were indulging in group sex fuelled by drink and drugs in his cell.

In the same month that Raquels started hosting rave nights, Tate was released from prison. All he possessed was his drug habit and a bad attitude. I call prisons hate factories because all they produce are people full of hatred. Tate came out of prison much that way. He wanted the world to know he was out and he wanted the world to know he was not happy about the way he had been treated. No doubt the prison staff who had encountered Tate were unhappy about the way he had treated them too.

Tony Tucker met Tate quite by chance with Craig Rolfe one morning at a café in Southend. Tate was with a man named Shaun Miller, who knew both Tucker and Rolfe. Tucker warmed to men like Tate; he was the sort of man he deemed 'useful'. Tate was 6 ft 2 in., extremely broad, 18 stone and fearless. He also had a glamorous bit of history. His fight with the police in court and escape on a motorbike were talking points in criminal circles. Tucker invited Tate to a night out and the same evening he became a member of the firm.

I had been made aware of Tate long before his release from prison. A teenage girl who regularly came into Raquels had told me during a conversation that her uncle was in prison and she visited him on a fairly regular basis. Over the following weeks and months, I'd always ask her how her uncle was getting on, let her into the club for nothing and get her the occasional drink. Having been in prison myself, I know how much it means to have your loved ones 'on the outside' taken care of.

When Tate was released he came down to the club to thank me and introduce himself since he had now joined forces with Tucker. He struck me as an extremely likeable person and when he invited me to a party that was being held later that night, I readily accepted. When I arrived, the likeable Pat Tate whom I had met just a few hours earlier had been replaced by a drugged-up, slurring zombie. He was in an alley that ran down the side of the house. His huge frame was propping up a wall. He was sweating so much, vapour was pouring from his head. The cold night air was visibly cooling him down, but his mood was a blazing inferno. He was rambling about people he wanted sorted out and other firms he wanted crushed. I put Tate's rant down to the fact he was celebrating his release and had taken too many drugs, but I was not the only one his behaviour had alarmed.

Tate's arrival was met with resentment by many firm members. A man named Chris Wheatley had returned from America some time before Tate's release. Tucker had latched onto him, becoming a 'close' friend and giving him control of the door of Club Art, one of his clubs in Southend. When Tate was released, however, Tucker dropped Chris as if he didn't exist. He also began to badmouth him to other doormen, casting doubt on his ability and sneering at the way he handled incidents that arose at the club. I really liked Chris and couldn't understand why Tucker behaved the way he did. There was no room for sentiment in the firm, though: Chris had fallen from grace and Pat Tate was to take his place.

Others who had no reason to dislike Tate felt their position was threatened. Few felt comfortable about his appointment because he had a domineering attitude and an explosive temper. Tucker, on the other hand, was loving every minute of it. He enjoyed pitching people against one another. On one occasion a doorman from Chelmsford mentioned in conversation that he thought another doorman named JJ was a police informant. JJ was a good, decent man who had known Tucker for years but that counted for nothing in our firm.

Tucker rang JJ and arranged a meeting with him outside McDonald's in Chelmsford. Then he told the other man that if he thought JJ was a grass, he should confront him and not talk about him behind his back. The accuser was allowed to arm himself with a machete and was taken to the meeting at McDonald's. Fearing he was going to lose face, he accused the unsuspecting JJ of being a grass in front of Tucker. JJ denied it, of course.

'He's just called you a fucking grass,' said Tucker. 'What are you going to do about it? I'd fucking hit him if he said that to me.'

JJ, an unwilling combatant, threw a half-hearted punch and the other man responded by slashing JJ's arm with the machete. JJ fled. You didn't get a P45 in our firm.

One evening, I received a telephone call from Steve and Nathan. They were with Thomkins. They told me they were having trouble with some doormen from Bristol who, seeing them driving round in a BMW and knowing they had a flat in London, wanted to get in on the act. I told them

I would make some phone calls and sort it out. I rang the doormen and told them to leave it out with Steve, Nathan and Thomkins otherwise they would have trouble. I gave them the impression the trio was working for a much bigger operation. We knew the Bristol doormen's names and where to find them. They didn't have a clue who we were or where we were from, which put us in quite a powerful position. The doormen argued that Steve, Nathan and Thomkins were the cause of the trouble, but they said it wasn't worth falling out over and the matter would come to an end.

The next morning, I got a frantic phone call from Steve and Nathan. They said they had been driving through Bath in their BMW when they had been flagged down. They were dragged from the car by two men, who informed them that they were taking the vehicle and keeping it. Steve and Nathan told me they wanted their car back, but they were scared of the thieves.

I said to them that if we were to go down to Bath to recover a car, we would have to go firm-handed because we wouldn't know what we were up against until we got there. I asked them how many men we'd need and they said if I could get ten down there, they would pay us all £300 each. I asked for a contact number for the man who had taken the car and said I'd be down that evening with ten people. I told them to stay out of the way until the matter was resolved.

The man holding the car was called Billy Gillings. He had a reputation in the area as a hard man and had just come out of jail for robbing a security van. I rang Billy and asked him if he had Steve and Nathan's car. He got all shirty at first, so I told him to calm down and listen. I pointed out to him that I knew where he lived and he didn't even know my name. I was coming to Bath to recover the car whatever. I had no particular loyalty to Steve and Nathan and therefore we could come to an agreement. 'Falling out over a BMW is hardly worth it,' I said.

Billy agreed. I told him for recovering the car I was going to be paid £1,000. If he would meet me at Bath railway station and give me the car, I would give him half the money. He would have to tell his friends that we had chased him, assaulted him and taken the car back. We'd both be £500 better off and everyone would be happy.

I rang Steve and Nathan and told them there were ten of us going down to Bath in two cars. They had to ensure that they stayed out of the way until I called them. I drove to Bath on my own and met Billy as arranged. I reminded him of the plot and said that I would meet him there again in an hour's time, but first he would have to give me the car. He agreed.

I phoned Steve and Nathan and drove to meet them. I said there had been a bit of trouble with Billy and so the other people with me had driven out of Bath because they feared the police may be looking for them. I added that I still had to meet them later as they wanted paying. I gave Steve and Nathan their car and they gave me the £3,000.

Thomkins, who had arrived with them, was going mad. He said another man, named Steve Woods, had burgled his house and stolen quite a lot of electrical equipment – televisions, videos, etc. – and covered his children's bedroom floor and walls with excrement. He was under the impression that we were to sort out Steve Woods as well for this money. He claimed that Woods and Gillings were in on it together: Gillings had the car; Woods, he alleged, had done the burglary and given the goods to Gillings to fence.

I told Thomkins it was the first I had heard of it, but if he wanted us to, we would resolve that matter for him. But it wouldn't get done today. Thomkins was adamant he wanted it sorted that night. 'Suit yourself,' I said. I shook hands with Steve and Nathan, jumped into a cab and went to meet Billy. I gave Billy his £500 and kept the £2,500 for myself.

Later that night, I got a call from Thomkins. He told me he couldn't stand the thought of knowing Steve Woods had robbed his house and covered his children's bedroom in excrement and got away with it. I said that Woods hadn't got away with it.

'Too right he hasn't,' he said, 'I've just fucking shot him.' He explained what he had done. After leaving me, he was in a rage. He had gone home and picked up a shotgun. He had gone to Woods's house and put on a balaclava before knocking on the door. Woods's girlfriend answered the door. Thomkins pushed her aside. Woods was in the hallway. It must have been a terrifying sight for him to see a man in a balaclava with a shotgun. Thomkins fired and hit Woods in the upper thigh. He then ran over to Woods, who had collapsed on the floor, put the gun to his head and shouted, 'I want my fucking television back.' Woods's girlfriend was screaming. Thomkins levelled the gun at her head and told her to shut up. Then he made his escape.

I remarked to Thomkins that that kind of behaviour was a bit over the top for the sake of a 14-inch Nicam television. He obviously did not think so. This was becoming the norm for more and more people in these firms. It was all about having front. Thomkins wanted people to know you couldn't take liberties with him.

Now Thomkins had calmed down, he didn't have a clue as to what he was going to do. It wasn't really my problem, but he was associated with us and you have to help your own. I suggested he conceal the weapon, jump in a car and meet me in Basildon as soon as possible. I didn't know if Woods still had Thomkins's television or not. Either way, it didn't really matter: according to the tabloids, everyone who is sent to prison these days gets given their own television anyway, so Thomkins was in luck.

I could have done without Thomkins's problem at that particular time. The police in Basildon, although maintaining their distance, were keeping a very watchful eye on my activities. Whatever, Thomkins was in trouble and I felt obliged to help. I wouldn't be able to keep him at my house because the police often watched those who came and went. I rang Pat, the landlady at a pub called the Owl and Pussycat in Basildon. I had sorted out a bit of trouble for her when she ran a pub in Southend. I asked her if she would put my friend up for the night. Pat asked me what the problem was. It was no good lying, so I told her Thomkins had shot somebody. At first, she was reluctant to help me, which is understandable – she had never even met the man and he had just attempted to murder somebody; the thought of spending the night alone with him must have been quite unnerving – however, in the end, she relented.

I met Thomkins in Basildon in the early hours of the morning and took him to Pat's pub, where he spent the night. We would decide what we were going to do in the morning when he had a clearer picture. The following day we contacted people in Bath to try and find out about Steve Woods's condition. We learned that Thomkins had blasted a large hole in Woods's upper thigh. It was unlikely that he would ever be able to walk properly again. His life was not in danger, but the police were treating it as an attempted murder.

We arranged for people to pick up the gun and dispose of it, and for Thomkins to go and stay with some people in Liverpool for a few days while the dust settled. The dust, unfortunately, in Thomkins's mind, didn't take long to settle. Within a week, Thomkins rang from Liverpool. He told me he had outstayed his welcome and had nowhere else to go. I had a friend in Edinburgh who would put him up, but Thomkins wanted to come back to Basildon. I sorted it out with the landlady at the pub again and he returned.

I knew Pat would not put up our fugitive for ever, so it

was decided that Thomkins's problem in Bath had to be sorted out sooner rather than later. It wasn't going to be easy because of the nature of the offence. Trying to persuade a man who had been shot that the person who had done it was not all that bad and didn't deserve to go to prison was going to take more than tact.

Woods had a bit of form himself, so he knew the score. It meant our task was not impossible. I rang Billy Gillings, the man who had done the deal on Steve and Nathan's car, and asked him if he would mediate and arrange a meeting between myself and Woods. If it made Woods feel safer, he could bring anyone he wished.

Billy went to see Woods and he agreed to meet at Leigh Delamere motorway services near Bristol. Woods insisted that his brother, who was nicknamed Noddy, should accompany him. When he was discharged from hospital I went to the meeting on my own. The Woods brothers and I all sat down at one of the cafeteria tables. Noddy Woods started getting a bit lippy about Thomkins, so I told him in no uncertain terms that we didn't have to sit there and discuss it. I was offering him and his brother a way out. 'If you persist with your lip,' I said, 'you'll get taken out of the game like your brother. I suggest you go and get some tea for us both, while I discuss this with Steve.'

It was important to let him know who was in the driving seat. I told Woods that we didn't normally do deals with people who inform on one of our number to the police but because he had suffered over a rather trivial matter we were making an exception. We were prepared to offer him £20,000 not to make a statement against Thomkins.

Woods said he had already made a statement. I said he would be paid the money if he retracted it. Woods wanted half upfront and half on completion, but I told him 'bollocks'. Our word is our bond. Do your part of the deal and you'll get your dough. He agreed and we went our separate ways. We didn't have any intention of giving him a penny.

A member of the firm named Mark accompanied me to the next meeting. Gillings and Woods met us at an out-of-town location near Bristol. Billy came over to our car and I asked if Woods had retracted his statement. Billy said he wouldn't unless he got half of the money upfront.

'Put Woods in your car and take him down the road,' I said. 'Then tell him to get out. Drive away and don't look back.' Billy asked why. I told him that Woods was going to be shot. Billy said he didn't want any part of it. 'OK. Tell Woods to get in our car because we want to discuss payment with him.'

Billy agreed, but he kept repeating that he didn't want to be involved in any shooting.

Woods came over. 'There's no problem, get in the car,' I said. We drove to a deserted lane. A gun was produced and Woods was told to get out of the car because we didn't want any of his 'shit or blood' messing up our vehicle. Woods was ordered to lie on a grass bank. The gun was put to his head. He was terrified. He had not yet got over being shot six weeks earlier. His whole body was shaking and he was weeping. He was told that the firm did not pay grasses. 'Now you are going to die.'

'I don't want any money, I just don't want any trouble,' he said.

'First you break into our friend's house and rub shit over the walls and now you come and demand £20,000. It doesn't work like that.'

'I'll retract my statement and that will be the end of it,' he said.

He was told that if he didn't, people would come back and he would vanish. The talking was over. Woods went away and within three hours he had retracted his statement. We returned to Basildon and Thomkins contacted a solicitor.

The solicitor said he would check to see if Woods's statement had been retracted. If it had, he would arrange for Thomkins to give himself up the following day. The solicitor was not aware that Woods had been threatened; he thought he had retracted his statement of his own free will.

The next day, I took Thomkins to Barking station in east London and we said our goodbyes. He travelled to Bath, where he gave himself up. What we hadn't counted on was Steve Woods's wife. She had not retracted her statement, so Thomkins was charged with attempted murder, threats to kill and possessing a firearm with the intention of endangering life. He was remanded in custody to await trial.

Obviously a lot of our conversation around that time was about Thomkins. Some liked him, some didn't. Once he was out of the situation, I was told that he had been talking behind my back about me. It was a hammer blow. I had done all I could to help him and yet he had been slagging me off to big himself up. I wasn't happy at all, but our world was overflowing with such people.

I contacted Steve Woods via a third party and told him Thomkins's protection had been removed. Woods and his friends could do as they wished. I went to visit Thomkins in Horfield prison in Bristol with two friends who were going to see him, while he was being held on remand. I told them I wanted to go and see him first. I would only be five minutes. They could wait outside. I went into the visiting room and Thomkins held out his hand. 'All right, mate,' he said.

'You're no fucking mate of mine. You've been slagging me off.'

A prison visiting room isn't the best place to settle one's differences. At that moment, I didn't really care. I went for Thomkins. The prison officers were alerted and Thomkins backed off to where they were. I walked out of the visiting room and have not seen him since. It is a shame because I considered him a good friend. Why he did what he did to me, I will never know. He was later sentenced to ten years' imprisonment for shooting Steve Woods.

With Thomkins, Steve and Nathan out of the picture, Tucker needed to recruit a new gang of drug dealers for Club UK. He telephoned me and asked how Murray was performing at Raquels. I told Tucker that he and his dealers were discreet, efficient and no problem. Tucker asked me to take Murray over to his house for a meeting.

When we arrived, he told Murray that he wanted him to take over the sale of drugs in Club UK. Murray would have to pay £1,200 rent each weekend, but in return, Tucker told him, he could earn in excess of £12,000. Murray stuck out his hand without hesitation. The deal was struck.

For the introduction to Tucker, Murray said he would pay me £500 a week once he started. I would have no further involvement. It was, he said, a drink for doing him a favour. It had been quite a lucrative ten-minute meeting.

In order to make Club UK pay, Murray would have to run a pretty slick operation. He would have to have enough dealers in the club to meet the demand in order to reap the rewards his predecessors had earned. Murray found the going hard. He couldn't earn any money because he couldn't recruit enough dealers. He was selling approximately 500 Ecstasy pills a night, nowhere near enough to reap any benefit. Needless to say Tucker demanded his rent regardless.

By the time Murray had paid for his stock, there wasn't anything left. Each week he remained there, he was simply getting deeper and deeper in debt. He begged Tucker for more time to pay, which he was initially granted, but he was never going to be given the time he needed.

Chapter 5

In January 1990, Steven Ellis had met Pat Tate in Chelmsford prison. Tate had just been extradited from Spain following his rather dramatic escape from Billericay Magistrates' Court. Ellis, known to many as Nipper because of his size, had been remanded in custody to await trial for an allegation of robbery.

Nipper was no stranger to trouble and knew his lack of size was a disadvantage in his dealings with fellow criminals and in an effort to overcome this he began training hard to bulk himself up. Tate, a knowledgeable and competent bodybuilder, agreed to train with Nipper and before long the two had become friends.

In April 1991, the prosecution dropped the robbery charge against Nipper citing lack of evidence and he was subsequently released from Chelmsford prison. Tate had by that time been sentenced to serve ten years' imprisonment for the Happy Eater restaurant robbery. This sentence was later reduced to eight years after he appealed. When Tate was finally released in the summer of 1994, he and Nipper began to hang around together in the pubs and clubs of Essex.

Tate was having problems with his long-term girlfriend, Sarah Saunders, mainly because his years in prison had diluted the love she once had for him. The fact that the couple were living in cramped conditions didn't help their situation, so, in an effort to rectify this and improve relations between them, Tate asked Nipper if he could rent out his flat, a spacious three-bedroom property. Tate assured Nipper that he only needed it for a few weeks because he and Sarah were buying a larger property together. Nipper agreed, but weeks soon turned into months and eventually he resigned himself to the fact that Tate was going nowhere in the foreseeable future.

Tate introduced Nipper to Tony Tucker, whom he described as being a 'great friend'. Tucker in turn introduced Nipper to Craig Rolfe, whom he also described as being a 'great friend'. Tate was constantly telling Nipper how 'brilliant' Tucker was, and Tucker was constantly telling him how 'brilliant' Rolfe was. They made Nipper feel as if he had really landed on his feet by meeting them. He thought he'd found three great mates and believed they would do absolutely anything for him.

Little did Nipper know, that's the way Tucker, Tate and Rolfe treated everybody initially. They would make someone feel as if they were the best friend they ever had. They would use them, then discard them, as if they had never existed. Tucker, Tate and Rolfe's excessive use of drugs began to concern Nipper. When the three men were out of their heads, they were very different to the warm, helpful men Nipper knew and respected.

One evening, Tucker called a drug dealer over to his table in a nightclub and asked the man if he had any cocaine for sale. The dealer smiled, thinking he was making a useful contact, and said he had. Tucker told the man he wanted three grams. When the man put his hand in his pocket and pulled out the drugs, Tucker grabbed him by the throat, slapped him across the face, took the parcel of drugs and told him to fuck off. Nipper was horrified and told Tucker that he was out of order. Tucker, as usual, just laughed.

In another incident, Nipper had been asked by a friend

if he knew anybody who would be interested in purchasing £250,000 worth of stolen traveller's cheques for £60,000. When Nipper mentioned it to Tucker, he said that he and Tate would buy them. Nipper was told to set up the deal and he would be given a 'drink' for doing so. Tate, Tucker, Nipper and four other men went to purchase the cheques at a meeting in a pub in Canning Town. When the man who had the cheques came out of the pub to greet his new business associates, Tate punched him to the ground and began beating him up. Tate made his bloody victim hand over the cheques and the gang walked off laughing. Nipper was mortified because he knew his friend would blame him for setting him up.

Concerned for his safety and disgusted by such behaviour, Nipper began to distance himself from the trio and they soon noted the fact. In an effort to sever all links, Nipper told Tate he needed his flat for himself. Reluctantly, Tate moved back in with his partner. This caused further resentment, and relations between the men began to fester.

The inevitable confrontation came one weekend when Tate, Tucker and Nipper went into a 7-Eleven store in Southend. Nipper threw a bread roll at Tate, who retaliated by throwing a cake at Nipper. The three men were all high spirited and were soon enjoying a full-on food fight in the shop. The male assistant kept telling them to stop, but they just got more and more carried away. Eventually, the assistant had had enough and told them he was going to call the police. Tate pushed the man and then ripped the phone out of the wall, shouting, 'You shouldn't say things like that!' Tucker said they would pay for the damage, but as they were talking, the police arrived. Tucker and Tate walked off down the street and Nipper was left to face the music. It was no big deal for people like them. They thought it was all a big laugh.

The following Sunday, Donna Garwood, Tucker's

teenage mistress, was trying to get in touch with him. She couldn't ring Tucker at home because she knew he would be with Anna Whitehead, his long-term partner. Tate was at home with Sarah, so Garwood couldn't call and ask him to contact Tucker either. Garwood, not for the first time, felt isolated and grew increasingly frustrated.

Tucker had installed Garwood in a small, one-bedroom flat that Tate owned in Basildon so that he effectively had 24-hour access to her. Being just a teenager, Garwood felt lonely and unable to cope when Tucker was not around. In order to try and alleviate the situation, Tate had moved a prostitute he knew named Paula into the flat so Garwood would have company. Paula was 18 and had just come out of prison with a fair amount of emotional baggage, not least her drug problem, but Tate had warmed to her. He used to call her 'Wild Child'. Such were his feelings for Paula, he eventually told her she was no longer allowed to work as a prostitute. Unfortunately for Donna, Paula rarely stayed at the flat.

Desperate to hear from Tucker, Garwood decided to telephone Nipper, who was at home but, unknown to her, asleep in bed. When Garwood asked Nipper, who was annoyed at being woken, if he had seen Tucker, true to form, he was sarcastic. 'He's probably at home giving his old woman one up the arse,' he said. Nipper hadn't said it maliciously. You could never get a straight answer out of him. He was always joking.

Feeling humiliated, Garwood couldn't wait to tell Tucker. When she did finally contact him, Garwood made it sound as though Nipper had said it with some venom. She told Tucker that Nipper had no respect for him.

The next time I saw Tate and Tucker, they didn't mention the phone call. But they did claim that Nipper had grassed them up to the police about the 7-Eleven incident. They said they were going to make him pay.

Tate had retained a key for Nipper's flat after he had been politely asked to leave. Over the next few days, Nipper began to notice that some of his possessions were going missing, despite there being no evidence of a forced entry into his home. Unknown to Nipper, Tucker, Tate and Rolfe were going to his flat when he was not there and helping themselves to items Garwood and Paula required for their flat. When Nipper telephoned Tucker and Tate about the thefts, they denied all knowledge and maintained a friendly attitude towards him. So much so, they attended a party at the flat the following weekend.

When Nipper was tidying up on the Monday evening, he noticed that his kettle, toaster, tea towels, bath towels, iron, even food out of the fridge, were missing. Feeling dejected and the worse for wear following the party, Nipper went back to bed where he remained until the Wednesday morning. When he got up, he surveyed the mess once more and began to tidy up. As he was doing so, his front door opened. Tucker, Rolfe and another man walked in.

'All right, Tone,' Nipper said.

'All right, Nipper, where's my gun?' Tucker replied. Two weeks earlier, Tucker had hidden a silver 9 mm handgun in Nipper's flat for safe keeping.

Nipper went into his bedroom and returned with the gun, which he handed to Tucker. As soon as he did so, Tucker gripped Nipper's face with his left hand, shoved him against the wall and lifted him off the ground. Tucker then rammed the barrel of the gun into Nipper's temple and began screaming, 'You little cunt! You little cunt! Fuck my bird up the arse! Fuck my bird up the arse! I'm going to teach you a lesson.'

After a few seconds, Tucker dragged Nipper into a bedroom and threw him on the bed. Tucker kneeled astride him and kept stabbing the gun in his head, all the while screaming, 'Fuck my bird up the arse, I'm going to show you what this can do!' Tucker's eyes were bulging and he was frothing at the mouth. Tucker was clearly out of his mind on drugs. Nipper told me later, 'All that was going through my mind was "I won't see my sisters grow up" and "I won't see my girlfriend again, I'm going to be killed here."'

Tucker continued to rant incoherently. He snatched Nipper's necklace from him and said he also wanted any jewellery his girlfriend owned. Nipper lay motionless on his back, repeating over and over again, 'OK, Tone. OK, Tone.' Nipper thought he had got through to Tucker because he suddenly stopped and put the gun in his jacket's inside pocket. But when Tucker brought his hand from inside his jacket, the gun had been replaced by a butcher's meat cleaver.

'You have got to pay, you cunt, you have got to pay!' he shouted. 'Your hand or your foot, which one do you want to lose, which one?' Tucker allowed Nipper to sit up on the edge of the bed. Nipper closed his eyes and held out his right hand.

After ten seconds, nothing had happened so Nipper opened his eyes again. Tucker stood before him holding the meat cleaver with a manic grin on his face. He put the weapon in his jacket and walked out of the room.

Foolishly, Nipper jumped up and shouted, 'What the fuck have I done, Tone?'

'Leave it, let him calm down,' the third man in the room said as he grabbed hold of Nipper's arm.

'I've done no wrong, he's a cunt,' Nipper protested, pushing the man away and trying to grab Tucker, who immediately pulled out the cleaver and swung it towards Nipper's head. Rolfe and the other man intervened and bundled Nipper back into the bedroom. Nipper was told that if he wanted to live, he would have to leave it and let Tucker calm down. Nipper slumped on the bed in shock and total disbelief at what had happened. The three men left.

84

Nipper turned to Tate, the man he had once considered a friend, for help. None was forthcoming. When Nipper rang him, he was told, 'You're a cunt. You insulted Tucker's woman and now you are going to die.' Nipper put the phone down and rang Tucker in the hope the drugs had worn off and he had calmed down.

'Have you sorted this out yet, Tone, what is going on?' he asked.

'Sorted what out?' replied Tucker, 'You're a piece of fucking shit.' Nipper asked what it was he had done. 'You told my woman I fuck her up the arse.' Nipper denied he had ever said such a thing to Tucker's partner. 'So you're calling her a fucking liar now, are you?' Tucker replied.

Nipper knew that it was an argument he was never going to win. Tucker told Nipper that he would be visiting him at his home that afternoon to sort it out, and then the phone went dead. Fearing for his life, Nipper went to the Army and Navy store in Southend and purchased a combat knife. He then telephoned a man to whom Tate had introduced him and who sold guns. Nipper told the man he had a problem and he needed a gun as soon as possible. When the man was told who the 'problem' was with, he said he wanted nothing to do with it and put the phone down.

That night, Nipper slept in his car because he was too frightened to return to his home. The next morning, after looking up and down the street for Tucker's, Tate's or Rolfe's cars, he entered his home via the back door. To his horror, he saw that the place had been ransacked. His TV, video, camcorder, microwave and clothing had all been taken. Anything that had been left was slashed, smashed or smeared with excrement. Even the walls and doors had huge holes kicked in them. Nipper was outraged. He rang Tucker and demanded to know where his stuff was.

'I want my fucking stuff back, you wanker. I'm going to fucking kill you,' he shouted.

Tucker didn't reply, he just laughed at Nipper. The line had been crossed now. Nipper knew he had to arm himself because Tucker would kill him when he found him. Nipper rang another man who bought and sold guns for the criminal fraternity, but when he heard who was involved he too declined to have any further involvement. That night, Nipper once more slept in his car, but he was no longer feeling afraid. He was filled with anger and a desire for bloody revenge.

The following morning Nipper was advised by a friend to purchase a bulletproof vest because word had got around that Tucker, Tate and Rolfe were going to shoot him. The friend also mentioned he knew where Nipper could obtain a machine gun, but Nipper could not afford the asking price. The only other weapon available was a .22 revolver that was at best useless for the task in hand, but Nipper purchased it regardless.

On the Friday night, Tate and Rolfe came down to Raquels. After talking about this and that, they asked me if I had seen Nipper. I told them he hadn't been in the club for a while. They said they wanted to check if any of his friends were in, so they walked around inside for about 15 minutes before leaving. Tate rang back later that night. He was obviously out of his head. He asked me if Nipper had turned up. I could hear him banging, as if he was punching a wall. He was shouting, saying that he was going to kill Nipper, and if he couldn't get hold of him, he would do his family. There wasn't a lot I could say to Tate. I just told him I'd pass on the message then put down the phone.

Nipper eventually managed to acquire a double-barrelled shotgun with which he decided to confront his tormentors. Nipper hid in a cupboard in his flat and waited with the shotgun resting on his lap. When nobody had shown up by 3 a.m., he went to lie on what remained of his mattress. At 6 a.m. the phone rang and Nipper answered it.

'Nipper?' Tate whispered.

'Hello, Pat,' Nipper replied, 'why are you doing this to me?'

'Don't worry, mate, it's all sorted out now,' Tate reassured him. 'We are going up to London to sort a bit of business. Give me a call around midday and Tony and I will come around and see you.'

Nipper sensed that he was being set up, but he didn't say anything to alert Tate to the fact. He simply said, 'OK, goodbye,' and then jumped up, grabbed the shotgun and ran out to his car, where he had the .22 revolver. As he reached the car door, Tucker's car screeched to a halt in the road and the occupants jumped out. They did not see Nipper, who had crouched down at the side of his vehicle. Nipper watched as they ran to his home and kicked open the front door. After a few minutes, they walked back out of the flat and Nipper stood up.

Tucker saw Nipper and the shotgun that was pointing towards him and Rolfe. Without saying a word, Tucker and Rolfe turned and ran. Nipper gave chase, but Tucker and Rolfe were in their car and speeding away before he could reach them. He went back into the flat and found a note written in Tate's handwriting. 'Nipper, don't let us lose all respect for you. I'm your mate, we want to help you.'

Nipper telephoned Tate, who asked him why he had laid in wait with a gun. 'Because you lot were going to fucking kill me,' Nipper replied.

'No, we just want to help you,' Tate said.

'So why kick my fucking front door in then?' Nipper asked.

There was no reply. Tate put the phone down. Unbeknown to Nipper and Tate at that time, after running away, Tucker and Rolfe had gone to the police and made a statement about Nipper confronting them with 'what looked like a sawn-off shotgun'. So much for wanting to kill Nipper for being a grass.

The following day, I telephoned Tucker, but, unusually, his number was unobtainable. He was due to hold his birthday party at a snooker hall in Dagenham that Sunday and I had been invited. I was going to tell him that I couldn't make it, but as his phone was unobtainable, I decided to leave it and try later.

At work that night, the doormen were telling me various stories about what was happening regarding Nipper Ellis. I was surprised to hear that even Nipper's father had been threatened. Tate, they said, was going berserk. That was the reason why I didn't fancy going to Tucker's party. I didn't want to listen to hours and hours of what he and Tate were and were not going to do to Nipper. I rang Tucker's house and left a message on the answering machine saying I was unable to go, as I had fallen ill. I later learned that only 20 people had turned up. I was obviously not the only one noticing the decline in Tucker and Tate's behaviour. A year earlier, there had been nearly 200 people at his birthday party.

On Monday, 21 November, I was contacted by two Basildon detectives, who said they needed to see me quite urgently. Because I was the head of security at Raquels I had to maintain some form of civil relations with both the police and the council. My gut instinct was to tell them I had no desire to talk to them, but Tucker and I would then have been out of Raquels and other clubs sooner rather than later, so reluctantly I agreed to see them.

When we met, they asked me if I had heard anything at all about Pat Tate being shot. I said I was not even aware that he had been shot. They also asked me if Craig Rolfe had been up to anything in the past few days and if Tony Tucker drove a black Porsche. I said he didn't, he had a BMW. They asked me if I knew anyone who had a black Porsche. I said I didn't. They said they knew I was mistaken because they had been watching me talking to a man in

88

a black Porsche a few nights earlier. I wasn't being very helpful, so they said I could go and they would be back in touch.

I immediately contacted Tucker. When I told him the police had been asking questions about Tate and Rolfe, he was very keen to hear what they had to say. He asked me to meet him as soon as possible. Less than an hour later, Tucker was telling me what had been going on over the weekend. He denied the problem with Nipper had arisen over comments made to Garwood and insisted it was because Nipper had grassed them up over the 7-Eleven incident. Tucker said on Sunday Tate had been at home getting ready for the birthday party. He was in the bathroom when somebody threw a brick through the window. Tate peered outside and Nipper opened fire from close range with a revolver. Tate put his right arm up to shield his face and the round hit him in the wrist, travelled up his arm and smashed the bones in his elbow. The gunman fled and Tate was taken to hospital. 'When Tate gets out, Nipper's going to die,' Tucker said.

Nipper was finally arrested for the shooting, but the case against him wasn't pursued because the judge ruled that the gun he had on him at the time of his arrest was not the one that was used to shoot Tate. Nipper received relentless death threats from the firm and was told there was a £10,000 contract on his head. His father, stepbrother and two sisters were also threatened. They were warned that Nipper's sister, who was only 15 at the time, would be abducted and raped and her fingers hacked off one by one until Nipper was man enough to face them. Nobody believed the rape allegation: however evil they may have been, Tucker and Tate would not have done that. The jury's out on whether or not someone on the payroll would have harmed Nipper's family. A hit man did go to Nipper's father's home after he had been released. His father looked out through an upstairs window and saw a large man in dark clothing standing at the front door. He opened the window and asked the man what he wanted.

'Is Steve Ellis in?' the man asked.

'No, he doesn't live here any more. Can I help you?'

'No, it's OK. I need to see Steve, I've got something for him.'

Mr Ellis says he clearly saw a gun protruding from the man's jacket pocket as he walked away.

Nipper eventually fled to Dorset where he remained until the trio were executed. He has since returned to Essex and lives a quiet life. When Nipper learned Tucker, Tate and Rolfe had been murdered, he told a reporter that he had danced with joy and he wished he could shake their killer's hand. It was a sentiment many people in Essex shared.

Chapter 6

The weekend Tate was shot was, by anybody's standards, an eventful one. Dramatic as they undoubtedly were, the assaults on Nipper and the shooting of Pat Tate paled into insignificance when compared to another incident that occurred that weekend involving members of the firm and a man from Basildon.

In early 1994, Kevin Whitaker thought he had turned a corner in his life. He had managed to kick his cocaine habit, secure employment and give up dealing in drugs. His long-term girlfriend, Alison, was also expecting their first child. The future, Kevin thought, looked bright. It was certainly very different to what many would have predicted for the former tearaway, who first came to the attention of the police aged 18. Kevin and two friends had drunk a large quantity of cheap lager and Pernod before breaking into Kingswood Junior school in Basildon and starting to fool around with matches. Soon, the half-dozen small fires they had lit had turned the school into an inferno. By the time the flames were brought under control, two classrooms were completely gutted. Kevin was seen fleeing from the scene by a witness and was arrested a few days later. He was acquitted but was sentenced to nine months' youth custody for his part in a series of burglaries that came to light during the arson investigation.

When Kevin was released, he returned home to live with

his parents, Albert and Joan, who did their best to put their wayward son on the straight and narrow. Kevin had a succession of menial jobs, none of which lasted more than a few weeks, and ended up spending most of his time on the dole. Despite his situation, Kevin never appeared to be short of cash or company, albeit of the shady variety.

'His friends would come around all the time,' his father commented at the time. 'They would have mobile phones and expensive cars, but none of them was working. Kevin had also started smoking cannabis. I told him I didn't want it in the house, but he just carried on regardless. Sometimes he would disappear for a few days at a time. And then there were times when we would get phone calls in the middle of the night. People would seem really desperate to get hold of Kevin, but they would only ever leave their first names, no numbers. At the back of my mind, I suspected he was involved in drug dealing, but there didn't seem to be anything we could do.'

Kevin had started dealing in drugs soon after being released from prison. He initially sold cannabis joints to his friends, but soon he was selling ounces of the drug to everyone and anyone and, combined with the dole, was earning enough money to be quite comfortably off. By the early 1990s, as with most, if not all, drug dealers, Kevin's profits from his illicit trade were not being re-invested, they were being shoved up his nose to feed his spiralling cocaine habit. Kevin had many sources for his supply of drugs, but the one he relied upon most was Craig Rolfe.

Just when it looked like Kevin was going to fall into a drug abyss, fortune smiled on him and he started up a relationship with a local girl named Alison Pickton. The relationship was initially rocky because of Kevin's drug habit and his dealing business, and after a few months the couple separated. But when Kevin realised what he had lost, he vowed to change his ways and the couple were reunited. Kevin and Alison got engaged and set up home together in Brackley Crescent, Pitsea. In late 1993, Alison fell pregnant and the couple announced their first child was due the following June. Kevin was really excited about becoming a father. He told his friends that he was never going to touch cocaine again because he wanted to be a good, decent parent. Kevin soon found a steady job working for a man named Ronnie laying crazy paving. His parents really thought their son had finally settled down: he was in a relationship, working and starting a family. They were both overjoyed. But then disaster struck.

In April 1994, Ronnie and Kevin had an argument over little or nothing and Ronnie sacked him. With a baby due within two months, Kevin suddenly found himself unemployed. Desperate for cash to support his family-to-be, he couldn't resist the temptation to go back to his old ways. When he picked up the phone and called his friend Craig Rolfe, it was to be the biggest mistake of his short life.

Rolfe agreed to help Kevin and said he could act as a courier on a cannabis deal between himself, Tucker and a firm from Manchester. It would be Kevin's job to go to Manchester, pick up the drugs and bring them back to Basildon. Kevin agreed. But the deal went horribly wrong for him. When he arrived back in Essex and handed over the drugs, Tucker noted there was a kilo missing. Since Kevin was the courier, the missing kilo was down to him. Tucker wanted to know how he was going to repay the shortfall. Kevin, who knew what was coming, had no means to pay and so he tried his best to avoid Tucker and Rolfe.

Towards the end of September 1994, he arrived out of the blue at his mother's workplace. He pleaded with her to help him because he was in serious trouble. Joan asked him what kind of trouble, but Kevin refused to elaborate. 'I will tell you one day, but I can't at the moment,' he said. Deeply concerned, Joan told her son that he would have to come home with her and explain things to his father.

Kevin's father, Albert, recalled that his son was 'white as a sheet' as he sat down to speak to them. He explained that he desperately needed £2,500 to pay for a kilo of drugs he owed. Albert commented at the time, 'He told us that if he did not get the money, he would kill himself; that he would jump off the multi-storey car park or something. He appeared nervy and in trouble. I'd never seen him in such a state. He'd never talked about committing suicide before, so we knew he was genuinely worried.'

Kevin's parents were due to go on holiday to the Far East in a few days' time, so they agreed to help their son in the hope that he would settle his debt and have no more to do with drugs. They certainly didn't want to go away and leave him alone in such a poor frame of mind. On 30 September, Albert wrote out a cheque for £2,000. Kevin told him to make the cheque payable to Russell Tate, Pat's younger brother. As well as the cheque, Kevin's parents gave him £500 in cash. The very next day, they left for their holiday. When they returned three weeks later, they learned that Kevin and Alison had split up and he was living with a friend named Simon Smith.

While staying at Smith's house, Kevin appeared to slip deeper and deeper into a depression. He never had a bath, or washed himself or his clothes. This was totally out of character in a young man who usually took pride in his appearance. Nobody knows if the separation from his girlfriend and their newly born son was the cause of his demise or if he had other problems on his mind. Everyone agrees that Kevin Whitaker was an extremely troubled man.

On Wednesday, 16 November, Kevin got up from the settee he slept on at Smith's and told his friend he was going out to meet someone. Smith asked him if he wanted a lift, but the offer was declined because Kevin said he was only going to nearby Rectory Road. When Smith got into his own car, he saw Kevin sitting in the passenger seat of a vehicle being driven by Craig Rolfe. Later that afternoon, Smith returned home to find Kevin asleep on the settee. When he awoke, the two talked about what they had been up to that day. Kevin appeared excited. He said Rolfe had agreed to let him get involved in another drug deal that would help him get back on his feet.

The following day, Smith dropped Kevin off at his parents' home. Every afternoon between Thursday and Monday, Alison would go to Kevin's parents' house so that he could see his son. This particular day, Kevin appeared happier than normal. He played with his son and received several phone calls. One of them was from Smith, who arranged to visit Kevin that afternoon. Later that day, Kevin spoke to Smith again, saying he would not be able to see him because he had to meet Craig Rolfe. Smith asked if everything was all right. Kevin assured him it was, adding, 'I'll talk to you when I get back.'

As the evening drew on, Kevin's parents became increasingly concerned about their son's whereabouts. 'Whenever he left us with the baby,' his father later said, 'he would call every hour or so to check everything was OK. This was the first time he had not done so. Kevin had seemed fine when he went out. He did not seem depressed or anything. The split with Alison had upset him but he seemed all right. There had been times in the week since the break that Kevin had been down, but he had not mentioned harming himself nor did he seem particularly stressed since he had asked for the money.'

Having escaped a severe beating over the missing kilo of drugs, Kevin had been careful not to get involved with Rolfe or drugs again. But after the split with his girlfriend, he had decided he would need to find money somewhere to live and get himself back on his feet. Kevin heard about a dilemma Rolfe was facing and, thinking he could help him out, he telephoned him.

A drug dealer had approached Rolfe and asked him to supply 25 kilos of cannabis for £60,000. Rolfe, unable to come up with such a large amount at short notice, stalled the potential buyer and frantically rang around everyone he knew, buying their stock in the hope he could supply the 25 kilos. Kevin knew where he could get his hands on a substantial amount of cannabis on short-term credit; in fact, not only could he get the drugs on credit, he could get them at a discounted rate if he bought in bulk. Kevin thought that this would be his chance to make some quick, easy, much-needed money. He worked out that he would make at least £5,000. Rolfe, however, convinced him he could earn more if he would once again act as a courier for the deal. Foolishly, Kevin agreed. When he met the dealer to purchase the drugs, the cash was taken from him but no drugs were handed over. Kevin had once more been ripped off.

Tucker and Rolfe had turned up for the meeting with Kevin in Rectory Road in Tate's cream-coloured BMW. As soon as Kevin joined Tucker in the back seat of the car, Tucker demanded the money. Terrified and with nowhere to run, Kevin blamed the drug dealer for the loss, so Tucker and Rolfe said they would take him to the man to confront him. The pair of them got increasingly annoyed as they headed down the A127 towards London. It was dawning on them that they weren't going to get their money.

Tucker later told me that he had grabbed Kevin by the throat and said, 'Thieve our gear, would you? If you like drugs that much, have some more of ours.' He had then injected Kevin with cocaine and Special K. He said Kevin had tried in vain to resist; he thought he was going to die, he was absolutely terrified. Kevin sobbed and pleaded with

Tucker and Rolfe to let him go, but they'd just laughed. Kevin was injected three times with massive doses of drugs. Tucker said Kevin had then passed out.

As they reached the Laindon/Dunton turn-off on the A127, Kevin was drifting in and out of consciousness. Rolfe drove up the slip road, as there didn't seem much point in taking him any further, and turned left towards Laindon. Kevin had completely lost consciousness by now. Rolfe pulled up at the Lower Dunton Road and ordered Kevin to get out of the car, but he got no response. Tucker and Rolfe pulled Kevin from the back seat, but he was unable to stand and collapsed on the side of the road.

They got into the car and drove off. Rolfe pulled up a short distance away and looked back. Kevin remained motionless. Tucker told me Rolfe had got out of the car and ran back towards him. He was standing over Kevin, telling him to get up, but still there was no response.

'Fucking leave him,' Tucker said.

'You can't leave him here,' Rolfe replied. It was about six o'clock and everyone was coming out of work.

Rolfe went back to the car, turned it around and drove to where Kevin lay. Tucker got out of the car with Rolfe and they both manhandled Kevin's lifeless body back inside. Rolfe then drove back over the A127 to Dunton Road. Tucker said they looked at Kevin and knew he was dead. They pulled him out of the car and he was put face down in a ditch strewn with bin bags and rubbish.

Nearly 30 hours after Kevin had left home, Albert and Joan's worst fears were realised. Just after 10 p.m. on Friday evening, Detective Sergeant Sharpe and Detective Constable Mayo knocked on their door and asked them to attend the mortuary at Basildon hospital to assist with an identification. After his distraught parents had positively identified Kevin, an autopsy was performed to determine the cause of death. There were no signs of violence but five puncture marks on his right forearm and elbow indicated he might have died after injecting drugs. A toxicology report found Kevin had cocaine, Ecstasy, ketamine and lignocaine in his bloodstream. Each drug was present in high enough concentration to have caused death on its own. The police began interviewing Kevin's friends and family to piece together his whereabouts in the hours leading up to his death.

Considering the amount of drugs detected in his body, it was obvious to the detectives that Kevin could not have made his own way to the secluded spot where his body was found. He could not drive and it was extremely unlikely he would have been able to walk anywhere.

A few days later, Craig Rolfe was arrested and taken to Basildon police station, where he made the following statement: 'I met Whitaker at a friend's flat five years ago. Over the years, I have got to know Kevin fairly well. Having said that, we were not particularly close, although I have done him a few favours in the past. We have only gone out socially together on one occasion and on average I would see him two or three times a month. The last time was on Tuesday, 15 November around mid-afternoon when I saw him standing in a telephone kiosk in Rectory Road, Pitsea, making a telephone call. I stopped the car I was driving and had a conversation for approximately ten to fifteen minutes. I then drove off and left him to walk to Simon Smith's house. The last time I spoke to him was between three and four on Thursday the 17th, when I phoned him from my home address to his father's address. The conversation lasted five minutes and I can recall that he said he had been to see his little boy that morning. At no time did he mention that he was worried about anything or that he had any problems other than the fact that he was a bit down having split up with his girlfriend. That evening, I went out to a friend's. I received a call on Saturday saying that Kevin was dead.'

Rolfe's girlfriend, Diane, who told police that she was with him at the time Kevin had died, supported his story. Diane said they had stayed in together watching a video. Nothing out of the ordinary had happened; it was just a quiet evening in.

The police investigation soon ground to an unsatisfactory halt. It was frustrating for Kevin's parents because they were sure Kevin had been murdered, but the police drew a totally different conclusion. They said the most likely explanation for Kevin's death was that he had accidentally overdosed at a friend's house. The friend, terrified of being implicated, would have put Kevin's body in a car and dumped it where it was later discovered. Joan and Albert could not accept this. A few years earlier, they said, Kevin had been bitten by a dog and they had tried to take him to hospital to have a tetanus injection. Kevin refused point-blank because he said he was terrified of needles. Despite his parents' protests, he never did go. Then there was the fact that the puncture marks were on his right arm and elbow – Kevin was right-handed. For him to inject himself in such a spot would have been extremely difficult if not impossible.

'There is no way my son died by accident. It was murder,' Albert told reporters at the time.

In January 1995, an inquest was held at Chelmsford Coroners' Court. Detective Inspector Peter Hamilton told the court that the police had investigated the possibility that Kevin had been murdered because of a drug deal that had gone wrong, but there had been no hard evidence to support this. The file, he said, had now been closed. The court also heard evidence from Craig Rolfe, who turned up for the hearing with Tucker in tow. Rolfe repeated what he had said in his statement. The coroner, Dr Malcolm Weir, had no choice but to accept what the police had to say about Kevin's death: depressed after the split with his girlfriend and the loss of his job, Kevin had started to inject hard drugs and had accidentally overdosed. An open verdict was recorded. Kevin's parents want to authorities to recognise the fact that their son was murdered. Having him labelled as a depressed junkie who overdosed is deeply upsetting.

Only one person can end Mr and Mrs Whitaker's torment. Everybody else who could assist the police is dead. I hope that person will look at their own child, understand what the Whitakers are going through and come forward. Only then can the Whitakers have closure.

Chapter 7

Tate had lost a lot of flesh from his upper arm after being shot by Nipper, but he remained in good spirits as he lay in his hospital bed. The firm made sure of that. Each evening, they would gather around him, listening to blaring house music, taking drugs and generally having a party. The other patients complained bitterly about the noise and bad language, and so Tate was soon moved to a private room.

When Sarah, Tate's long-suffering partner, would take their son, Jordan, to visit him, the nurses used to say to her, 'What's a nice girl like you doing with someone like that? As soon as you walk out with your little boy he has girls sitting on his bed.' Embarrassed, Saunders made her excuses to Tate and stopped visiting him.

A cocktail of prescribed and non-prescription drugs had made Tate paranoid. He would ramble incoherently about setting up Nipper so that he could kill him. It was obvious to everybody present that Tate was troubled and embarrassed by the fact that Nipper had not only stood up to him but also fought back. In his paranoid and confused state, Tate would think that Nipper was coming to the hospital to finish him off and so he asked Tucker to give him a firearm to keep in his bed. He was supplied with a handgun, which he hid under his pillow.

Before Nipper had gone on the run, he had telephoned Tucker and left a message on his voicemail. 'Hey you, you cunt,' he said, 'this is Steve Ellis. I've fucking just shot Pat Tate and you're next. Now fucking leave my family alone, you fucking wanker.'

Tate advised Tucker to phone Nipper and say there was no need for any more violence. Tucker was to tell Nipper that Tate wanted him to visit him in hospital so that they could resolve their differences. Nipper was no fool, he sensed that he was being lured to his death and refused to go anywhere near Tate or Tucker. Tate's intention had been to blast Nipper in the head when he walked up to his bed. The gun would then be taken away from the crime scene by another firm member and destroyed. Tate would then tell the police that a hit man had shot Nipper and fled.

It was while at Tate's bedside that I first met Darren Nicholls, the man Tate had met in prison and who considered himself a bit of a face in the drugs world. Nicholls had been released from prison on 17 May 1994. Despite ringing all of his 'friends' to announce his release, not one of them took him up on his request to give 'the big drug baron' a lift back to his home in Braintree, Essex. Feeling humiliated and desperate, Nicholls telephoned Jack Whomes and pleaded with him to give him a lift. Never one to refuse anybody in need, Jack agreed. When Jack asked Nicholls why none of his friends and family had met him out of prison, Nicholls told him that he hadn't informed them of his release because he wanted to surprise them.

In an effort to help Nicholls return to the straight and narrow, his mum had pestered his brother, Graham, to employ him as a labourer. Graham had a landscape gardening business and he agreed to let Darren join him. The venture was doomed from the start. The brothers argued constantly and they parted company after only two weeks. Nicholls then tried to set up his own business, but he could not attract any customers as nobody seemed to trust him. Another brother, Jonathan, offered him a job, but his wife and father-in-law objected to the proposed partnership because they did not want their family to have anything to do with him. After several heated arguments, Jonathan withdrew his offer.

Finally, Nicholls managed to secure employment as an electrician with a friend of his named Ricky Snell, who had his own electrical business. The hours were long and the pay was poor, so Nicholls began selling cannabis around Braintree to subsidise his income.

Since being released from prison, Steele and Jack Whomes had visited each other regularly. Jack would take a mechanical problem he had to Steele and Steele would do likewise. John Whomes remembers their conversations about mechanical matters as boring him 'to the brink of suicide'.

One afternoon, Nicholls turned up at Whomes's yard with his wife Sandra and their children. He told Jack he had 'been passing' and had decided to pop in to say hello. Jack and John were taking a speedboat they owned down to Felixstowe, so they invited Nicholls and his family to join them. Jack and John were keen sportsmen who enjoyed water skiing, parascending and diving. Nicholls said he would love to try it and they all spent the day together on the boat in which, John recalled, Nicholls appeared to take a great interest. 'He kept asking Jack how it could be navigated at night and what speed it could do. Jack thought nothing of Nicholls's questions and answered them the best he could.'

Around the same time, Nicholls heard on the grapevine that Tate had been shot and he thought it would be in his interest to contact him. In prison, Tate had been the man to arrange things. Nicholls was sure Tate would be able to help him expand his drug-dealing business by selling him cheaper stock and introducing him to more customers. Nicholls rang Mick Steele and asked him if he had a contact number for the man he had once described as a 'great bloke'.

When Nicholls finally got through to Tate, he learned he was in Basildon hospital. Tate sounded pleased to hear from him, and so Nicholls arranged a visit the very next day. When he arrived at the hospital, he was carrying four bottles of lager, which he said were a 'well done for not being dead' present. Within a minute of being in Tate's company, Nicholls realised the 'great bloke' he had met in prison was no more. An attractive teenager named Lisa was sitting on the bed and Tate asked Nicholls if he wanted her to perform oral sex for him.

'She's just here to give me a blowjob, so I don't have to trouble Sarah when she comes to visit me,' Tate said. 'Lisa doesn't mind, she does it for a living; she's fucking good at it too,' he laughed. To emphasise the power he had over this 17-year-old girl, Tate started ordering her about, telling her to sort his pillows out, sending her to fetch drinks and generally treating her like a servant. Nicholls was embarrassed and changed the subject by asking Tate if he could supply drugs to a friend of his. Tate, always one to relish the prospect of making money, began to reel off what and how much was available. 'I can get fucking truckloads. I can get the lot: Ecstasy, speed, cocaine, cannabis. Tell him, no matter how much he needs I can get it. I'm the man.' I could see Nicholls was regretting visiting Tate, who was making it clear he considered Nicholls 'nothing more than small-time'.

'What you after, then, Darren?' Tate said laughing. 'A joint? We tend to deal in lorry loads.'

Tate was enjoying every minute of ridiculing Nicholls. Though Nicholls was seething with anger, he knew he couldn't say anything because he didn't want to upset Tate or his friends, who were gathered around the bed. He left eventually, looking like a scolded child.

Within a couple of days, a nurse discovered Tate's gun while making up his bed. She contacted the police and Tate was arrested. Because he was still out on licence for his robbery sentence, he was automatically returned to prison for being in possession of a firearm, as this broke his parole conditions.

Tate was not the only firm member with problems. Rolfe too was experiencing difficulties. His partner, Diane, had told him that she had had enough of his drug habit and drug deals, and she and their daughter moved out of their home. About three weeks later, Diane returned after Rolfe promised her he was going to make an effort to kick his drug habit. Diane believed him and the couple took their daughter away on holiday to the Norfolk Broads for a week. When they returned, Rolfe did have one lapse back into the use of cocaine, but generally he did try hard to stick to his promise. Rolfe went out most weekends and Diane guessed he took small amounts of cocaine and used Ecstasy but not on the scale that he had done. It seemed the couple had reached a happy medium.

With Tate in prison and Rolfe off drugs, normality began to return to life within the firm. Perhaps 'normality' is the wrong word to describe debt collection, punishment beatings, the supply of controlled drugs and robbery but that was 'normality' to its members. Conflict with other gangs or individuals was minimal and rarely descended to the use of firearms – when Tate had been out, every incident had been settled with the threat of guns or murder. This period of normality was not to last; in fact, it turned out to be the calm before the storm.

On 31 October 1995, Pat Tate was released from Whitemoor prison. In his absence trade had been very good at Raquels. Tucker's drug dealers had capitalised on the trouble-free environment and he had done very well out of it. So much so, in fact, he had been able to purchase Brynmount Lodge, a luxury hacienda-style bungalow with stables on the outskirts of Basildon with stunning views of the countryside.

To celebrate the success of the club, the promoters held a party at the Cumberland Hotel in Southend and we were all invited. It was an excellent do. Tucker, Tate and Rolfe were there. From the excited look on Rolfe's face it was clear that his promises to stop using or dealing drugs were about to come to an end. He idolised Tate and if his hero asked him to do something, I knew he would do it. The boys were back in town.

At the party, everybody was talking about an article that had appeared in the local papers. Half a million pounds' worth of cannabis had been found in a farmer's pond near a village called Rettendon. It was believed that the 336 lbs of cannabis wrapped in 53 different plastic parcels about the size of video tapes had been dropped from a low-flying aircraft. Instead of the drugs landing in the field, they had landed in a pond and the dealers had been unable to find them.

A farmer named Yan Haustrup found one parcel while cutting his hedges. He didn't know what it was and threw it on a fire. He said he then found another one near the pond and contacted the police. Divers recovered the haul. Tucker and Tate were saying what an idiot the man was to throw it on the fire and then hand over £500,000 worth of gear to the police. Tate thought it was worth looking to see if any of the shipment had been missed. He asked me to get in the car with him and go straight to Rettendon, but I declined – I knew it was the drugs talking. Rettendon village consisted of a roundabout, a church, a post office and probably 50 or so houses. There wasn't anything else there. We were hardly going to scour the fields after the police had crawled all over them.

But Tate kept on about it. He couldn't believe that someone could be that honest and hand over anything to the police of that much value. Tucker said he was going to find out who the drugs belonged to. He didn't like the idea of people trading on his manor if he wasn't getting a slice of the profit. He also knew that as the drugs had been lost, there would be a replacement shipment arriving soon.

Within a short time of arriving at the party, Tate's excessive drug taking had left him out of his mind. He was boasting about the prostitution business he was going to build across London and the South-east. He said he was also going to flood clubs and pubs with drugs he was going to import from abroad. Rival firms that dared to threaten us would be smashed. Anybody who could be bothered to listen to Tate would have thought he was on the way to the top of the criminal heap. But in reality, he was barely scraping the barrel.

Beneath his tough exterior, things were not going well for Tate. He realised that he had become addicted to heroin. The drugs were now controlling him, rather than him controlling his use of them. Tate knew that if Sarah found out, she would sever all links with him and that would mean he would not be able to see his son.

Tate had been to see his brother Russell and had admitted he had a problem, but swore him to secrecy. Russell decided that the only way his brother would get help was if he was open about the fact he had a problem. Fearing for Tate's physical and mental health, Russell had told Sarah. He asked her to help her partner, so she took him to see a drug rehabilitation expert-cum-psychiatrist in Southend, thinking that it would help him. To Sarah's horror, Tate sat with the man for an hour and came out laughing. He told Sarah he had been talking to the man about how to take different drugs and the expert had seemed impressed he knew so much about them.

Undeterred, Sarah tried in vain to help Tate get out of the mess he was in. She wanted the relationship to work, but Tate liked the debauched life he was living too much. Sarah preferred to stay at home with their son, but Tate wanted to go out with Tucker and Rolfe and have a good time. She even tried going out with them a couple of times, so she could keep her eye on Tate, but his friends were not her sort of people. She made excuses whenever he invited her out again. It wasn't a problem for Tate, he just replaced Sarah with one of the many prostitutes he had working for him.

When the clubs closed and the drugs wore off, Tate would briefly return to reality. He would turn up at his bungalow in Gordon Road, where Sarah was living, and sit and cry. He would say that he was sorry and he was not going to be like that any more. He would promise Sarah that he was going to change, get help and go back to how he used to be before he was sent to prison. Sarah, wanting to believe him, would allow him to stay, but the very next day Tate's phone would ring and shortly afterwards Tucker and Rolfe would be knocking at the door to take him away. The rows between Sarah and Tate intensified and eventually, in a drug-induced rage, Tate threw Sarah out.

Sarah telephoned the boyfriend of her closest friend, who lived nearby, and asked if she could stay with him that night. The man drove round to Tate's, who had since gone out, helped Sarah collect her possessions and drove her back to his home. When Tate heard about the man picking up Sarah, he immediately telephoned Tucker and Rolfe and asked them to meet him. Moments later, Tucker and Rolfe pulled up outside Tate's bungalow. Tate was insane with rage. He told Tucker and Rolfe that the man who had moved Sarah out of his house was responsible for the separation and he was convinced the man was sleeping with her. Tate got in the car, Rolfe slammed it into gear and they sped off in search of the man. It didn't take them long to find him. He was walking along the street totally unaware of the impending danger. The car containing the trio pulled up behind him. Tucker and Tate jumped out and bundled the terrified man into the car. Rolfe was ordered to drive back to Tate's home. Once inside, Tate produced a combat knife and threatened to cut the man's throat.

Tucker, recalling the way he and Rolfe had murdered Kevin Whitaker, had a better idea. 'Make the cunt do coke, Pat,' Tucker hissed. 'Make the cunt do coke.' Rolfe prepared six generous lines of cocaine and Tate ordered the man to snort them. The man was sobbing, begging Tate not to cut him with the knife. Tate told him that if he didn't comply, he would cut his throat. The man, who was on his knees, leant over the coffee table and started snorting the cocaine. When he had finished, Rolfe prepared more lines and the man was ordered to snort those. This continued until eventually the man passed out.

But his ordeal was far from over. They stripped him naked and began burning his body with lighted cigarettes in an effort to wake him up. When he eventually did, they forced him to snort more cocaine until he passed out again. Once again, he was burnt until he came round. Fortunately for him, they ran out of cocaine. Tate grabbed him by the hair and dragged him out of the house, kicking him as he and the others went. He opened the boot of his car and Tucker helped him put the man inside. Rolfe was told to clean up the blood in the house and Tucker and Tate drove to where the man lived. When they arrived, they reversed onto his drive and dumped his naked body in the garden. His girlfriend found him rolling around the front room of their home some hours later. He had so much cocaine lodged in his nose he was having difficulty breathing. He was gasping for air through his mouth, crying and in a state of total bewilderment. He did not know who she was, who he was or where he was. His girlfriend called an ambulance and after being seen at the hospital he was transferred to a psychiatric unit where he remained for three days. Tucker, Tate and Rolfe had completely broken him. When the man was released, he refused even to talk to the police, let alone press charges.

Word soon reached Tucker that the drugs that had been found in the pond at Rettendon had been destined for a heavy firm from Canning Town in east London. Tucker and Tate approached those concerned and said they were interested in purchasing any future shipments. The Canning Town firm told Tucker and Tate that they were due to receive a replacement drop soon and they would keep them informed so a deal could be struck when it arrived.

Tucker and Tate had a better idea – they were going to rob it. They telephoned me and we met in the car park outside the entrance to Accident and Emergency at Basildon hospital, a place where we often met. Tucker said they wanted me to act as a backup driver on a scam they were pulling off shortly. They had arranged to intercept a large shipment of drugs. They had done this type of thing loads of times before but, they said, this was different. This was the big one.

Before Tucker and Tate's suicidal dive into excessive drug use, they had been my friends. The drugs had turned their brains into porridge and they were oblivious to any danger. Tate was driving on Tucker with his constant talk of riches. I warned Tucker to be careful, but as usual he just laughed and turned my advice into ridicule.

'Nobody can fucking touch us,' he boasted. 'This is money for nothing.'

'That may well be the case,' I replied, 'but I can't do it because the police are watching me. I've got to keep my head down.'

Tucker looked at Tate and rolled his eyes, and the pair walked off. As I watched them swagger across the car park, I knew our firm was reaching the end of its reign. Tucker and Tate would either get locked up for killing somebody or they would be killed themselves. Robbery, drugs and murder were all they ever talked about. They thought they were invincible.

On a morbid high because he had got away with the murder of Kevin Whitaker, Tucker decided on a whim to kill JJ, the man he had lured into a confrontation in Chelmsford.

Tucker had known him for years, however, his drug-induced paranoia had turned him against JJ. Unsure that he could take him on alone, Tucker had turned Carlton Leach and a number of other friends and associates against JJ by saying he now knew for sure he had been giving information to the police. One drug-crazed night, Tucker, Tate, Rolfe and a fourth man went to Epping Forest Country Club with the intention of carrying out Tucker's murderous plan. They filled two syringes with a cocktail of drugs they called 'champagne'. A third was plunged into Rolfe's vein so blood could be extracted. This was then topped up with pure heroin, which they shook so it resembled the contents of the other two syringes. The plan was to get JJ in the car, let him see Tucker and Tate injecting the 'champagne' and then offer him the syringe full of pure heroin. If he refused, they intended to jab him with it. If that failed, the fourth man, who was sitting in the back of the car, had agreed he would shoot JJ in the head. When they arrived at Epping, they found out that Carlton Leach, who knew nothing of the murder plot, had arrived there earlier with his firm and JJ had decided it would be best to leave.

Back in Basildon that night, Tate was so drugged out of his mind and hyped up by the thought of killing somebody he had tried to shoot Rolfe. Tate's aim was poor and Rolfe had fled in a state of sheer terror. The following day, Tucker and Tate were laughing about it, saying Rolfe had been so scared he'd climbed out of a window to escape. The pair later told him to forget about it, it wasn't personal – Tate was just hallucinating. Everybody knew it wasn't right, whatever Tate's excuse. Murder, it seemed, was now an acceptable party trick. A meaningless joke that the victim shouldn't take personally.

Chapter 8

There was plenty of money to be made for everyone in the drug world – but plenty was never going to be enough for Patrick Tate. However much money Tate earned, he would always want that little bit more.

As soon as he had been released in 1995 he'd started talking about importing drugs from Holland. Most of the people he approached to assist him made their excuses and declined, but one person was extremely enthusiastic. Darren Nicholls needed money. Darren Nicholls wanted to be a somebody. And Darren Nicholls craved to be associated with his hero, big Pat Tate. The one thing both men lacked when they decided to join forces was money.

Tate, as usual, had a solution. He approached Tucker and Rolfe, shady car dealers, villains and dodgy businessmen to put up the cash to import large shipments of cannabis from Amsterdam. He assured them that however much they invested, they would get a good return within ten days. One evening, Tate telephoned me and asked me what I was up to. I had nothing planned.

'Give me a lift, Bernie,' he said, 'I've not got a motor at the moment and I need to go over the bridge to see a mate.' Over the bridge was a reference to the QE2 Bridge that separates Essex from Kent.

'Look, Pat,' I replied, 'I don't mind giving you a lift, but I need to be back at a reasonable hour, is that agreed?'

Half an hour later, Tate and I were driving down the A13 towards the M25, which we would join and then cross over to Kent via the bridge.

'Where we going then, Pat?' I asked.

'Near Brands Hatch racetrack. My mate lives there,' he replied. Tate didn't elaborate, so I knew he didn't wish to discuss 'his mate'.

We spent the 40-minute journey talking about Raquels and the various characters who went in there. We laughed together about some of them and for a short time the old Tate who everyone spoke so warmly about was back. After we crossed the bridge we continued along the M25 until we reached the A20 exit. Tate told me to leave the motorway and head for West Kingsdown. After about ten minutes, Tate pointed to a pub coming up on our right and said, 'We have to meet him in here.'

We sat in the corner of the lounge, Tate with an orange juice and me with a Coke. Tate began laughing, saying, 'I bet that barmaid thinks we are a couple of queers, sitting here together sipping soft drinks.' Every few minutes, Tate would get up and look out of the window and on to the car park. 'He's fucking late,' he kept repeating, 'but he will get here.'

It sounded to me like Tate wasn't sure if his friend would turn up, so I reminded him I wanted to be back in Essex at a reasonable time. After half an hour, I said, 'Look, Pat, he isn't going to show. Let's call it a day.'

'He will, he will,' Tate insisted. 'There is no way that he will let me down.'

Ten minutes later, Tate's friend walked into the pub. I recognised him immediately. It was one of Britain's most infamous villains, Kenny Noye. In January 1985, Noye had been acquitted of the murder of Detective Constable John Fordham, who had been deployed to keep him under surveillance because he was suspected of being involved with an armed gang that had stolen £26 million worth of gold from a warehouse at Heathrow Airport two years earlier. The robbery became known as the Brinks Mat robbery. DC Fordham and his colleagues, dressed in balaclavas and dark clothing, were on Noye's property one night watching his house. Noye saw DC Fordham crouching in the bushes, assumed he was a villain up to no good and confronted him. A struggle ensued in which Noye, who was carrying a torch and a knife, was being overpowered, so he repeatedly plunged the knife into DC Fordham. When the struggle ended, Noye summoned help. Moments later, the area was swarming with police. DC Fordham died of his injuries. Noye was charged with murder but pleaded not guilty, saying he had acted in self-defence.

The fact Noye was acquitted of murder left a very bitter taste in many officers' mouths. Shortly afterwards, Noye was imprisoned for 14 years for his part in the Brinks Mat heist. When the jury announced their guilty verdict, Noye turned to them and said, 'I hope you all die of cancer.' It was while serving this sentence that he had met Tate. Noye was gym orderly at HMP Swaleside in Kent and when Tate arrived there the pair had become friends.

Tate expected Noye to sit down with us and have a drink, but he made it clear he did not intend to hang around. He took a canvas satchel out of his coat and handed it to Tate. 'You'll find it's all there, Pat,' he said. 'Gotta go, catch you later.' With that, Noye turned and walked out of the door. I could see Tate felt let down. When we got in the car to drive home, Tate was unusually silent. I asked him if everything was OK.

'Yes, sure,' he said. 'I just don't like people who think they can treat me like a mug. That geezer's invested a bit of money in my business – he can fuck himself if he thinks he's getting it back.' And that was that; Tate never mentioned Kenneth Noye, his money or the meeting again.

Darren Nicholls had no such influence over people nor did he have affluent friends: he was going to contribute to the operation by travelling to Holland and purchasing the drugs. He would then use 'suicide jockeys' he had recruited to bring the drugs into the country. Suicide jockeys were people obviously desperate for money, who were prepared to drive cars laden with drugs from the Continent to England for between £6,000 and £8,000 a trip. Nicholls assured Tate that two out of three cars would get through Customs without being caught – more than enough profit to cover the occasional loss. Tate didn't care how many got caught because he was not even risking his own money. He felt he couldn't lose.

Tate, Tucker, Rolfe and the syndicate managed to raise £124,000. On 6 November, this was given to Nicholls in a holdall. He and one of his sidekicks then left for Harwich to catch the ferry. When they arrived, Nicholls got right into his gangster role. He insisted that he would purchase the tickets, he would carry the bag of cash through Customs and his 'mate' would have to keep a discreet distance from him at all times. He obviously did not realise that all he was doing was leaving a paper trail of evidence with his name stamped all over it.

Nicholls really thought he had arrived in the big-time. He told his associate to remain in their cabin with the money while he spent the journey in the bar and the casino, where he lost most of the spare cash he had. When they arrived in Holland, Nicholls carried the syndicate's cash through Dutch Customs and booked the train tickets, again in his own name. Upon arrival in Amsterdam, Nicholls's bravado began to falter. He had no idea if he was going to be robbed or even murdered by the drug dealers he was about to meet, so he told his friend it was his turn to carry the bag. Nicholls made his way to a bar called Stone's Café, where he had been told he could purchase some grass. The dealer, a man named Harris, told Nicholls there was no grass available, but he could supply him with cannabis resin. Harris switched on the television and searched Teletext for the current exchange rate. He tapped figures into his calculator before telling Nicholls he could sell him the resin at £1,125 per kilo, roughly half of what it would sell for in England. Nicholls stuck out his hand: the deal was done.

Harris, Nicholls and his friend took a taxi over to Europcar, where Nicholls had pre-booked a Toledo. Nicholls completed the necessary paperwork and handed over his credit card. The assistant swiped it through the machine, but it was declined. Harris knew at once that he was dealing with a fool. Embarrassed, Nicholls asked Harris if he could use his phone.

The three men went back to the bar and Nicholls called his bank, the TSB in Braintree. Nicholls was told that he had exceeded his £250 limit and they were not prepared to extend it. He was advised to contact somebody in England who could go into a TSB bank for him and deposit further funds. Nicholls telephoned his wife, who spent an hour running around, trying to borrow money from people. Eventually, she managed to get £300, which she deposited at the bank. Harris called another taxi and the three men went over to the Europcar depot.

As the taxi drove off, Nicholls realised he had left his luggage in the boot and had to run after the taxi, waving his arms and shouting until it stopped. Harris was beginning to regret the moment he had set eyes on Nicholls; he certainly wasn't the type of man he wanted to do regular business with. Nicholls finally managed to hire the car and was told by Harris to park it around the corner from the bar and await delivery of the drugs. Ten minutes later, Harris and another man appeared carrying large cardboard boxes. There were five in total and they were placed in the boot. Nicholls drove away and met up with his suicide jockeys, who were going to bring the drugs back to England. On this occasion, there were two of them. One vehicle was loaded with two boxes, the other carried three. Nicholls's friend was ordered to travel back with the driver whose car carried the three boxes to ensure the haul was safe.

His work finished, Nicholls drove back into the centre of Amsterdam and returned the hire car. He then booked into the Delta Hotel before returning to Stone's Café, where he drank himself into a stupor. Nicholls should have delayed any celebrations until the drugs were safely back in England and had been examined. Harris, who had dealt with heavyweight drug dealers for years, was the man who should have been celebrating. He had ensured Nicholls wouldn't be dealing drugs for much longer and it was unlikely there would be any comeback on him.

Back in Basildon, Tate was also celebrating the success of his first major drug importation. The £124,000 he had given to Nicholls was going to be turned into almost £250,000 overnight. He thought that if he could do a drug run twice a month, he would be a millionaire by Christmas. If any of the investors who had given Tate money honestly believed they were going to get it back, they must have been mad. It just wasn't the done thing in Tate's world. A kindness was a weakness, an investor a fool. Even Noye, a man few, if any, would mess with, was due to be knocked. Tate assumed he had the right to take anybody's money or possessions, including those of his friends.

Tate didn't have a car of his own so had borrowed Tucker's black Porsche. He had arranged to take a young girl named Lizzie Fletcher out clubbing in Southend as part of his celebration party. Throughout the day, he had been taking large amounts of cocaine, Ecstasy and Special K. High on drugs and high on the thought of becoming rich, the inevitable happened. Tate misjudged a mini-roundabout on the edge of the A127 and converted Tucker's gleaming Porsche into a heap of twisted scrap. In the early hours of the morning, Tucker was woken by the sound of his phone ringing.

'This had better be good,' he told the caller without even asking who it was.

'It's me, Pat,' said Tate. 'I'm sorry to have to tell you this, but I've totalled your fucking motor. Don't worry, though, Tone, I will pay for it.' Tucker remained silent. 'I've been nicked,' Tate explained. 'They think I stole your car.' Tate, still out of his mind on drugs, began to laugh uncontrollably. 'They're also going to do me for no insurance and driving under the influence. You couldn't come and give me a lift home could you, Tone?'

Tucker put the phone down and rang Craig Rolfe. 'That silly bastard Tate has wrote my car off,' Tucker ranted. 'He was showing off to some silly little tart. I need you to go down to Southend police station and pick him up.'

Tucker didn't give Rolfe time to reply. He slammed down the phone and rolled over in his bed. Rolfe roused his girlfriend Diane and informed her that they had to go to Southend to pick up Tate.

After the couple had secured Tate's release they were both surprised by his demeanour. They had expected him to be remorseful about Tucker's car and thankful that they had got up in the middle of the night to help him out. They couldn't have been more wrong. As soon as Tate got in the car, he wanted to know if Rolfe had any cocaine or Ecstasy on him. When Rolfe said he hadn't, Tate insisted they go round to a dealer's house to get some. Diane objected and said that she and Rolfe were going straight home. Tate exploded into a fit of rage. He began punching the dashboard and screaming that he was going to have a good time regardless of what they wanted. Then, almost immediately, Tate seemed to calm down. He began telling

Diane that he had loads of big drug deals in place and he was going to make Rolfe rich. Diane just looked at Tate and nodded in agreement.

The following morning, Tucker got out of bed in a foul mood. A man who had been paid to fit the kitchen at his home had the misfortune to telephone soon after he had woken up. 'Get around here now, Jeff,' Tucker screamed down the phone. 'There's a problem with this fucking kitchen you fitted.'

The man, who knew Tucker well, assured him that any problem would be rectified without charge; there was no need to be aggressive. He would come straight round. When Jeff arrived, Tucker grabbed him by the throat and dragged him through the house into the kitchen.

'See this! See fucking that!' Tucker shouted, as he pointed to minor faults. 'I've fucking told you to fix them and you keep mugging me off. You treat me like some sort of fucking dog, now I'll treat you like a dog until you learn some manners.'

Jeff was slapped and punched and dragged out to the back of the house where Tucker's Alsatian dogs were kept in a kennel. Tucker opened the kennel door and shoved Jeff inside. 'Stay in there with the fucking dogs until I decide you can come out.' Jeff lay whimpering next to two Alsatians. He was covered in their urine and faeces, but he did not dare move until Tucker released him the following day.

The morning after the accident, Tate got up and went to see an old friend, ex-Metropolitan policeman Barry Dorman. The pair had met in the '70s at the various car auctions that were held around London and Essex and had soon become friends. Tate, despite his age, 19 or 20 years old at that time, owned his own car front on London Road in Southend. Dorman had left the police service by this time and, although he was working full time, he subsidised his income buying and selling second-hand cars. In 1984,

Dorman was involved in a very serious car accident and as a result of his injuries had to give up work. The following year, as he made a slow recovery, Tate urged Dorman to go into the second-hand-car trade full time.

Through Tate, Dorman managed to rent a forecourt located at the junction of the old A13 and One Tree Hill in Basildon and it was here Tate arrived that morning, asking his old friend for a favour. He told Dorman that he had crashed his friend's Porsche and it had been extensively damaged.

'Could you get it fixed up for me, please, Barry?' Tate asked. 'He's a really good friend and I've given him the hump.'

Dorman agreed and gave his daughter the time-consuming task of trying to locate cheap second-hand spares for the repair. Dorman also arranged for quotes to carry out the bodywork. As a result of the work that needed doing on the Porsche, Dorman was in touch virtually every day with either Tate, Tucker or both – the majority of the time they were together and were accompanied by Rolfe. At that time, Dorman had a blue Range Rover 3.5 Vogue SE on his forecourt that he had recently taken as a part exchange. As Tucker was now also without a vehicle, he and Tate showed interest in purchasing the Range Rover, which Dorman had for sale at £10,995. After some negotiation, Dorman agreed to sell it to them for £9,800.

Dorman knew that neither Tate nor Tucker would be able to get finance on the vehicle. When he pointed this out, Tucker said that his friend would be buying it on his behalf, but he would be using it. Dorman agreed to accept a £2,000 deposit and put the remainder on finance. A friend of Tucker's named Peter Cuthbert visited Dorman's site and provided sufficient details for him to complete the finance agreement. They then took the keys from Dorman and drove away the vehicle. Little did they know they had just invested in the perfect vehicle to assist their would-be assassins. If Tate had not crashed Tucker's Porsche, they would still have been driving around in it three or four weeks later. A Porsche would never have made it down the rough, potholed farm track at Rettendon because the chassis sits too low to the ground. Only a Range Rover or similar 4x4 could have possibly delivered them to the spot where they were to meet their deaths.

The same morning, after Nicholls had awoken from his drunken slumber at the Delta Hotel, he made his way to Amsterdam Central Station and caught the train to the ferry. Upon his arrival, he booked a cabin but spent most of the journey losing even more money on the roulette wheel in the casino. When the ship docked in Harwich, Nicholls purchased some duty-free lager for himself and several boxes of cigarettes for his wife. He then made his way to his car and drove home.

The drugs and Nicholls had made it safely back to England. All Tucker, Tate and Rolfe had to do now was distribute them to the dealers and wait for the money to come rolling in. Nothing could possibly go wrong.

Rolfe had been involved with a drug dealer named Gary from north London for about five years. When the cannabis from Amsterdam arrived in the country, Rolfe immediately contacted him and agreed to sell him £10,000 worth of the load. No money would change hands: Rolfe was going to give the cannabis to Gary on credit and collect the cash when the drugs had been sold. Rolfe trusted Gary. The pair had originally met in the Astoria nightclub in the West End of London. Rolfe started off buying Ecstasy from Gary for the friends he took to the club. Although theirs was really a business relationship, if Gary was in the club at the same time as Diane and Rolfe, they would spend the evening together. Rolfe enjoyed Gary's company and they would talk for hours. After Rolfe had become involved with Tucker, the situation turned around and Rolfe ended up selling cannabis to Gary. This was Gary's most frequent purchase, although he would buy whatever drugs he required from Rolfe, including cocaine, usually a half-ounce or an ounce at a time, depending on what was available and what was required.

Because of Rolfe's cocaine habit, if he was going to see Gary, Diane would generally ask him to wait for her to finish work so she could go with him. This was to prevent Rolfe from getting any cocaine and either using it there and then or bringing it home. On average, Rolfe visited Gary up to three times a week. Initially, Gary would meet Rolfe at a roundabout off the North Circular Road near Leytonstone. There was a small Greek grocer's shop nearby, and the meetings took place in the car park. Later on, Rolfe would drive directly to Gary's home and the deals would be done there.

On the day Rolfe was due to deliver the cannabis to Gary, Diane, as usual, accompanied him. Diane watched as Rolfe walked to the front door with a holdall and knocked. Gary answered, acknowledged Diane in the car, then both he and Rolfe went inside. About five minutes later, Rolfe came out. Diane noticed he had left the holdall there and when she asked him what was going on, she didn't really get a reply.

In Braintree, Nicholls was also waiting for the money from the cannabis to start rolling in. He had supplied numerous dealers, who had been waiting for the consignment to arrive. Within a few hours, all the drugs Nicholls had for sale were gone. Pleased with himself that things had eventually worked out after several mishaps in Amsterdam, he sat back and prepared himself for a long, hard drinking session in his local pub to celebrate. Within minutes of his celebration starting, his phone began to ring.

Elsewhere in Essex, Diane became aware that Rolfe was receiving an unusually high number of phone calls. When she asked him what was going on, Rolfe told her that the calls were regarding the cannabis being of poor quality. Diane could hear people shouting down the phone and could see that Rolfe was very aggravated. Eventually, Rolfe told her that all of the cannabis was being returned because it was rubbish.

Nicholls was being told the same thing as Rolfe, although he initially refused to believe the callers. He said that he was not worried; in fact, he was pissed off. He accused the dealers of trying to rip him off. 'You always get someone who wants to try it on,' he later stated. 'They buy some puff on credit, have a few joints and then try to pull one over on you by saying that it isn't any good and they want you to cut the price.'

Nicholls began to get aggressive with the callers, but they were equally vocal. They were adamant that Nicholls had sold them 'shit, complete unsmokable cack'. Two in particular were extremely upset and threatened to have Nicholls bashed up. Nicholls finally realised that nobody was trying to rip him off and agreed to look into it for them. His celebrations were put on hold. When he sat back to think about the numerous mishaps in Amsterdam and Harris's attitude towards him, he realised that Harris, annoyed by his lack of professionalism, must have loaded the boxes with dud cannabis.

This was just the beginning of the firm's troubles. Shortly before Nicholls's trip to Amsterdam, the police had raided Club UK in south London. The whole operation was televised. There were more than 1,000 people in the club. Mark Murray's dealers had thrown all of their pills and powders on the floor in order to escape arrest. Murray lost 800 pills in total – pills for which he had not yet paid Tucker. Already in debt, it was estimated that Murray owed Tucker approximately £20,000. Prison would have been salvation for him.

There are no financial advisers in the drug world and there are certainly no overdraft facilities. Tucker wanted his money and he wanted it immediately. He came round to my house with Rolfe and asked me where Murray was. I said I assumed that he was at home, so we all got into a car and went round to his house. His girlfriend answered the door. Rolfe pushed past her, went into the front room and asked, 'Where's Mark?' She said she didn't know. He asked if he had taken his phone with him. She said no, that he had left it at home. Rolfe picked it up, switched it on and started making calls.

Tucker was sitting on the settee next to me. He was laughing. He pointed at the television and asked the girl, 'Are you watching this programme?' She said no, so he ripped the plug from the wall, wrapped it round the TV set and told Rolfe to go and load it and the stereo in the car, which he did. He then told Murray's girlfriend she was coming with us. She was very frightened and said Mark would be home soon.

'Don't worry about that, get in the car,' said Tucker. We all drove round to another man's house. Fortunately, Tucker had forgotten why he had taken Murray's girlfriend with us, that's if he'd ever had a reason. I think he just did it to ensure she didn't forewarn Murray that he was looking for him. Whatever, tired of waiting, we all went home.

That night, Tucker and Rolfe returned to Murray's flat. Tucker pulled out a huge bowie knife, grabbed Murray by the face and pressed the point into his throat. 'I want my money, Murray,' he said. 'And for every week you owe me, you pay £500 on top. If I don't get it, you're dead.'

Murray, terrified in the knowledge Tucker was more than likely to carry out his threat and equally concerned that his debt now carried interest, contacted everybody he knew asking for financial assistance. When people learned that Tucker was Murray's creditor, they didn't want to know. In desperation, Murray turned to a man he had recently met on the Essex club circuit.

John Rollinson was a small-time drug dealer whom I had met once or twice when he had visited Raquels with Murray. He was a scruffy, overweight individual who worked during the day as a hairdresser. By night, he gave himself the rather grand title of 'Gaffer'. He peddled drugs and sat in the quieter pubs telling anybody who would listen that he was not only a face in the Essex underworld, he was 'the most dangerous man in the country'.

It was John, or Gaffer, who came to Murray's aid. Although he didn't have the capital to settle his debt in full, Gaffer scraped together £2,000 for Murray – a generous amount by most hairdressers' standards. Murray, who still feared Tucker was going to damage him or worse, asked me to arrange a meeting with him at Raquels so he could pay him the cash and ask for the interest agreement to be dropped.

At the meeting, which was held upstairs in the diner, Murray pleaded with Tucker to give him more time and to drop the interest charge because he had only been able to raise two grand. 'I will have what I owe you soon,' he said. 'If you don't let me carry on dealing, I won't be able to get the money to pay you.'

Tucker reluctantly agreed and dropped the interest clause but said Murray must purchase all of his drug supply from him and the cost would be inflated so that his debt could be paid off sooner rather than later. Unfortunately for Murray, there was another but – Tucker had recently acquired a batch of Ecstasy pills, which had been named 'Apples' because they had an apple motif imprinted on them. Tucker said that they were extremely strong and people who had taken them had complained of headaches. 'The dealers can't get rid of them once everyone knows what they're like,' he said. 'Sell them.'

He took the £2,000 that Gaffer had given to Murray and handed the Apple Ecstasy pills to him. Breathing a sigh of relief as Tucker strode off, Murray felt safe for the moment. He was back in business: soon those extra-strong pills would be in the hands of his dealers and being distributed in Raquels. Soon, he thought, his troubles would all be over. Little did any of us know the firm's dud cannabis and dodgy pills were the beginning of the end for us all.

The following Friday night, I was standing at the bar in Raquels talking to Tucker and Rolfe. The assistant manager was also with us. One of the barmaids telephoned the assistant manager and asked him to go and see her because she had a problem. Tucker and I were asked to go with him to resolve whatever it was. We went to the bar near the main dance-floor area and the barmaid told us she knew that a girl in the club was under age. She had refused to serve her and now the girl was getting stroppy. We called the girl over. She looked distressed. I asked her if she had any identification so that she could prove her age.

'I haven't, my purse has been stolen,' she said.

'I'm sorry, if you have no ID, then you will have to leave because the barmaid says she knows you and you are under age.'

The girl became very irate. 'I've had my purse stolen,' she said. 'I showed you my ID on the way in, why are you asking for it now?'

'You may appear to be 18, but the barmaid says you aren't,' I said. 'Therefore you must show your ID or leave.'

'I have had my purse stolen,' she said. 'There is £300 in it. My dad's a policeman, I'm going to get him and you'll all be in trouble.'

'Look, any story you tell me, I've already heard,' I replied. 'If you haven't any ID, you will have to leave.'

'My dad's a policeman,' the girl began shouting. 'I've had my purse stolen.'

'I'm sorry, you will have to leave. If your dad is a policeman, he will understand that if you haven't got ID we cannot let you remain here.'

Eventually, the girl left. To be honest, I couldn't have cared less if the girl was 17 or 18. I have always judged people on the way they behave. Most 17-year-old girls who came into the club were trying to act older than they were anyway, so were usually no trouble. It was the 30-year-old men who behaved like 12 year olds that I objected to. If the barmaid hadn't said anything, I certainly wouldn't have asked the girl to leave.

At closing time, I was putting the chains on the fire doors and waiting for the staff to leave before going home myself when I heard a commotion. I thought somebody was being attacked, so I went to see what the problem was. I found the barmaid who had told me the girl was under age at the front door. The girl had waited outside the club to have it out with her and they had ended up fighting. I told the barmaid she had better wait inside until the girl had gone.

Half an hour later, when I was satisfied the incident was over, I went home and thought no more about it. It wasn't until some time later that I found out the truth about what had happened. Somebody who had objected to the way the girl had been treated told me that the barmaid had stolen the girl's purse from the toilets. The girl knew the barmaid had her purse and demanded that she return it immediately. The barmaid had then telephoned the assistant manager to say that the girl was under age so that we would eject her and the accusations would cease. Leah Betts, the girl who had her purse stolen, was rightfully upset. She had waited outside the club after being ejected. She confronted the barmaid and was assaulted. Because of this incident, Leah was barred from coming into Raquels.

Chapter 9

On Friday, 10 November, it was business as usual in Raquels. Ecstasy, cocaine and amphetamines were being sold discreetly near the top bar. Because of his financial problems, Murray was selling the drugs himself that night. A nervous teenager sidled up to Murray and asked him if he could score. Murray nodded. The teenager, a friend of Leah Betts, held the folded notes in his hand, Murray the Ecstasy pills in his. They pretended to shake hands. Murray took the money, the teenager the pills. Leah Betts's fate was sealed. That deal was going to end her life and change a lot of other people's.

Unfortunately for Leah, the drugs that were purchased from Murray were the Ecstasy pills with the apple motif that had come from Tucker. The following night in her father's home, Leah, against the advice of her closest friend who had been given a warning about the strength of these particular pills, took one, thinking it was going to give her the best night of her short life.

On Monday, 13 November, I was filling up my car with petrol at a garage. I was thinking about Christmas, of all things: 1995 had been a bad year for the firm and myself. Once Christmas was out of the way, I could concentrate on the New Year – a fresh start and hopefully a new beginning. As I walked to the garage kiosk, I glanced at the news-stand. Every paper had a picture of a girl on the front page. Her eyes were closed, her mouth slack, agape, and there were tubes everywhere. I picked up a tabloid out of curiosity and paid for the petrol. I looked at the picture and thought to myself, 'What a waste.' I turned the page and a picture of Raquels leapt out at me. The article said an 18-year-old girl named Leah Betts was on a life-support machine after taking an Ecstasy pill that had been purchased in Raquels. My heart sank. I knew this was going to cause serious grief.

When I got home, I sat on the stairs and put my head in my hands. I wasn't sure what to do, but I knew I had to do something, as it was more than a possibility that the police would want to talk to me, along with Murray, Tucker, Tate, Rolfe and all of the other members of the firm. In the end, I rang Murray, but his phone was unobtainable. I tried ringing Tucker, Tate and Rolfe but, like Murray, they had obviously heard the news and gone to ground.

Despite the problems we were now all undoubtedly going to be facing, Tate continued to rampage through Essex, drawing unwanted attention to everyone connected to the firm. He was desperately trying to locate Darren Nicholls over the dud cannabis. Tate was seething with rage and swearing bloody revenge. He rang Mick Steele, whom he knew could contact Nicholls, and explained the situation: either Nicholls pays back the money or he suffers an unimaginable death.

Steele didn't believe Nicholls would have the bottle to deliberately give Tate dud cannabis. 'Fuck me, Pat,' he said. 'You know what Nicholls is like, he was full of himself in prison, but he wouldn't rob you, he's shit scared of you.'

Tate would not accept this and continued to rant about killing Nicholls. Eventually, Steele said he would contact Nicholls to try and resolve the problem. When he got hold of him, Nicholls told Steele that he had spoken to the dealer in Amsterdam and after explaining that the dud drugs had been purchased by a firm of 'very heavy Essex villains' the dealer had offered to return the money on the condition the drugs were returned to him. Nicholls had agreed. Steele explained this to Tate over the telephone. Tate, forever suspicious, insisted Steele meet him so that he could ensure Nicholls was not trying to pull 'another stroke'. They met at the Carpenters Arms pub near Basildon, where Tate said he would pay Steele £2,000 if he would 'chaperone' Nicholls on the trip back to Amsterdam to recover the syndicate's money. Rather foolishly but with good intent, Steele agreed.

Nicholls, concerned he might get caught in possession of such a large amount of cannabis, albeit dud, decided to purchase a cheap car in which to keep the drugs. He bought a red Mark 2 Granada, loaded it with the drugs and left it in a pub car park in a village called Great Sailing in Essex.

Nicholls breathed a sigh of relief when he heard from Steele that an agreement had been reached with Tate. Nicholls truly believed that everything was going to be OK once he had returned Tate's money. What he did not know was that Tate had decided to rip him off in revenge for supplying the dud cannabis. Unbeknown to Nicholls, one third of the cannabis shipment had been good. Tate had sold this third for £80,000 and smashed up each block of the poor quality cannabis so that when the drugs were returned to Nicholls, he would be unable to count the cannabis bars and realise some were missing.

With the drugs safely stored, Nicholls booked the tickets to travel to Amsterdam and then telephoned Steele to say he was ready to leave. The pair travelled from Harwich to the Hook of Holland on a ferry and then caught a train to Amsterdam. When they arrived, they made their way to Stone's Café and met the dealer. Nicholls discussed the money and how it was going to be paid back. He said he wanted it repaid in sterling. The dealer said it would take a bit of time although he could pay it in guilders straight away. Nicholls declined and said he would wait.

Nicholls and Steele went for a walk around Amsterdam before Nicholls returned to the bar alone later on that day, where he collected about £30–£35,000 in sterling. The dealer asked Nicholls where the drugs were that he was supposed to have returned. Nicholls assured him that once all of the money had been reimbursed, he would get the drugs back. 'I'm hardly going to run off with a load of dud cannabis, am I?' he told the dealer.

Nicholls was told that there was no more sterling available that day and he would have to return the following morning. When Nicholls left the café, he met Steele and took him to the Delta Hotel, where he had stayed previously. Nicholls booked one twin room in his name and paid in cash.

The next day, Nicholls returned to Stone's Café but was told there was still no sterling available and he should return later. That evening, Nicholls was given a further £40–45,000, but a similar amount remained outstanding. When he returned to the café the following morning, Nicholls was told that the balance would be available within the hour. The dealer then unwittingly delivered a hammer blow to Nicholls. 'I asked you yesterday when you are going to return the drugs.'

'And I told you,' Nicholls replied, 'when I get the money. I'm hardly going to rip you off. It was dud cannabis anyway.'

The dealer glared at Nicholls. 'Two thirds of it was shit, one third of it was good. We require you to return it.'

Nicholls realised that he had been double-crossed. The Dutch villains had intentionally supplied him with dud drugs. How else would they know what percentage of the batch was good or bad? Tate, Tucker and Rolfe had also ripped him off: they had kept and sold the good third of the haul. They had then insisted that all of the drugs were worthless. Nicholls now realised why the drugs had been broken into small pieces before being returned. He had no idea how many bars of cannabis were in the bag they had given back to him. Nicholls went back to the hotel, told Steele to get his things together, then returned to the café. Shortly afterwards, Nicholls returned with a sports bag into which he put all of the cash before telling Steele they were going home immediately.

Nicholls was becoming paranoid after realising the Dutch dealers had deliberately duped him. He told Steele he believed they were going to have him set up to be robbed. 'He sold me dud drugs,' he told Steele. 'Why wouldn't he have me attacked now I've got a big bag of fucking money?'

Steele tried to calm Nicholls down, but he wasn't having any of it. When they reached the railway station, Nicholls leapt out into the road and hailed a taxi. 'Take us to Ostend,' he pleaded.

'But that's miles away,' the driver replied.

'I don't care, just take us,' said Nicholls. When the taxi pulled up outside the ferry terminal, the total fare was £400. Nicholls paid it without blinking. He had escaped from one dangerous situation, but he knew he wasn't safe just yet.

He told himself all he had to do was hand over the money as agreed with Tate and that would be the end of the matter. There was no 'end of the matter' if you crossed the firm. Kevin Whitaker and Nipper Ellis had been given similar worthless assurances. They had been taught a hard lesson which Nicholls himself was about to learn.

When Nicholls and Steele arrived in Ostend, Tate was pacing up and down outside the railway station with Rolfe. They had wanted Tucker to travel with them too, but he had told them that he had made 'prior arrangements'. The truth was, Tucker second-guessed that Tate was going to pull some sort of stroke and didn't relish upsetting any Dutch gangsters on their home soil. When Tate saw Nicholls swaggering towards him, he turned and walked away. Rolfe sneered at Nicholls before he too turned and followed Tate into a nearby café. Nicholls looked nervously at Steele and asked him if everything was going to be OK.

'Stay here,' said Steele. 'It's obvious Tate is not in the mood for talking to you.'

Steele went into the café, while Nicholls hung around outside to try and see what was going on. Through the window, he could see Barry Dorman, the car dealer, sitting with Tate, Rolfe and Steele. There were also four women present: Donna Garwood, Lizzie Fletcher and her friend, and Dorman's girlfriend. Dorman and his girlfriend were present because Dorman had unwittingly loaned Tate £10,000, thinking it was intended for a car deal. Tate, of course, had invested the money in the drug shipment. Fearing one person may be stopped by Customs with such a large amount of money, Tate had recruited Dorman, his girlfriend and the teenage girls to travel to Ostend, where the money would be divided into smaller amounts and carried through Customs by several people rather than just one.

When Steele came out of the café, he told Nicholls that everything was going to be OK. 'You upset him. He wanted the money back. We have it and so he says this is the end of the matter. But be careful, you can't trust him, his mind is messed up with all of the drugs he takes.'

Steele took the sports bag from Nicholls and began to walk up the road slowly. Tate came out of the café, caught him up and took the bag from him. Tate walked back into the café and as soon as he did so, Rolfe and the others got up and left. Nicholls said he needed a drink, so he and Steele went into a nearby bar.

Tate, Rolfe and their entourage booked into the nearby Burlington Hotel where the money was divided into smaller amounts. Barry Dorman took the money he was owed and returned to England immediately with his girlfriend. Tate,

Rolfe and the three girls started to celebrate their windfall. During the night their smoke alarm went off and a hotel porter rushed to their room. When he arrived, Tate was drugged out of his mind. The room was wrecked and the smoke detector was hanging out of the ceiling. Rolfe promised the porter that the damage would be paid for, so he went away. The following morning, before leaving, Tate peeled £100 from a huge roll of banknotes and told the manageress they were sorry.

By the time Tate and Rolfe had crawled out of bed, Steele and Nicholls had returned to England. The swagger was back, the attitude had returned: Nicholls thought the matter was closed. All he had to do now was dispose of the poor quality cannabis, which was still in the boot of his car. He drove to a disused gravel pit in Church Lane, Bocking, which is known locally as the ARC pit, and threw the haul into the deep water. He had never intended to risk returning it to the Dutch.

The day Tate, Rolfe and the others returned, I was out of town. I had a court case in Birmingham I had to attend, various driving offences, nothing serious. I was banned for 12 months and fined £330. Driving back down from the court case, I heard nothing on the radio but reports about Leah's condition and the police inquiry.

Four addresses were raided that morning in Basildon. One of them was Tate's flat, where Donna Garwood was living. A quantity of amphetamine was found, not a lot, just a bit of personal, but the fact that they'd raided Tate's flat indicated the police knew the firm was involved in the supply chain. Donna was a regular in the club; Tate was a member of the firm and had only been out of prison for two weeks. It seemed the net was closing in. My big concern was that all the main players were running a mile, leaving me to face the music. So much for loyalty. I didn't think it would be too long before they rounded us all up for questioning.

I finally managed to speak to Tucker about Leah Betts collapsing and Raquels being named as the source for the Ecstasy that she had taken. Tucker made it quite clear that he wanted his name kept out of any police inquiry; in fact, he told me that he didn't even wish to hear his name mentioned in the same sentence as Betts. He said he'd got the hump over Donna Garwood being arrested for the amphetamines that had been found at the flat, even though she had not been charged. Tucker said Garwood was claiming a doorman from Raquels had grassed her up. At that time, though, the police hadn't talked to any of them. The pressure was getting to Tucker: if he was arrested over the Betts incident, he knew he would be ruined. He could see his empire crumbling and now he was panicking. A menace fuelled by paranoia was growing. Everyone was putting his or her back against the wall and somebody else's name in the frame.

The Piano Bar had been closed since the weekend when Leah had collapsed, but reopened that Wednesday night. I went into work at about eight-thirty. There was an eerie atmosphere in there. It was as if everyone had their eyes on me, half-looking for a reaction, I think. I felt like a condemned man. What made it even stranger was the fact that in the bar there were four television screens. Every time there was a news item, images of Leah lying in bed with tubes coming out of her were coming up on these screens. We had this dark room full of kids Leah's age – some on drugs, some not – loud music and pictures of Leah lying in hospital as a result of what went on in this very building. Strange, very strange, and unnerving really.

There were the usual fools, who were coming up asking for my opinions on Leah. A couple of reporters were in there trying to buy drugs. So obvious: long raincoats; short, tidy hair; middle-class accents; going up to people asking if they could 'score'. I was just glad to get out of work that night.

The following day, Debra and I were due to move. I could see the firm was on the brink of self destructing and I was preparing to leave before I too was destroyed. We'd bought a house on the Essex coast in a village called Mayland. It was a beautiful house, surrounded by woodland and a stone's throw from the sea. We both hoped it would be our sanctuary from the madness we had endured over the past decade. I had my doubts. A fresh start, a new beginning and no more trouble were all the things I'd hoped for on my train journey to Essex from prison almost a decade earlier. Debra had gone to the house to wait for the removal van and I took the children to school. I was driving back to Mayland when I heard on the car radio that Leah had died in the early hours of the morning. I felt saddened when I heard her family sobbing with grief and pleading for people to name the drug dealer responsible for supplying her.

When I arrived, Debra was standing at the front door. 'Have you heard what's happened?' she asked. I told her I had. Debra was very upset by Leah's death. She had no idea of the firm's involvement and I couldn't bring myself to tell her.

Around lunchtime, Tucker rang me. He was going mental. He was saying he wanted the 'fucking mess' sorted out and he wanted it sorted out 'today'. There was too much police attention both on him and on the firm in general, he said. Now Leah had died, the shit was going to hit the fan. Tucker was stressed out because he feared the police attention from the Betts inquiry would unearth the dud cannabis deal with Nicholls and jeopardise the robbery he was planning at Rettendon.

After Tate and Rolfe had returned from Ostend with the syndicate's £120,000, they were still feeling mugged off by Nicholls's incompetence. Tucker, Tate and Rolfe discussed the matter and decided to seek revenge on Nicholls for embarrassing them and making them look like amateurs.

They told the members of the syndicate that Nicholls had not only delivered dud cannabis in an attempt to con them but he had also failed to reimburse any of their money. Some members of the syndicate were hardened criminals who said they were going to kill Nicholls; others, not so violent, still wanted some sort of vicious penalty imposed. Tucker, Tate and Rolfe were quietly confident that Nicholls would soon be dead or at least in hiding, and they could keep the syndicate's money as well as the £80,000 they had made selling the third of the haul that had been of good quality.

Now holding enough ready cash to convince any drug dealers they were serious players, the trio once more approached the Canning Town firm who were waiting for the replacement drop at Rettendon. They were told that a shipment was due any day now and they would be the first to know when it was available. Tucker, Tate and Rolfe knew that they weren't dealing with fools, so they decided to invest in some firepower for the robbery.

One afternoon, Rolfe told his partner, Diane, that he was going to pick up a machine gun with a silencer and ammunition for the firm and asked her to accompany him. Rolfe explained that the gun was coming from a man known as 'Mad' Mick Bowman, who lived in south London. When Diane asked Rolfe how much such a gun was going to cost, Rolfe told her that he was borrowing it and would return it to Bowman when they had done the job. Rolfe said that he had to meet Bowman at Thurrock Services on the M25 to collect the gun. Diane travelled with Rolfe in the blue Range Rover that had been purchased from Dorman. When they arrived, they went into the restaurant for something to eat while they waited for Bowman. When he eventually arrived, Rolfe walked outside alone and returned shortly afterwards. He told Diane to leave her drink and join them outside.

When Diane walked out into the car park, she saw that Bowman was there in a white Volkswagen Corado and there was another male with him in an old green Vauxhall Cavalier. Bowman was behaving like he was paranoid. Diane assumed that he had taken cocaine and was acting that way because of the machine gun. Bowman was concerned he was being followed and was unhappy about driving off to a different location. Rolfe suggested that he would lead, the Cavalier would go in the middle and then Bowman could follow on at the rear. After scouring the car park for the 100th time, Bowman finally agreed. Rolfe drove the Range Rover to the A13 and along to the Five Bells roundabout. He drove around it once and stopped at Barry Dorman's car lot. The Cavalier pulled up behind Rolfe and Bowman parked behind that. They all got out and Diane walked away in order to appear discreet. A blue/grey holdall was taken out of the boot of the Cavalier and was placed in the boot of the Range Rover. Rolfe called Diane back to the car and the pair then drove off to Tate's bungalow on Gordon Road, Basildon. When they arrived there, Tate and Tucker were sitting in a Suzuki Vitara. Rolfe took the holdall from the boot, and Tucker and Tate followed him into the house.

Rolfe was in the house for about ten to fifteen minutes before he returned to the car with the holdall. He put it back in the boot and drove to a safe house in Basildon where it was put into the loft. On the way from Tate's home, Rolfe was telling Diane how pleased Tucker and Tate were with the gun and how much damage it could cause anybody who fucked with them. Diane had heard it all before. She wasn't impressed. In her heart, she knew the machine gun could only mean there would be more trouble.

A couple of days later, Rolfe, Tucker and Tate tested the gun in a field at the back of Tucker's home. They took it in turns to blast imaginary enemies. They had then cleaned it and Rolfe had taken it away to store at his house ready for the Rettendon robbery.

Tate and Tucker were concerned the police would raid their homes and find the syndicate's money. The police had, after all, already been to Tate's flat where Donna Garwood was living. They decided to put the money into a Head sports bag and give it to one of Tate's lifelong friends, a man named John Marshall – one of the few people Tate said he could trust to look after so much money. With the proceeds of one scam now safely stored, they began planning the Rettendon robbery.

Tucker knew most, if not all, of the players in Canning Town, so he set about recruiting a man with inside knowledge of the other firm to find out what he could about the incoming shipment. He wanted the man to tell him when, how, where and at what time the drop was going to be made. Tucker knew that everyone in the drugs world has a price: there is no loyalty when there's hard cash on offer. Before long, Tucker had his Judas.

Chapter 10

Whatever happened regarding the Leah Betts inquiry, common sense told me that the management at Raquels would want to show that there had been changes, i.e. changes in security. Matters were coming to a head. There was the death of Leah Betts, the dud cannabis saga and Tucker and Tate's plan to commit a robbery with the machine gun. Without telling me, Tucker had already consulted a solicitor about the Betts case, despite the fact he hadn't been questioned. Murray had disappeared off the face of the earth. It was plain to see it was now every man for himself. The Essex Boys' empire was crashing down around us.

It was very quiet the next time I went into work, as I recall it. I just sat at the bar and had a drink. The more I thought about the life I had immersed myself in, the more I realised just how stupid I had been. Sure, I had enjoyed some of it, but, in the main, life in the firm was violent and depressing. You never knew if you were going to be the next person to fall out of favour and end up dead or in hiding. I had to face facts. I'd had enough. I hated it, loathed it. My plans to leave and make a fresh start would have to be brought forward – with immediate effect. About eleven o'clock, I thought, 'Fuck this, I'm going.' I went to Maurice, a doorman from Bristol, and said, 'I want you to be head doorman. I'm going.' He looked rather puzzled but thanked me. We shook hands and I went up to the office. 'I'm leaving,' I told the manager.

'What's the problem?' he asked.

'There ain't no problem. I'm leaving. See you later,' I said and walked out.

I had no idea how I was going to support my wife and children from there on in, but I didn't care. My leaving had to be a total departure. No occasional acquaintances from memory lane. The firm, the violence, the police, the grief – I wanted it to mean nothing now. It had to become a thing of the past.

The night I walked out on Raquels and the firm, I decided I would go out and celebrate, so I drove over to a club in Southend named Ad-Lib. I walked in the door and down a flight of three or four steps. To my dismay, I saw Tucker and Tate standing at the bar with two girls. Tate smiled and put his arms around me. 'It's great to see you, Bernie, how are you?' he said, patting my back. Tucker grunted something. He looked as if he had the hump.

'What's the matter?' I asked him.

He shook hands with me and said, 'Nothing.' Then he added, 'Can I have a word?'

We went out of earshot of the others and he repeated the story about one of the doormen grassing up Donna Garwood. Donna was constantly causing problems. In Raquels, she would come downstairs and say to me that such and such a man was giving her grief, such and such a man was staring at her. Tucker, she said, had insisted that if she had a problem, I had to throw out the person who had upset her.

'No doorman has grassed her,' I said. Tucker got annoyed and said one of the doormen must have because she was in Tate's flat when the police found some whizz. 'That's bollocks, the police haven't even spoken to the doormen,' I said. He told me another doorman had confirmed it.

'Well, who's this other doorman then?' I asked. 'We'll go and see him.'

'I've got to go now,' he replied.

'Fair enough,' I said. 'Ring me up and we'll discuss what has been said.'

He walked out of the door. Tate turned round and put his arm round me again. 'Don't worry about him,' he said. 'He's just got the hump.'

We shook hands and Tate left to join Tucker. I waited a minute and thought, 'I'm not having this, I am going to clear this bollocks up.' I went outside. They were sitting in the Range Rover. I leant against the driver's door and said to Tucker, 'I'm telling you, no doorman's grassed Donna up. Someone's just saying it to cause trouble. And as for this doorman who confirmed it, why don't we go round and see him tomorrow and if you think he's lying, we'll bash him?'

'Fair enough, we'll fucking bash him,' Tucker replied. Tate slammed the vehicle into gear and they roared off up the street. I didn't know it at the time, but it was to be the last time that I was ever going to see them.

I don't know why I said what I said. I had just decided to walk away from the firm and its grisly business. I had told myself I wanted nothing more to do with them. I suppose old habits are hard to break.

The following morning, I rang Tucker. As usual, he wasn't in or wasn't answering his phone, so I sent him a fax telling him I had quit Raquels the night before and Maurice was taking over. The fax read: 'There are no problems, it's safe, it's sorted.'

The next day, Monday, 20 November, Tucker rang. I wasn't in, so he left a message on my answering machine. He was being abusive and threatening. He said I couldn't just walk out of Raquels. He wanted an explanation. 'I'm going to fucking do you,' he said.

My problems are my own: nothing would have made me involve Debra and our children. And I knew what might happen; I didn't need to ask Nipper Ellis, Kevin Whitaker or their families. When my children came out of school, I booked them and Debra into a hotel near Rettendon. If Tucker did come to my home, at least my family would not have to witness whatever occurred. I wasn't the only one being threatened with violence. Nicholls had been getting lots of grief from members of the syndicate who still believed he had not repaid their money. In desperation, he approached Tucker and Tate, pleading with them to come clean and admit he had given them the money back. Tucker told Nicholls that Tate wasn't in any position to pay anybody back for the time being. 'The fucking car dealers and their ponces can wait. When we pull off this job at Rettendon, they will get their money back,' he said.

Tate and Tucker were telling people they were relying on the Rettendon robbery to solve all their troubles. Tucker had to pay off his new Brynmount Lodge home, which was plunging him deeper into debt. They had made promises to pay the syndicate and the car dealer for the Range Rover, but in reality they had no intention of paying anybody. They never did – perhaps because nobody ever pressed them for money.

I was still owed a week's wages, because we were paid in arrears at Raquels. I rang the door staff and told them I would be down on Friday to collect it. 'You had better ring me before you come,' one of the doormen said. 'I've heard that Tucker has got the hump.' I told him I didn't care, but I didn't want to involve him and the other doormen and so I agreed. Always cautious, I tooled myself up. I put a huge combat knife in the back of my trousers and a bottle of squirt in my pocket, and went down to Basildon town centre to collect my money.

Maurice and Gavin met me near Raquels and advised me not to go round to the club. 'Tucker's there now with Tate, Rolfe and a few other people we haven't seen before,' said Gavin.

'Tucker's told me he's holding your money and if you want it, you should get it yourself, but I wouldn't advise it – he's firmed up. I'll give you my wages and get yours off Tucker. You can go round if you really want to, you know I'm with you, but I wouldn't advise it.' I'm many things but stupid isn't one of them, so I agreed. Gavin gave me his money and went back to the club. When he arrived, Tucker asked Gavin if he had seen me. 'I know he's your mate, but we've got a problem with him,' he said.

'I have seen him,' Gavin replied, 'and I've given him my wages, as you've got his. Now I need you to pay me.'

Tucker hesitated, apologised and gave Gavin his money. As far as I was concerned that was the end of the matter. Everyone was happy. I was out of Raquels and out of the firm. There was no need for anyone to continue with a vendetta.

The following night, Saturday, 25 November, I was told that Tate and Rolfe had been in the club looking for me. I don't know what Tate's problem was. He and I had always got on well. I suppose, as with Nipper, because Tucker had the hump with me he had to follow suit. It was always the way with these morons. Gavin was in the club when Tate and Rolfe had arrived and Tate had asked him if he had seen me.

'Tell Bernie he can't hide for ever,' he added. 'And when we see him, we are going to take lumps out of him.'

'He's my mate. I don't pass on messages like that,' Gavin replied. Tate should have learned from his experience with Nipper that he shouldn't go around making threats. He and Tucker started telling everybody they were going to shoot me. If they were intent on doing so, they knew where I lived and I was hardly going to try and hide for ever. Nor was I going to give them for ever to carry out their threats.

I had no idea why Rolfe was involving himself either.

He had nothing to do with Raquels or my arrangement with Tucker. At that time he was having enough troubles of his own. On Tuesday, 28 November, WPC Ponder was on duty in a marked police vehicle with PC Barham. At approximately 11.25 p.m., they were driving along High Road, Pitsea, when their attention was drawn to a blue Range Rover. They followed the vehicle into Pitsea Road and into Beambridge. The Range Rover then pulled into a parking spot. PC Barham stopped behind it, got out of the police car and had a conversation with the driver, who was very annoyed at being stopped. The Range Rover contained three passengers, a blonde female about 25 years of age and an older couple whom the driver referred to as Mum and Dad.

'What the fuck do you want?' the driver said initially. 'I ain't done nothing wrong, there's nothing wrong with my driving. You're the one who has fucked up. You didn't indicate coming into this road.' He then said, 'You should read the fucking Highway Code because you're supposed to indicate!'

'I just want to talk to you about the speed you were driving,' PC Barham replied.

'Just give me a ticket. I'm getting cold out here, let me go inside.' The driver then told his mother and the others to go inside the house.

'I'm not going to give you a ticket, I just want to talk to you about the way you came round a bend on Pitsea High Road,' PC Barham said.

In a calmer voice, the driver replied, 'I came off the roundabout and there were cars parked there, so I had to pull out.'

PC Barham asked the driver his name, address and date of birth.

'Michael Andrew Rolfe, 403 Long Riding, 29–9–66,' the driver replied.

PC Barham wrote these details down and then walked around to the front of the Range Rover. 'The vehicle's got no tax,' he said.

'Yeah, I only bought it a couple of days ago,' came the reply.

PC Barham looked closely at the driver. 'Aren't you the guy I nicked last year in a stolen Honda?'

'No.'

'I'm sure it was you.'

'No, it was my brother, Craig Rolfe.'

The officer completed the paperwork and explained what was required. He asked the driver to sign the papers and then gave him a copy, saying that he would be reporting him for not having any road tax. The driver made no reply and elected to produce his documents at Basildon police station. He then walked to a nearby house.

PC Barham was not convinced that the driver to whom he had given the ticket was Michael Rolfe and after making enquiries at Basildon police station, he and WPC Ponder visited an address in Calshot Avenue, Chafford Hundred, Grays. There, parked alone on the drive, was the blue Range Rover. It was now 2.20 a.m., less than three hours after they had stopped the vehicle in Pitsea. The officers went to the door of the house, where PC Barham knocked repeatedly.

After a short time, they heard a male voice coming from a first-floor window above the door. 'Yeah, what?'

The officers stepped back and PC Barham pointed his torch at the man. 'Hello, Craig.'

'Yeah, what do you want?'

'I stopped you driving earlier on tonight.'

'You didn't stop me.'

'I am reporting you for driving while disqualified.'

Craig Rolfe didn't answer, he simply closed the window.

The following morning, I rang Tucker about the threats

he, Tate and Rolfe had been making about me. 'I hear you want to speak to me,' I said.

'Why didn't you tell me you were leaving Raquels when I saw you in Southend?' he asked.

'I had had enough of everything,' I explained. 'I admit I was wrong not to discuss it with you, but I just wanted to walk away. I told the manager Maurice was taking my place and the door was safe. You've not lost out. It is still your door. In fact, you have complete control now instead of going down the middle with me.'

'But people are talking,' he said.

'I don't give a fuck about people,' I replied. 'I'm out of it.'

'I don't believe you,' Tucker said and the line went dead.

On 5 December, I was contacted by a detective from Basildon police station. He told me the police were taking the threats Tucker and Tate had made to shoot me seriously. People within the firm were discussing it and, inevitably, the police had got to hear about it. He also told me that Detective Chief Inspector Brian Storey wanted to talk to me about events leading up to the death of Leah Betts.

'I've moved away from Basildon now. I don't need this shit,' I said.

It was impressed upon me that I could attend the police station voluntarily or be taken there under arrest. If I wanted to move away and start a new life, then I would have to clear up any outstanding matters with the police first. It would be an informal chat. I could then go off and begin my new life, no strings attached. He also asked if Debra would be willing to talk.

'She has nothing she can tell you,' I said. 'She knows nothing. She only worked at the club occasionally, searching females as they entered.'

The detective said they would be speaking to every member of staff, so it was in both of our interests to get it over and done with. In the end, I agreed that we would both attend South Woodham Ferrers police station the following day at about 2 p.m.

I was due to see a mutual friend of Tate and Nicholls's the following day at 2 p.m. in Great Blakenham, near Ipswich. He was going to give me an update on what Tucker and Tate were up to. I wanted to know what, if anything, they were planning for me, but there seemed little point now. The police had told me what their intentions were. That afternoon snow began to fall heavily. Soon everywhere was covered under a white blanket.

That night, Tate was up to his old tricks. He was at home with Lizzie Fletcher, who had called the London Pizza Company in Wickford and asked for a pizza with different toppings on different sections. Roger Ryall, the manager, told Lizzie they didn't do that type of pizza. Tate grabbed the phone and started swearing at him. Mr Ryall said later, 'I wasn't going to take that, so I said, "Get rid of that attitude and I will send you a pizza."'

He obviously didn't know the type of man he was talking to. Tate became more irate and slammed down the phone. Half an hour later, he turned up at the pizza shop, picked up the till and hurled it across the room at Mr Ryall. Fearing for his life, Mr Ryall backed out of the office and pushed the panic button which was linked directly to the police. It was his second mistake of the evening. Tate, fearing arrest and a return to prison, overreacted. He punched Mr Ryall in the face, grabbed him by the hair and smashed his head into a glass plate on the draining board. Tate told him not to call the police or he would come back and smash up the place and hurt his staff. However, the panic button had already been activated and officers arrived after Tate had left.

When Tate was identified, and the police told Mr Ryall who he was and a bit of his history, Mr Ryall decided not to press charges after all. Only Tate could turn ordering a pizza into an orgy of violence.

Now I had spoken to Tucker myself, I wasn't too concerned about the rumours that were flying around. He hadn't, after all, threatened to shoot me in any conversation I'd had with him. It was probably just wannabes stirring it up, gloating over the fact Tucker and I had fallen out. I thought that once I had spoken to the police, my purpose would have been served and nobody would have any further business with me. I could at last see light at the end of the tunnel. I was awakening from the nightmare.

The following day, Tucker, Tate, Rolfe and their friend, Peter Cuthbert, sat at table number 50 in TGI Friday's restaurant at the Lakeside shopping centre in Thurrock, Essex. As soon as they sat down, Helen Smith, a staff member, approached the men and asked them if they wanted a drink. They ordered three bottles of Beck's beer and a Diet Pepsi. When Helen Smith walked away to sort out the drinks order, another member of staff, Linda Wolfe, walked over to the table and asked them if they wished to order any food. Rolfe said they were all hungry and that they wanted to order straight away. Tucker and Cuthbert ordered fajita baguettes, Tate ordered steak and mushrooms with a baked potato, Rolfe ordered Pasta Santa Fe with garlic bread. As they sat in the restaurant, Tucker received the call he had been waiting for. The Rettendon drop was being made the next day. The Canning Town cartel advised him to get the money organised. Everything, Tucker thought, was coming together. They just had to wait for Tucker's Judas to call with the exact location and the time of the drop.

Cuthbert sat quietly waiting for his food and drink but after receiving the call, Tucker, Tate and Rolfe seemed excited. They began fooling around and generally taking the piss out of the staff. They kept asking the waitress to let her hair down and eventually, after their constant pestering, she did.

'Oh, yeah, nice. You've got to come to the Berwick Manor on Friday. Ask for Tony Tucker. Tony Tucker, it's easy, it rolls off the tongue,' Tucker shouted out.

She said she might but she had no real intention of going because she had to work on Friday evenings. She mentioned to Tucker that she knew a man who worked at Hollywood nightclub in Romford. To her surprise, Tucker said he ran security there and he would ring the club and find out who this man was, as he had never heard of him. He tried dialling the number, but his phone wouldn't work, so he used Tate's. When he finally got through and asked if they had a bouncer called 'Boysey', somebody must have given him the man's name because Tucker started laughing and said, 'What? Mick! Fucking sack him.' Although he continued laughing, he assured the waitress he was only joking. At the end of their meal, the bill came to £56. Tucker threw £70 on the table and Tate threw down £10. All four left shortly afterwards.

Around the same time as they were having their lunch, Debra and I were driving to the police station. We were met at the door by four detectives. Two wished to speak to Debra. DCI Storey and another detective wanted to speak to me. Debra knew nothing and therefore could say nothing, so I said I had no objection to her talking to anybody. However, if, as they had said, this was an informal chat, then I would only be prepared to talk to DCI Storey on his own. Storey, in my opinion, knew the score. I think he knew the pressure I was under. He agreed to see me alone.

As I was meeting the police, Tucker received a second telephone call. This time it was from his Judas in the Canning Town cartel, who was calling from a payphone near Great Blakenham. The caller told Tucker he wanted to meet him, along with Tate and Rolfe, later that evening to show them where the drop was going to be made so they could rehearse the robbery at the scene. Moments later, the same caller telephoned Darren Nicholls from the same payphone. It's not known what was said, but phone records confirm that both of these calls were made.

Storey soon made it clear to me that he was well aware of the firm's involvement in just about everything. He also knew what he could prove and, despite knowing the facts, what he couldn't. He knew the pill that had taken Leah's life had come via Mark Murray. Murray had been arrested the morning after Leah had collapsed. Murray had been questioned, but nobody was going to give evidence against him. I could see Storey's task was painful, but he knew at that time the only people he could realistically prosecute were Leah's friends, whom he knew had purchased the drugs in Raquels.

Storey had heard that the firm had threatened to shoot me. These were serious people. He knew it wasn't an idle threat. He asked me if I would make a statement about the sale and use of drugs in Raquels. I didn't have to implicate anyone. I explained that I had enough problems with Tucker without him hearing I had assisted the police. 'He's threatening to shoot me now,' I said, 'what do you think he will be like if he hears I've given your mob a leg up?' Storey assured me that if I made a statement, police protection would be given to my family should Tucker and Tate try to carry out their threat. He added that there was always the possibility that if I refused I may be subpoenaed to court, although he made it clear he wasn't offering me an ultimatum, he was just being honest with me. I told him I understood my position. I couldn't put my family at risk for things I had done, but I wouldn't rule out the possibility of doing what he asked. I told him I would give it some serious thought, discuss it with my family and speak to him again in a couple of weeks.

Our conversation lasted until about 4 p.m. When I came

out, Debra was waiting. She said they had kept her for half an hour and had only asked about who was working on the night and other trivial matters, facts they already knew. I left the police station feeling a little better about everything.

Debra and I had asked her mother to look after the children whilst we were at the police station. It was approximately ten past four when we left South Woodham Ferrers to pick them up. The snow had continued to fall and was now perhaps three or four inches deep. We arrived at Debra's mother's house at about five o'clock and stayed for a cup of tea. Then we drove on to Wickford, where we had something to eat, before heading towards the Rettendon Turnpike, the main roundabout on the A130. By now, it was about 6.30. It was a miserable night. The snow was still falling and it was pitch-black.

At around the same time as we were nearing the Rettendon Turnpike, Tucker, Tate and Rolfe were approaching it from the Southend arterial road to rehearse the Canning Town cartel's cocaine robbery with a man they thought was their co-conspirator. We must have negotiated this busy roundabout at around the same time, but we didn't see each other. I was concentrating on getting home with Debra and the children. They were no doubt focusing on the drugs they would steal and then sell, making them millionaires.

Chapter 11

Detective Superintendent Dibley had been with Essex Police for 31 years. During that period, Dibley had investigated twenty-five murders: only two had remained unsolved. He had joined the force at the age of seventeen and was only four months away from retirement when on 7 December, just after 8.30 a.m., he received a call asking him to take charge of the biggest case of his entire career. Three men had been found shot dead in a Range Rover that had been parked down a farm track in Rettendon. Although Dibley was on leave that day, a colleague had followed protocol by telephoning him to offer him the case, as the murders had taken place on his patch.

Never one to turn down a challenge, Dibley told his colleague that he would take charge of the investigation, but first he had go to his daughter's house to change an electrical fitting. Considering the crime scene was covered with a blanket of snow that had footprints and tyre marks embedded in it that were melting before the officers' eyes, it may not have been a wise decision to delay the investigation for a faulty electrical fitting.

When Dibley had completed the work at his daughter's home, he made his way to Rettendon. There were no houses overlooking the scene or even any close enough to consider conducting house-to-house enquiries. It was so remote there was no chance of a witness having seen or even heard anything. Dibley stood in the lane and thought, 'Christ, where do we start?'

At that stage, Dibley had no idea who the three dead men were. Nobody had telephoned the police saying they were concerned about a missing son, boyfriend or husband. The Range Rover provided no clues regarding their identities either. The man in whose name the vehicle was registered was found to be alive and well but he was unable to throw any light on the occupants because he had sold it on some months earlier; however, police records did show that the vehicle had been stopped the previous day.

When the two officers who had stopped the vehicle, DC Pullinger and DC Williams, were contacted, they said that at approximately 4.30 p.m. they had been on duty in plain clothes in an unmarked police vehicle. As they left Grays police station and drove into Brooke Road, they had noted a blue Range Rover travelling in front of their vehicle. The Range Rover parked adjacent to the front entrance of the police station, and they parked directly behind it. As DC Pullinger got out of the car, the sole occupant of the Range Rover did likewise. The officer recognised the driver as Craig Rolfe and called out to him. They then had a conversation regarding a future appointment to obtain a statement from his partner concerning a motoring allegation. Dibley had his first name.

It was only when local news bulletins about three men being found dead in a Range Rover started being broadcast that relatives and friends began reaching for the phone. At 2 p.m. Tucker's partner rang. 'My boyfriend, Anthony Tucker, was out last night in company with Pat Tate and Craig Rolfe. They were in a blue Range Rover part index NPE, which is jointly owned by them but not registered in their names. They were due to take me and two others out for dinner last night but didn't come home.' Before the officer who took the call could answer, the woman became hysterical, saying that she knew they were the deceased and that they had been murdered. She went on to say that unless action was taken quickly 'it wouldn't end there'. She also said that by the time the police got the killers, they would need to 'dig them up'.

Totally distraught, in hysterics, she demanded to be allowed to identify the bodies. When the officer asked for her name and address, she refused to give it.

At 2.20 p.m., Craig Rolfe's mother called the police. Mrs Rolfe said, 'My son is missing. He has an F-registered Range Rover 3.9 Vogue, colour blue. I don't know any other details concerning the car. I last saw him yesterday between 3 p.m. and 4 p.m. at my address, when he picked his daughter up.'

DS White, who took the call, told Mrs Rolfe, 'Our inquiries are at an early stage. If we have any positive information, someone will speak to you.'

At five past seven, Tucker's brother, Ronnie, called the police. 'Can someone call me if one of the deceased is my brother, Tony Tucker. I suspect that it is him, so a phone call will do.' At 9.35 p.m., DC King took a call from Marie Tate, who asked if her son, Pat, was one of the three dead men. The officer was unable to give her any information but said someone from the incident room would make contact with her.

When Tucker's father Ronald, aged 63, of Folkestone, Kent, heard the news of his son's death, he suffered a heart attack, collapsed and died. God only knows what Mrs Tucker went through that day and has undoubtedly been through since.

As the identities of the dead men became known, the nature of the executions began to make sense to DS Dibley. Especially when it came to one of the dead men. DS Dibley had met Tate several years earlier. Dibley was a detective inspector at the time, investigating a number of armed robberies that Tate was rumoured to have been involved in. Before Dibley could interview Tate, he had escaped from the magistrates' court, fled to Gibraltar, been brought back and imprisoned. Undeterred, Dibley had gone to visit Tate at Swaleside prison in the hope he could persuade him to confess to the unsolved robberies. Dibley was sitting in the visiting room staring at the doorway through which Tate was going to enter. As it was an unarranged visit, Tate would have no idea whom the visit was from or what it was about. Dibley hoped the element of surprise would help him talk Tate into assisting him. When Tate appeared, it was Dibley who was surprised. He later said, 'I have never seen such a big man in the whole of my life. He actually took all the light away from the room, that's how big he was. His arms, chest . . . everything was just enormous.'

When Tate sat down, Dibley said, 'Hello, Mr Tate, you don't know me, but I'm investigating some armed robberies . . .'

For the next half-hour, Dibley talked, talked and talked. He was telling Tate what he suspected him of being involved in and was saying the only way he would get parole on his current sentence would be if he came clean about everything. Tate did not even blink. The whole time he just sat staring at Dibley without saying a word. Then Tate got up and walked out of the room. The next time Dibley set eyes on him, Tate was lying dead in the Range Rover.

That morning, I'd arranged to meet my brother, Paul, in London. I travelled on the train, as I didn't fancy battling through traffic in the snow. At about eleven o'clock, I rang home to see if there were any messages on the answering machine. There was one. A detective was asking me to contact him as soon as I got his message. It sounded urgent. I rang him from a call box at King's Cross station.

'We've found a Range Rover with three bodies inside,' he said. 'They've all been shot through the head. We think it's your mates.'

'What do you mean?' I asked.

'Do you recognise this registration: F424 NPE? I am sure it's them.' He told me he had seen them in the car before.

'I don't know what you're talking about,' I said. 'Tell me what's happened.' I was confused.

He repeated that they had found a Range Rover. Tucker, Tate and Rolfe were inside, but they had not been formally identified at that stage.

'Are they dead?' I asked.

'They're very dead.'

The policeman asked where I was, but I didn't answer. I said I would ring him later and put the phone down. I rang Tucker's mobile number. It rang and rang and rang. He wasn't going to answer. Unbeknown to me at that time, his mobile phone was still in his hand. The police had not yet removed it from his grip. Nor had they taken the body from the Range Rover. I rang home. Debra wasn't in. I left a message on the answering machine saying I had been told that 'those three' had been found murdered. I told her not to answer the phone if anyone rang. I walked around London in a daze. I really couldn't believe what I had just heard. I even began to wonder if I had actually had the conversation. Debra never did get my message. She had gone straight to the school at 3.30 p.m. to pick up the children and two detectives met her there.

'Are you Bernard's Debra?' one asked, having walked across to her. When she said yes, he replied, 'You and the children better come with me.' They were put in an unmarked car. Nothing was said in front of the children, but Debra was told what had happened. The police feared a revenge attack of some type might be carried out on my family or me, so they were going to remain with them until I had been located. The police – and others – obviously thought that I was somehow connected or responsible for the murders when in fact I had been as shocked as anybody when I heard the news.

The following morning, DS Dibley held a press conference where he told the gathered media: 'All three men have been shot in the head twice at point-blank range. The weapon, which has not been found, is thought to be a 12-bore shotgun. The men had criminal records, including armed robbery, drugs offences and car theft, but were not convicted drug dealers. Our intelligence is that they were moving into the drug field and that's the line we are currently trying to develop.

'They were higher in the scale than street dealers. It may be that this has occurred over higher drug dealers trying to find a greater position of power. Perhaps there has been a falling out in that connection. My view is that there could be a power struggle going on. There could have been a double-cross and someone has sought retribution or it might be that they owed money and they did not pay their bill. I think these are valid theories. Because drugs offer quick money and easy money there is this power struggle among the larger dealers.

'Inevitably, there are going to be incidences, such as this, occurring. I don't think Essex is any worse than anywhere else. However, I anticipate that someone will try to fill the void these deaths have created and that there could be more violence. There has been a lot of speculation that this killing was connected with the tragedy of Leah Betts. I must say that this is pure speculation. There is nothing factual to link these men with the tragedy of Leah Betts. I am afraid if that is allowed to continue it may well divert attention from my inquiry on this murder and will take me away from the real investigation. I would appreciate it if the connection between Leah Betts and this triple murder were dropped. At this moment in time, there is nothing to suggest that they distributed drugs to Leah Betts or any of her associates.'

When Dibley had finished, Diane Evans, Rolfe's partner,

Police examine the crime scene with the bodies
still slumped in the Range Rover.

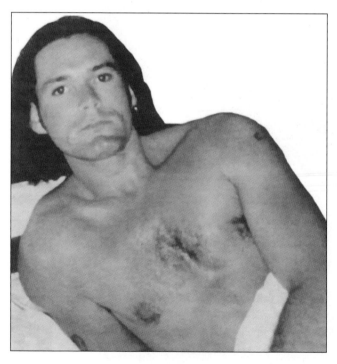

Craig Rolfe.

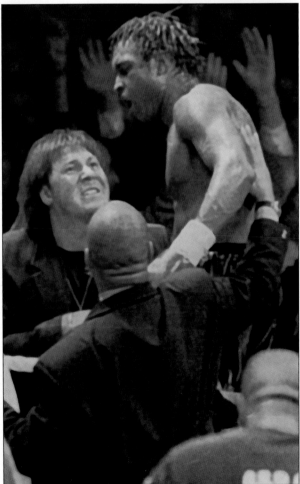

Above: Pat Tate
weightlifting in HMP
Swaleside prison, Kent,
where he met Kenneth
Noye.

Left: Tucker in the ring
congratulating his friend
Nigel Benn.

Mark Murray (left) with me in Raquels shortly before
Leah Betts's death in November 1995.

With Steve Curtis and Nathan Kaye at Epping Forest Country Club
the night I introduced them to Tony Tucker.

John (left) and Jack Whomes at home in Suffolk prior
to their imprisonment for car ringing.

Tate, Jackie Street and Mick Steele.

Happier times: Steele (left) and Tate relaxing on a beach.

Police surveillance photo of Jack Whomes fuelling his boat in a garage.

The most dangerous man in Britain, John 'Gaffer' Rollinson, flees from a knife-wielding Bernard O'Mahoney outside an Essex nightclub.

John Whomes and associate protest above the M25, causing traffic chaos around London.

Above: Jack's mother, Pam Whomes, with Emma O'Mahoney.

Left: With Larry Barrett (partner of Jayne Whomes) and John Whomes, protesting the Rettendon Two's innocence outside the High Court, 2006.

Jack Whomes being led back to the cells after
his and Steele's failed appeals. (Empics)

made an emotional appeal to the public for help. 'I would just like anyone who was with them on Wednesday afternoon or who knows anything about what happened, or has seen anything, to just come forward. We need all the help we can get.'

That same morning, John Whomes was working at the establishment in Haverhill for the mentally handicapped where he had worked while he was a prisoner at HMP Highpoint. A contract to build an extension had been advertised and John had managed to secure the tender. John heard on the radio that three men had been found shot dead in a Range Rover. When a few hours later they were named as Patrick Tate, Craig Rolfe and Tony Tucker, John immediately telephoned Jack and said, 'Tate's dead. I've just heard on the radio he's been shot.'

'Don't be daft, John, he was shot last year and locked up,' Jack replied.

'I'm telling you, Jack. It's just been on the news.'

'Fuck me!' Jack replied. 'I can't believe it.'

Few could believe what had happened to the seemingly invincible trio; even fewer were upset about it.

Two days after the bodies had been discovered, Darren Nicholls answered his front door to a gypsy named Matty. 'I hear you want to buy a shotgun,' he said. 'I've got one in my van.'

Without hesitation, Nicholls replied, 'OK, great, I'll have a look.'

The pair went to the back of the van and Matty opened the doors to show Nicholls a nine-shot single-barrelled pump-action shotgun with three cartridges. Nicholls purchased the weapon for £350.

At that time, Nicholls had been working at Mick Steele's home. The premises had an old barn that Steele had refurbished and Nicholls had agreed to rewire it. For reasons known only to Nicholls, he drove over to Steele's home with the shotgun hidden in a canvas bag. When he arrived, Steele was not home, so he went into the barn to continue doing the electrical work he had started. At some stage during that day, Nicholls hid the shotgun and cartridges in Steele's barn behind some bamboo poles before leaving for home.

Over the Christmas period, Rolfe's brother moved Diane Evans's belongings from the home she had shared with Craig in Chafford Hundred to a new address in Basildon. Diane had only been in the house for a couple of days when she decided that she was going to have to do something about the machine gun Tucker, Tate and Rolfe had stored at her home.

Diane spoke to Rolfe's mother and she suggested that Diane bring it round to her house. Diane removed the holdall containing the gun from its hiding place and put it on the dining-room table. When she opened the bag, she saw the machine gun for the first time. She was terrified. She knew that she had to make a decision as to what she was going to do about it. She then took it to Rolfe's mother's house.

A couple of days later, Diane contacted DI Florence and told him that she wanted to see him but didn't say why. The following day, the police officer went to see Diane and she told him about the gun. Diane took him to Rolfe's mother's home. Mrs Rolfe retrieved the holdall from the shower room on the ground floor and put it on the dining table for DI Florence to see. Diane explained in detail how the machine gun had ended up in her possession. The officer asked if either of them had handled the gun and when both said they hadn't, he took it away to be examined.

As the New Year dawned, the management at Raquels decided to close the club. Publicity linking it to the death of Leah Betts and the Rettendon murders had dramatically reduced trade. The firm had lost its leaders and a prestigious door, and the end was in sight. On 13 January 1996, rival firms, aware that Tucker's vice-like grip had slipped from running the drug deals that went on in the clubs he supplied security for, took advantage of the free market brought about by his death. Tucker's dealers in Club UK had fled with Murray after Leah had collapsed but were soon replaced by others wishing to make their fortunes.

Andreas Bouzis, a 19-year-old boy of Greek descent, purchased an Ecstasy pill outside the club and took it while he was queuing up to enter. Shortly afterwards, he died. The tablet he had taken exacerbated a congenital heart defect. The club was closed down in the aftermath of his death and Tucker's once-powerful door firm was finally no more.

On 25 January, I had another meeting with DCI Storey, who said he wanted me to make a statement in relation to the Leah Betts incident. He could see that I was still struggling with the very thought of it. The murders had added additional pressure to my thought process, and so he told me to go away and think hard before I made my decision. For two or three days, I wrestled with my conscience. But I knew what I had to do, this nightmare had to end sometime. I realised that if I wanted to shed the criminal make-up I had worn for so long, the only decision that I could make, which would not allow me to return to my criminal associates and lifestyle, would be to agree to cooperate with DCI Storey's request. I contacted him and we arranged to meet at Maldon police station.

I will never forget sitting in that room, which overlooked a row of quaint shops. Below, people were going about their everyday business and I sat there watching them while I talked about the deaths of young people. I sat astride two worlds. I knew which one I wanted to inhabit. I made the statement. The door to my previous life was closed firmly behind me.

My former friends would never have me back now that I had assisted the police. As the Betts and Rettendon investigations got under way, villains fearful of being implicated in either matter began informing on their rivals to deflect attention away from their own illicit businesses. The police were inundated with anonymous tip-offs: some factual, some outright lies.

Because of the amount of trouble Nicholls had caused drug dealers over the dud cannabis, it was not long before his name and, by association, Mick Steele's were given to the police as persons somehow involved in the Rettendon murders. When the police researched Steele and Nicholls, they learned of Steele's drug importation conviction and Nicholls's boasts to undercover officers that he would blow people's heads off if he were ever ripped off. When they discovered both men had been in prison with Tate, they decided that Nicholls and Steele would be worthy of further scrutiny.

Instead of arresting Nicholls and Steele, the police set up an elaborate sting to try and find out what, if anything, they had done. Nicholls was put under surveillance and Steele started to receive menacing telephone calls. These were made from Belfast by two undercover officers who claimed to be members of the IRA. It's incredible even to consider that officers who are paid to uphold the law in a civilised country are permitted to make threats to suspects in any of their inquiries, but that is exactly what these officers were sanctioned to do. The first call came just after the news at nine o'clock on Thursday, 15 February 1996. The voice was that of a softly spoken Irishman, who said he had been trying to track Steele down for weeks.

The caller said his name was 'Billy' and that he and his brother 'John' were part of an organisation that had worked closely with Tate. Unbeknown to Steele, Billy explained, all the drugs he had smuggled for Tate were destined for Ireland. When the enterprise had started up, Billy and John had been led to believe that supplies would be reaching them on a regular basis. With that in mind, they had invested a lot of their own money in the venture. Now, with Tate dead, the brothers had found themselves severely out of pocket and totally out of stock. Billy's initial question was simple enough: would Steele be prepared to supply them with the drugs directly?

Up until that point, Steele had said no more than 'Hello'. When Billy had finished talking, Steele simply replied, 'I haven't got the faintest idea what you're talking about, mate.' Then he put the phone down.

The second call was made two days later. 'Pat owed us £40,000,' ranted Billy. 'We want our fucking money. Where is it? This isn't a fucking game.'

Steele remained calm. 'I think the police have got it. Why don't you talk to them?' Once more, he hung up.

Since Billy didn't appear to be getting anywhere with Steele, his brother, John, decided to have a go. When Steele picked up the phone for the third call, John hissed, 'We want our money or you'll be sorted out just like Pat was.' The threats became more sinister. Steele was warned that his car would be blown up, but he just listened rather than inflame the situation by arguing.

Eventually, Steele grew tired of being threatened about Tate's money and said, 'I haven't got a clue about it. Now then, I wonder what's happened to it. Perhaps I've got it under my floorboards, eh?'

John, laughing, replied, 'Now there's a thing.'

'Aye?'

'There's a thing. Have you?'

'Well, I haven't got floorboards, for a start; I've got a concrete floor,' Steele replied.

'Right.'

'And I wish I did have that sort of money about me because I'd be a very happy man.'

'Right.'

'Now then, what I want to say to you—'

'Right.'

'Is the fact that you keep ringing up here; I mean, every fortnight or so.'

'Yeah.'

'I mean, your Billy, was it? Billy, was it, on the phone making all sorts of threats? You know, like I said, I'm one of these people, I'm a little bit laid-back. Nothing really worries me.'

'Mmm.'

'And Billy was saying to me he's got A levels in – what is it he said? – A levels in whacking people, I think his expression was. I honestly don't give a fuck.' Steele replaced the receiver.

The calls became more and more frequent and the threats more and more serious. Billy and John talked about the recent IRA bombing at Canary Wharf, implying they were members of that terrorist organisation. 'You'd better watch your back,' John told Steele. 'The ceasefire has gone, Mickey, and your ceasefire's gone.' During one of the calls, Billy said, 'You're going to have to emigrate one day, that's the only way. I'm going to have to follow these matters up.'

Steele's response was short and to the point. 'Why don't the pair of you just fuck off and bother someone else.'

A few days later, Sarah Saunders received similar threats from Billy and John. Sarah, fearing for her safety and that of her young son, immediately reported the threats to Basildon Police. Their response brought Sarah little comfort. The contact number Billy and John had given Sarah, they said, was the number of a well-known IRA bar in Belfast. Billy and John, they added, had been identified as known members of a major terrorist cell that had recently moved to mainland Britain. They had been tracked entering the country, but the officers watching them had now lost them. Sarah was naturally terrified but almost as soon as the threatening calls had started, they stopped.

Chapter 12

On Friday, 1 March, I was asked to attend South Woodham Ferrers police station, where the Rettendon murder inquiry team was based. DS Saunders and DC Chapple led me through the back to an interview room. In the corridor outside was a storeroom and on the door a sign read: 'Risk of health hazard, Rettendon exhibits'. In that cupboard, behind that door, were my friends' clothing and personal effects, no doubt soaked in their blood. I don't know if I had been shown it deliberately for effect, or if it was a mere coincidence, but it made the whole horror story real.

When the detectives sat me down, they asked me about my military career, adding that the gunman had executed the trio with ruthless efficiency. 'Someone who knew what they were doing, Bernie. An ex-military man, perhaps?' I said I knew what it looked like, but I had not murdered my friends. I was told that I had to understand that a lot of people believed I was involved. 'Even if you didn't pull the trigger, Bernie, you had good reason to see the back of them. They were threatening to shoot you. Maybe it was a case of you or them? You could have done it out of fear.'

All the time they were 'chatting' to me, I was aware that one of the detectives kept his gaze fixed firmly on my eyes, as if he was looking for a reaction. When they had finished their 'chat', which had lasted for an hour and forty-five minutes, they said they would need to see me again. They gave me their names and numbers on a piece of paper – 'Just in case you remember anything, Bernie,' they said – and told me to go.

As we walked past the storeroom again, I felt myself reaching out to touch the door. Tucker's thick gold neck chain with its solid-gold boxing glove, I knew, would be in there. He always wore it. I imagined it caked in blood and the police having to clean it before they returned it to his loved ones. These morbid thoughts saddened me and made me feel deeply depressed. I found it hard to accept that I would never see them again, though I felt annoyed at myself for feeling sorry for them. Those three bastards would have murdered me at the drop of a hat. How on earth did we arrive at all this?

The detectives couldn't resist a parting shot. 'Keep your head down, Bernie. You know some people think you had a hand in this and they aren't happy.'

It wasn't a threat. I knew as well as they did it was a fact. Whether they actually cared about my well-being was another matter. When I got outside, I had an urge to run, to get away from this bloody mess, but I thought the detectives would be watching me from the police station windows, so I walked around the corner before running to the nearby gymnasium car park where I had left my vehicle – I was still on the 12-month driving ban I'd picked up in Birmingham. I felt stupid. I felt hunted by the police and hunted by the people who, according to the police, were plotting my murder. For others in the murky drug world I had left behind, it was business as usual.

Twenty miles away in Braintree, Darren Nicholls continued to use his suicide jockeys to import cannabis. He had also become heavily involved with an Essex detective. One day, he had been in the Sailing Oak public house having a drink when somebody tapped him on the shoulder. A voice said, 'I know you're a drug dealer.' When Nicholls turned around, he saw DC Wolfgang Bird looking at him with a big smirk on his face. Nicholls had never spoken to the detective, but he knew who he was because their paths had crossed twice in the past. The first time had been in that very pub. DC Bird had lent his car, a Ford Escort XR3i, to three friends, who had crashed it and one of them had ended up in intensive care. Nicholls and a group of his friends had mocked the detective about the incident. On the second occasion, in the same pub around Christmas time, Nicholls had seen DC Bird unloading bottles of spirits from the boot of his car and taking them into the pub. Enquiries by Nicholls among the regulars revealed the detective was a friend of the landlord and supplied him with booze he bought cheaply at police auctions.

As Nicholls stared back at the detective, who had just accused him of being a drug dealer, he was trying to think of something to say. Before he had a chance, DC Bird said, 'I suppose you're going to deny it? Everyone always denies it.'

'I don't know what you're talking about,' replied Nicholls. 'All of that was a long time ago. You're out of date.' He turned and walked away.

Two days later, Nicholls received a call on his mobile from DC Bird. Paul, the boss of an electrical company Nicholls worked for, was a friend of the detective's and he had given him Nicholls's number. 'What do you want?' Nicholls asked.

'I'm only telling you this because you're a friend of Paul's,' DC Bird replied. 'You're about to get spun. The drug squad is planning a raid on your place because they reckon you've got a load of gear stashed there.'

Nicholls laughed. 'I didn't think the drugs squad was that slow. I've told you, mate, that was all in the past.'

DC Bird was persistent. He told Nicholls that he was looking at a note on the CID office wall that had details of a raid that was going to be carried out at Nicholls's home address. 'Tell you what,' DC Bird said, 'if you're telling me the truth and you're not at it any more, I will stop it from happening.'

A few days later, DC Bird telephoned Nicholls again. 'I told you, Darren. I stopped it happening. Your home didn't get searched, did it?' Nicholls was far from naive: he knew the officer had probably made up the whole story just so Nicholls felt in his debt. He also knew what would come next – a meeting to talk to the officer about how he could repay that debt. DC Bird did not disappoint. A few days later, at his request, the pair met. The detective made it clear from the outset that he wanted Nicholls to be his informant. He knew Nicholls was a major supplier of drugs on his patch.

At first, Nicholls was reluctant to comply, but he soon realised that he could use DC Bird instead of being used himself. If anybody threatened or upset him, he could simply get them removed by setting them up and informing on them to his police handler. In order to test the water, Nicholls told DC Bird about the dud cannabis that he had dumped in the gravel pits lake. Nicholls said that he used to smuggle cannabis, but those days were long gone. He then told the officer that he had imported a load that had turned out to be dud, so he dumped it in the lake. As soon as Nicholls mentioned the drugs, DC Bird grew visibly excited. He told Nicholls to get in his car and the pair drove to the lake, where Nicholls pointed to the spot where he had dumped the drugs.

'This will look blinding on your record,' Nicholls told DC Bird. 'You'll have this find because of your initiative.'

DC Bird told Nicholls that he would get a reward if the cannabis was still in the lake, but first he would have to come up with a story of how it got there. If Nicholls was the one who smuggled it and then dumped it, he could hardly expect the police to do anything other than arrest him. They certainly wouldn't reward him. Nicholls concocted a story about the origin of the drugs. He blamed two innocent men whom Nicholls claimed he had overheard talking in a Braintree pub. When it came to collecting the reward, Nicholls was told that he would have to become a registered police informant and meet a senior officer. At the meeting, he was handed £400 for his 'public spiritedness' and was told that from now on if he had any contact with his police handlers, he would have to use the name Ken Rugby. This was to protect him from people eavesdropping on police conversations or dubious officers seeing his real name on informant sheets at the police station.

Two years before Nicholls had become involved with DC Bird, the sister of his wife Sandra had been going out with a local man named Alan Richards. Sandra, Nicholls and Richards all got on well until one drunken night when Richards gave Sandra a lift home. Instead of taking her to her own home, he took her to his, where she stayed the night. When Nicholls found out, he went berserk. A few days later, he confronted Richards, who told him he had been too drunk to drive Sandra home, so she had slept on his settee. Nicholls refused to believe him. From that day onwards, the atmosphere between the two men was dire. It was obvious that eventually they would come to blows.

That night came in the Sailing Oak pub, where DC Bird was also drinking. Nicholls, who was drunk at the time, began calling Richards names. Eventually, Richards lost his temper, stood up and suggested they both go outside to resolve the matter once and for all. Before Nicholls could reply, Richards sat back down awkwardly and fell off his chair. Everybody in the bar burst out laughing. The landlord quickly appeared on the scene and accused Nicholls of causing the trouble. Nicholls flew into a rage, badmouthed the landlord and walked out of the pub.

Seconds later, DC Bird was at Nicholls's side. He said he had spoken to the landlord and he had apologised. If Nicholls returned to the pub, he could have free drinks all night. At that moment, Nicholls realised DC Bird could be more than his handler, he could be his friend and protector. Instead of returning to the pub, the pair stood in the car park talking about Nicholls importing drugs, selling them, telling DC Bird who had purchased them and DC Bird then arresting them.

'That's a bit strong,' Nicholls replied when DC Bird had first suggested it. 'You are kidding, aren't you?'

DC Bird paused momentarily. 'Of course, I'm serious,' he said, 'of course, I am.'

Unbeknown to Nicholls and DC Bird, Alan Richards, still smarting from being humiliated, was watching them from the pub window. It all made sense to him now. When Nicholls started being abusive to him, DC Bird had remained in his seat and said nothing. When Nicholls had a go at the landlord, DC Bird had gone out of his way to smooth things over on Nicholls's behalf. Watching them talk in the car park, Richards felt uneasy. A voice in his head told him that they were talking about him. That same voice warned him that Nicholls might be thinking about setting him up.

Early the next morning, Alan Richards presented himself at Essex Police headquarters in Chelmsford and asked to speak to a senior officer. He told them he had information about one of their officers who he believed might be involved in criminal activity. 'I think I can prove it,' he said.

When the police realised who DC Bird was involved with, they had little doubt that the allegations needed investigating. A massive surveillance operation codenamed Operation Apache was mounted, which involved tailing Nicholls and DC Bird and taping all of the phone calls DC Bird made and received. In all, 35 officers were assigned to Operation Apache. It remains the biggest internal investigation ever undertaken by Essex Police.

All Customs officers have some sort of system to relieve the boredom of watching hundreds of cars, then pulling one over at random. George Stephens had several, but his favourite was to add together all of the figures in that day's date and then count off the passing vehicles until he reached that number. On 14 April 1996, vehicle number 43 happened to be a white Mondeo that was passing through Dover at 9.45 a.m. Stephens flagged the car down and asked the driver his name, where he had been and why. The driver, Craig Androliakos, appeared nervous. 'I've been to Paris,' he said. 'I was visiting a girl I met a couple of weeks ago.'

'Is this your car then, sir?' Stephens enquired.

'No, it's hired, a friend of mine hired it,' Androliakos replied.

'Who was that, then?' Stephens asked. 'I need to know the name of your friend.'

Androliakos was visibly sweating. He paused for a long time before answering, 'Nick Reynolds, Nick Reynolds hired it.'

Stephens had been in his job long enough to know that Androliakos was hiding something, so he asked him to get out of the car so that it could be searched. The first place Stephens looked was the glove box, where he found the rental agreement from Budget car hire. 'This car's been hired by somebody called Darren Nicholls,' Stephens said. When he searched the boot, he found a pair of fisherman's waders. They were still wet and were covered in sand. In Androliakos's luggage, Stephens found maps of Holland and Belgium, and scraps of paper with mobile phone numbers on them. Although suspicious, the items were not illegal and so Stephens had to let him go.

As soon as Androliakos had departed, the Customs officer dashed back to the office and ran a few names through the computer. Darren Nicholls's name flashed up on the screen and below was a memo that asked anybody who came into contact with him to get in touch with Essex Police.

On 30 April, DS Ivan Dibley retired and handed over the Rettendon murder investigation to DS Brian Storey. The latter soon realised that he would not be conducting a lengthy investigation because, shortly after taking charge, the taps on the phone of DC Bird began to reveal some startling conversations.

On 10 May 1996, DC Bird and Nicholls talked about a Jaguar that Nicholls wanted to sell for £3,000. Nicholls told DC Bird that drug dealers were going to use the vehicle to transport £150,000 out of the country so that they could purchase drugs on the Continent.

'Righto, oh that's goodo,' DC Bird said. 'Oh, right, so really all I've got to do is steal that car when it goes abroad next time and keep the loot.'

'That wouldn't be a fucking bad idea, would it?' Nicholls replied.

'No.'

'That would be a bloody good idea. Wouldn't that be nice between us?'

'Yes.'

'It would be like a hundred and something-odd thousand pounds. No, it would be more than that, actually . . . no, it wouldn't, it would be about a hundred and fifty grand, I reckon.'

'Mmm.'

'It buys a lot of gear down there where they are going.'

'Yeah, exactly.'

'No, it would be more than that. I reckon they're paying seven and a half this time, they said.'

'How many people go driving abroad with the cash then?'

'Only two.'

'What, they leave it in the car, or do they go—'

'Leave it in the car.'

'Good grief, that's very remiss of them, isn't it?'

'Yeah, they used to carry it on, you know, used to get it out of the boot, and then they decided that it's probably worse walking round with a couple of hundred grand like a dickhead in suitcases on a boat than just leaving it in the motor.'

'Yeah.'

'Which is a shame, if you know what I mean.'

'Exactly. It's a shame you haven't kept a spare key.'

'Oh, fuck me, I'd get into it.'

'It would be better with a key because all you would do is drive on with them, make sure you follow somewhere near them, you hang around when they go up on deck.'

'Yeah.'

'Swap from one boot into the other and just drive off with them at the same time.'

Ultimately the gang didn't think the car Nicholls had for sale was reliable, so they hired a vehicle instead.

As well as discussing what drug dealers were up to, DC Bird and Nicholls talked about making amphetamines. Nicholls had told DC Bird two pints of a chemical known as BMK (benzyl methyl ketone, an essential ingredient in the production of amphetamine sulphate) were available. DC Bird told him more would be needed. 'Say a gallon, Darren,' he said. The pair were recorded laughing about dishing out the drugs they planned to make to people 'like sweets'. Thankfully, this scheme never went ahead.

As proof of the corruption and drug dealing mounted, DS Storey organised a briefing involving not only Essex Police officers but also Customs officers, so that they could trade information and discuss tactics. When the evidence had been processed and compared with other intelligence,

DS Storey was amazed to discover that Craig Androliakos, who had been stopped in the Mondeo hired by Nicholls, was working for a gang headed by none other than Pat Tate's younger brother Russell.

Customs spotter planes were put on standby and dozens of undercover officers were earmarked for duty. Intelligence reports showed that Russell Tate and other members of his gang had just left for Spain. When Nicholls had said to DC Bird, 'It buys a lot of gear down there where they are going,' police officers hadn't initially understood what he had meant. It now dawned on them that 'down there' meant Spain, and the money Nicholls and DC Bird had talked about stealing from a car had belonged to Tate's gang. DS Storey decided to have the gang's mobile phones monitored, and when transmissions from those phones showed that they were heading north, back towards England, police and Customs would swoop into action.

On Monday, 13 May, Nicholls was driving along the A120 near Colchester in the blue Jaguar that he had failed to sell to Tate's gang. One of his friends, Colin Bridge, was following behind in Nicholls's Transit van. Always cautious when 'working', Nicholls was convinced that he was being followed. He picked up his mobile and rang DC Bird. 'Oi, am I under surveillance? Are you lot following me?' he asked.

'Nah, don't be stupid, Darren,' DC Bird replied. 'You're just being paranoid.'

'I don't think so, mate, I'm sure I'm being surveyed. I've been paranoid before and it doesn't feel anything like this.'

'I'm telling you, Darren, you're not being followed. If you were, I'd tell you, wouldn't I? I mean I'm not going to fuck you up, am I? You're on our side, just relax.'

'All right. Listen, though. The shipment came in last night. I'm just going over to pick up my share.'

'I know. Don't worry, everything's under control. Relax.'

A short while later, Nicholls and Bridge arrived at Steele's house, and Nicholls asked Steele if he could pick up some tools he had left there. Steele, who was sitting on a deckchair sunning himself, said, 'Sure, help yourself.'

Nicholls took a toolbox from the Jaguar's boot and walked off. A short while later, he returned carrying the toolbox and put it in the back of the van. The Transit, driven by Bridge, then left Steele's home with Nicholls in the Jaguar behind.

At just after 2 p.m., uniformed police officers stopped the two vehicles on the B1053 at Broad Street, Bocking, near Braintree. When the vehicles came to a halt, Bridge got out and began talking to the officers; however, Nicholls refused to open the door of his car and began talking on a mobile phone.

First, Nicholls telephoned his wife Sandra. 'I won't be home, after all,' he shouted. 'I'm being stopped by the police. I'll try and call you later. Bye.'

By now, officers were hammering on the window, telling him to put the phone down and open the door. Nicholls chose to ignore them because he had one last important call to make.

'DC Bird's message pager,' said a woman's voice. 'Can I take your message, please?'

'Yeah, the message is, "I'm being fucking nicked."'

There was a long silence and then the woman said, 'I'm sorry, sir, I don't think I can send that particular message.'

The officers outside the car had pulled out their truncheons and were threatening to smash the window. Nicholls looked at them, sighed and said to the woman, 'All right. Just tell him that Darren has been arrested.'

As soon as Nicholls stepped out of the car, the officers snatched his mobile phone from him and handcuffed his hands behind his back. As he looked up the road, he could see Bridge, also handcuffed, being put in a police van.

'Do you know why you have been stopped?' asked one of the officers.

Nicholls said nothing. He just shook his head.

'Where have you come from?' asked the officer.

'Colchester,' Nicholls replied.

'Well, there have been a number of burglaries in Colchester and you've been stopped today because we would like to search your van in connection with those burglaries.' Nicholls nodded, 'OK, fair enough, but everything in that van is mine. Colin is just driving it for me. He has nothing to do with anything. It's all down to me.'

Because the back of the van was empty except for the toolbox, it didn't take the officers long to find the ten kilos of cannabis inside. 'What are these, then?' asked the officer.

'They look like chocolate bars to me,' Nicholls replied. 'What do you think they are?'

A huge grin broke out on the officer's face. 'I think they're drugs and you're under arrest.'

Bridge was taken to Chelmsford police station and Nicholls was taken to Braintree, where he remained for three hours. Nobody is quite sure why he was taken there or what he may have been questioned about because his custody record was never found. It is assumed he was questioned about his relationship with DC Bird, who had also been arrested, but nobody other than the police and Nicholls know if that's the case.

Earlier that day, Jack and John Whomes and their brother William were driving lorries used to shunt trailers on the docks at Felixstowe. The night before, Jack had telephoned his brothers and asked them to stand in for a couple of drivers who had telephoned in sick. As the brothers were working, Mick Steele entered the dock in a rigid inflatable boat. John asked Steele if he had enjoyed a good day out and Steele replied that he had. Moments later, a large crane lifted the boat out of the water and onto a trailer attached to

Jack's van. Steele drove the van and boat back to Jack's yard, where he unhitched the trailer and pushed it and the boat into Jack's workshop. Steele then headed home to Clacton to pick up his partner, Jackie Street, and get changed. When they were ready, Steele and Street drove them back to Jack's yard. A friend, Peter Corry, followed in Jack's van.

At approximately 3 p.m. as Steele drove along Ranelagh Road in Ipswich, an unmarked police vehicle pulled in front of him and the two vehicles collided. One of the police officers approached the driver's door of Steele's vehicle and opened it. 'I am DC Chapple from Essex Police,' the officer said. 'I am arresting you both on suspicion of being involved in the importation of controlled drugs.'

'Has he fucking damaged my bumper?' Steele shouted after the caution had been read out. One of the other officers put his hand on Steele's shoulder as if to try and calm him down. Steele turned and fixed his gaze on the officer. 'Take your fucking hands off me, boy,' he said. The officer immediately removed his hand. Jackie Street remained silent throughout.

DS Sandford meanwhile had stopped the Transit van and run to the driver's door. 'You're nicked,' he said as he opened it. Peter Corry was then taken out of the vehicle and handcuffed. 'You are under arrest for conspiracy to supply controlled drugs,' he was told, then cautioned.

'I don't know what you mean, mate,' countered Corry.

Steele, Street and Corry were put into police vehicles and transferred to Colchester police station. Jack Whomes was at his yard cleaning the boat Steele had left there when Customs officers and police, some of whom were armed, approached him.

'OK, Jack,' one of them said, 'put down the power washer.'

'Actually, it's a pressure washer,' Jack replied. As he turned, he saw armed police officers crouching down, their weapons pointing at him. 'Fucking hell, this is a bit heavy, isn't it?'

Jack was arrested, cautioned and transferred to Clacton police station. Nicholls meanwhile had been taken from Braintree police station to join Colin Bridge at Chelmsford. All the way there he was expecting his friend, DC Bird, to appear and tell the officers they had made a terrible mistake. Nicholls could imagine him saying, 'No, this one's OK, he's on our side.' But DC Bird was never going to come to his rescue: he too was going to be facing some awkward questions. Nicholls soon realised the only man who could save him now was himself. He decided he would give 'no comment' answers to all of the police questions until he knew exactly how strong their case was. Only then would he decide what path he was going to take. One thing was for sure: saving himself was top priority.

At 9.16 p.m., Nicholls asked if he could speak to a nominated police officer who was known to him, but DS Storey declined the request. At 11.26 p.m. on the day of his arrest, Darren Nicholls was interviewed for the first time about the importation of cannabis. He said 'no comment' to all of the questions that were asked. At the end of the interview, DC Winstone, who was asking Nicholls the questions, said, 'I don't intend to say any more about the possession with intent to supply at the moment. The time by my watch is 23.35 hrs and you're now going to be arrested for being involved in the murders of Pat Tate, Craig Rolfe and Tony Tucker. Do you wish to make any comment to the fact you've now been arrested for those murders?'

After a pause, Nicholls replied, 'No comment.'

The following day, as the extent of the evidence against him began to be revealed, Nicholls realised he was in a hopeless position, but he still refused to comment when each question was asked. In addition to all of the Customs and police surveillance records – which now included video footage and still pictures – the police had access to his phone records. Additionally, Nicholls was the only person who had been caught in possession of drugs. Colin Bridge had been released after just two or three hours because it was clear to police he had played no active part in the drug-smuggling operation. Nicholls had told the officers that everything in the van was his so prosecuting Bridge would have been impossible.

At the end of his second interview, DC Winstone said to Nicholls, 'Last night you asked if you could speak to a police officer. Would you like to tell me who the police officer was?'

Nicholls looked at DC Winstone and said, 'No comment.'

'All right, I can tell you that at the moment two police officers from Essex have been arrested and are currently in custody.'

Nicholls's jaw dropped. 'Oh, fuck, I don't believe it . . .'

DC Winstone continued, 'The officers have been charged with a number of offences including some linked to the possession of controlled drugs. We have evidence that you have had numerous dealings with one of the officers. Is there any comment you wish to make now?'

'No, no fucking comment,' Nicholls replied.

As soon as the tape had been switched off, Nicholls asked to see a senior police officer. DS Barrington was summoned and Nicholls asked him if he were to give him the name of the police officer who had been arrested, would he confirm it? DS Barrington said that he would.

'Is it DC Bird?'

DS Barrington confirmed that it was.

Nicholls told him that DC Bird was the reason he had got into all of this trouble. 'I've been set up,' he said.

Nicholls knew that he was now facing the toughest decision of his life. If he managed to escape prosecution by the police, which was extremely unlikely, the fact that he was Ken Rugby, police informant, would come out and if he were sent to prison he would undoubtedly be in extreme danger. Even if he escaped imprisonment, all of the people in Braintree he had grassed on and set up would find out and he would have to move. There was no way out for him. Whichever path he took, he faced ruin.

It was an established fact that Nicholls was DC Bird's informant, so the police knew he wasn't averse to informing on people, even friends. They also knew he had nowhere safe to turn, so they threw him a lifeline. If Nicholls could tell them who had murdered Tate, Tucker and Rolfe, he would become a witness and not a defendant. If he told police about the drug importations he was involved in and gave evidence against fellow smugglers, they would put him and his family on the witness protection programme. This deal would give him and his family a new identity, a new home in a new area, a completely fresh start in life. Nicholls didn't hesitate: it was time to start talking.

Chapter 13

At first, Nicholls would only talk to the police about his association with DC Bird – how he had met him and how he had led him to the cannabis in the gravel pit, how the two innocent men had been set up for putting drugs there and about the reward he had received for his information. When it came to Nicholls's own involvement in smuggling and selling drugs, he lied through his teeth. He claimed that he had only travelled abroad once and then his passport had expired, that he had never spoken to Harris, the Dutch drug dealer, and had never made any money from drugs. When Nicholls was asked whom he was working for, he blamed the men he had met in prison: Jack Whomes and Mick Steele.

During one interview, Nicholls said that he had only become involved with DC Bird because he wanted Steele and Whomes – the men he was to allege had carried out the Rettendon murders – out of the way because they scared him. 'I wanted them out of my life,' he said. 'I wanted to set them up.' Until that point, Steele and Whomes had not been serious suspects in the murder investigation. An intelligence report compiled in the weeks after the murders had 167 entries. My name appeared more than a dozen times. Steele's name appeared twice, with informants suggesting that he, as an associate of Tate's, might know who carried out the killings. Jack Whomes's name did not appear at all.

Nicholls knew that almost any story he told concerning

Steele and drug importation would be plausible because Steele was a convicted drug smuggler and Whomes was a good friend of Steele's who happened to own a boat capable of crossing the Channel at speed. Add the fact that Nicholls had been seen picking up a toolbox containing drugs from Steele's home address, and Nicholls had undoubtedly produced a believable story.

After two days, Nicholls was moved to Rayleigh police station, where he began to tell detectives his version of events concerning the murders of Tucker, Tate and Rolfe. When asked why Steele and, in particular, Whomes – who had not even met Tucker and Rolfe – would want to murder the men, Nicholls said it was because when Tate was asked by 'Billy and John', the 'IRA' men, for their refund, Tate had insisted that Steele had their £40,000. The IRA men had then rung Steele and threatened him. Nicholls had learned of the calls while carrying out electrical work at Steele's home. Unfortunately, neither Nicholls nor the interviewing officers realised the IRA men were undercover police. Nor did they remember the IRA men had only materialised six weeks after the murders. When this error was spotted, the IRA motive disappeared from Nicholls's statements.

Nicholls quickly offered the police a second motive. He claimed Steele was having an affair with Tate's girlfriend, Sarah Saunders. Steele didn't like the way Tate treated Saunders, so together they had decided to murder Tate. Saunders, the mother of Tate's child, could claim his life insurance into the bargain. Of course, Sarah denied any affair or plot with Steele. No explanation was given as to why Tucker and Rolfe had to be murdered in this particular plot or why it would involve Whomes. In total, Nicholls made 20 separate statements. The police refused to disclose all of them to the defence because some were deemed not to be in the public interest.

Eventually, it was decided that the dud cannabis that Nicholls had picked up in Amsterdam and later dumped in the gravel pit was the motive behind the murders. Nicholls told detectives it was Steele who had masterminded the importation of the cannabis that turned out to be dud. Nicholls merely worked for him, travelling to Stone's Café in Amsterdam to purchase the drugs before Steele brought them into the country in an inflatable boat. Whomes, he said, met Steele when the boat arrived back in England. Following the importation of the dud cannabis, it was Nicholls who was given the job of dumping the drugs in the lake and he who was asked to travel to Amsterdam by Steele to recover Tate's money.

These were hardly 'voluntary confessions' about himself and his crimes. They were details Nicholls could not deny because he had used his credit card to pay for the trips. The telephone calls concerning his dealings with the detective had been monitored. The £400 reward for telling the officer where he had dumped the cannabis was a recorded fact and satellite signals for calls to and from his own mobile phone, which placed him at the murder scene at the relevant time, had been recorded by a nearby transmitting station. But for everything that couldn't be pinned on himself, Nicholls blamed Steele.

He said it was Steele who had fallen out with Tate, not him. 'Tate was telling people he hadn't received his money back from Steele and he was going to make Steele kneel down before shooting him.' This particular claim made Steele very brave or very stupid because, according to Nicholls, it was Steele who travelled down the deserted lane in the Range Rover with Tate and two equally dangerous men, Tucker and Rolfe, whom Steele would have been aware had already murdered their friend Kevin Whitaker.

Nicholls said Steele had told Tate a light aircraft was going to land a shipment of cocaine at Rettendon. Steele, Tucker,

Tate and Rolfe were then going to rob it. This robbery was the job Tucker and Tate had asked me to assist them with when we met at Basildon hospital. I am pleased I turned down their offer and wasn't in the Range Rover with them that night. Nicholls did tell police that there should have been a fourth man in the car, but he said it was to be a man named Spindler: somebody Tucker and Tate had no doubt recruited in my absence but who had also had the sense not to turn up. But, again according to Nicholls, there was no shipment: it was a baited hook and the trio took it. All this information was widely known amongst the criminal fraternity because Tucker and Tate had talked about the robbery to numerous people, including Nicholls.

In the final interview, Nicholls said that at 5 p.m. on 6 December he met Whomes and Steele outside a motorbike shop in Marks Tey near Colchester. Nicholls got into Steele's Toyota and they set off towards Brentwood. Whomes followed the pair alone in another car. At about 6 p.m., all three arrived at Thorndon Country Park. They parked their cars and Nicholls moved into Whomes's car, on which he was trying – unsuccessfully – to stick false number plates. Steele drove off in his Toyota, and Whomes and Nicholls soon followed. At 6.15 p.m., the Toyota pulled into the car park of the Halfway House pub on the busy A127. Steele parked and told Whomes and Nicholls to find a space where they could watch him but couldn't be seen.

At 6.17 p.m., the Range Rover containing Rolfe, Tucker and Tate swept into the car park and pulled up next to the Toyota. Whomes and Nicholls then drove off and headed down the A127 towards Chelmsford. At 6.30 p.m., according to Nicholls, Steele pulled into the Hungry Horse pub car park at Rayleigh. Rolfe, Tucker and Tate had followed him there in the Range Rover. Steele climbed into the back of their vehicle with Tate and the four headed off to Rettendon.

At 6.35 p.m. Nicholls dropped Whomes off at Workhouse Lane. Nicholls described Whomes as wearing overalls and new wellington boots, and carrying a large canvas tool bag. Nicholls turned the car around and parked at the nearby Wheatsheaf pub car park to await further instructions. At 6.47 p.m., the Range Rover turned into Workhouse Lane. Nicholls said the plan was to allow the Range Rover to drive into the open field under the pretence of showing Rolfe, Tucker and Tate where the 'aeroplane' was going to land. Once the men were in the open with nowhere to run, they were going to be gunned down.

It was pitch-black as the Range Rover edged its way down the track. The vehicle eventually pulled up in front of a locked gate. Nicholls said Steele thought they had blown it, as he was expecting the gate to the fields to be open. Steele got out of the back of the Range Rover just as Whomes, who had been lying in wait near the gate, emerged from the bushes.

Through the open rear door, Whomes fired the first of three shots, which would leave Tucker and Rolfe dead and Tate seriously wounded. Steele and Whomes, according to Nicholls, had made a pact whereby both men would fire shots into the victims' bodies so one could not give evidence against the other. Whomes is said to have handed Steele a second shotgun and the orgy of violence continued. Nicholls said that during the shootings, Steele's weapon fell apart. He took Whomes's pump-action shotgun and shouted, 'Give me some cartridges! Give me some cartridges!', before shooting Tate through the head.

When the shotguns fell silent, Tucker, Tate and Rolfe lay lifeless in pools of their own blood. Flesh, bone and brain tissue were splattered throughout the car interior. It was a horrific scene.

Whomes is then said to have phoned Nicholls on his mobile. It is alleged he said, 'All right, Darren. Come and get us.' When Nicholls arrived at the lane, Whomes climbed into the back of the car. He was wearing surgical gloves and they were splattered with blood. Steele was delayed due to his shotgun falling apart. When he finally arrived, he got into the front passenger seat.

Nicholls claims Steele said, 'That's sorted those fuckers out. They won't be threatening me again.' It was at that moment, Nicholls says, that he realised somebody had been killed. He said he was so shocked he nearly crashed into an oncoming car as he pulled out of the lane.

Steele began handing over pieces of the gun to Whomes and repeatedly asked Nicholls if he was OK. Nicholls said Whomes laughed as he described Steele's gun falling apart during the shootings. 'Mick told me that Jack was a cold-hearted bastard because once Mick had got out of the Range Rover, Jack had shot them all immediately,' he said. 'Then he reloaded without any emotion and shot them all again in the back of the head.' He said it looked as if it meant nothing to Jack. 'Micky said he felt like the "angel of death". Then he said, "We have done the world a favour. Nobody will miss them."'

Throughout his time in police custody, detectives were keen to keep Nicholls happy, particularly as he was being so helpful with their inquiries. They gave him a daily choice of takeaway meals: Kentucky Fried Chicken one day, taco chips the next. In his cell, they provided him with a colour TV, tables, chairs, a cabinet for his clothes and a multi-gym. He was even given a cup of hot chocolate before he went to bed at night. This special treatment was totally unwarranted when one considers that this was the man who had told police that he had plotted to have two innocent men locked up for the dud cannabis he had dumped.

Once the police had taken Nicholls's initial statements, he was told he would have to go to prison until the case reached court. Nicholls told the police that he was terrified of being kept in custody among the other inmates because he would

be attacked and killed for being a grass. The police explained
to Nicholls that his family had been moved to a safe house
and he would be going to a special unit within the prison
system. This unit is for supergrasses only and the dozen or
so inmates it houses are told to keep their identities from
one another by staff. Instead of their real names, everyone is
referred to as Bloggs followed by a number. Darren Nicholls,
the drug dealer, and Ken Rugby, the grass, ceased to exist and
in their place was born Bloggs 19.

On 20 May, Steele and Whomes appeared at Chelmsford
Magistrates' Court charged with three counts of murder
plus the importation of cannabis. Steele was also charged
with possessing a pump-action shotgun. Tight security,
involving armed police and dog handlers, surrounded the
town centre court throughout the day. The road in front of
the court was closed to traffic as Steele and Whomes, their
heads shrouded with blankets, were taken to and from the
building. Both were remanded in custody to appear before
Southend Magistrates at a later date.

Misery, misfortune and tragedy appeared to be affecting
all the firm's members and those who had worked alongside
us at Raquels.

On Thursday, 23 June 1996, Larry Johnston, a former
fellow doorman and friend, fulfilled my grisly prediction
and murdered a man. Larry stabbed a 31-year-old doorman
named Stephen Poultney at a pub in Rush Green near
Romford because he had been refused entry. An ambulance
crew rushed to the scene where Mr Poultney lay bleeding to
death from a stab wound to his left side, but they were too
late to save him. Larry, himself only 32 years of age, was
later sentenced to life imprisonment. Another waste of two
young lives, and for what? A poxy argument about being
let into a poxy pub. I was glad I was no longer inhabiting
that world.

The week that Nicholls, Whomes and Steele were charged

and Larry committed murder, Tate's friend, John Marshall, went missing. John had been holding the syndicate's money for Tate in the Head sports bag. I knew John well; I often collected debts for him. He made his living in the motor trade, but he wasn't averse to the occasional drug deal. On the day he disappeared, John told his wife he was going to Kent to 'do a bit of business'. He had £5,000 in cash with him and was carrying the Head sports bag. The police have never been able to establish what was in the bag because it was taken by his killer. John's wife made various appeals for him to come home or to at least get in touch, but there was no response.

A week after John left home, his body was found in his car on Roundhill Road, Sydenham, south London. A parking ticket had been slapped on the windscreen, indicating that John's metallic-blue Range Rover had been there for some time. John was under a bale of straw in the back of the motor. He had been shot once in the chest and once through the head. The £5,000 in cash remained in the glove compartment. The only thing missing was the sports bag.

And so another blue Range Rover with a dead occupant was put on a police transporter. It was taken to Essex, where the murder inquiry team was based. Despite appeals from the police neither the bag nor its contents have ever been recovered and John's killer has not been brought to justice. Jack Whomes and Mick Steele certainly weren't responsible – they were in police custody at the time of his death. Could it have been members of the syndicate recovering their money? An empty Head sports bag was found in the Range Rover at Rettendon. The police considered it to be of no significance. It was never tested for traces of drugs or other evidence. The police have always denied there was any link between the murders, but if there wasn't, why would Essex Police investigate a murder committed in Kent or London? The area certainly doesn't fall under their operational jurisdiction.

As Nicholls, Steele, Whomes and others faced their own particular dilemmas, the spectre of Raquels and the firm's grisly affairs decided to visit me. On Thursday, 20 June 1996, two detectives, whose job it was to escort me to court for the committal proceedings concerning the Leah Betts case, picked me up from my home. The night before, I could not sleep. I sat at the end of my bed in the dark, wrestling with my thoughts. I had made the agreed statement about the illicit drug deals in Raquels, but I knew that today was the day that mattered. If I didn't turn up, the case would collapse and I could face three months' imprisonment for ignoring a witness order. It almost seemed worth it. It would solve many of my problems and I would be back on side with my associates. I looked in at my sleeping children. I could not betray them. Any chance I had of making my life worthwhile lay with them. I had to do what was right despite the fact that doing right felt so wrong.

I walked out to meet my escort. I wasn't stupid: they weren't there for my protection, they were there to make sure that I turned up at court. On the journey to Southend Magistrates' Court, the detectives made casual conversation, most of it about Tucker, Tate and Rolfe. One of the detectives had been present at Broomfield hospital in Chelmsford when the three had been laid out in the morgue. He told me that Tucker and Rolfe had been badly disfigured. 'Big fucking geezers, weren't they, Bernie? Their heads were a right mess.'

I wanted him to shut up. I didn't want him to make conversation with me. I didn't even want to hear him speak. The thought of getting friendly with the police made my stomach churn. It wasn't the men – I had known decent police officers – it was their authority, their uniform and the past experiences I had endured that filled me with loathing. When we arrived at Southend, I was driven straight into the police station via a back entrance. I was told they didn't want the press or cameramen getting anywhere near me. 'Let's keep it low-key, Bernie,' one of them said.

Once inside the police station, I was led through a maze of corridors, the detectives flashing their warrant cards to get numerous locked doors opened. We passed through the custody area and eventually into the court building. We climbed a dozen narrow, wooden steps and emerged into the dock of the court. The proceedings had not yet started, so the court was empty. I looked across from my more familiar position in the dock to the witness stand. I was going to have to stand on that platform and publicly assist those I had spent my life hating.

I was once more in turmoil. If I walked out now, I would be condemned as the man who had brought about the collapse of the trial concerning Leah Betts, a girl who, in death, had become a national icon in the war against the evil drug trade. The papers would have a field day speculating as to why I would rather face prison than awkward questions. The bitter finger of suspicion would once more be levelled at me. I could face prison, I could put up with the press and the gossip, but could my family and my children? They didn't deserve to have to endure anything since they had done nothing. The detectives must have sensed my anguish because they suddenly decided that we should all leave the court and get some tea that had been sent up to another room. I laughed out loud, but I didn't tell them why. I was thinking of my mother. Whatever the crisis, however dire the situation, she always resorted to saying, 'We had better make some tea.'

At 10 a.m., I was called into court. Old-style committals are, in effect, dress rehearsals for a Crown Court trial. The magistrates listen to the evidence and the witnesses under cross-examination and decide whether the matter should proceed to a full trial with a jury. I was in the witness box for an hour and three-quarters. At the end of it, the magistrates decided that the case would go to trial.

I felt dirty leaving the court, but the police were jubilant. It was a real kick in the teeth when they actually thanked me. I couldn't wait to get home. I wanted to get away from these people. I wanted the events of 1995 to have some sort of closure.

The police dropped me off, wished me luck and disappeared down the drive. I knew that they would be slagging me off and laughing. Paranoid? I doubt it. If 1995 had been a bad year, 1996 was proving to be no better, if not worse.

Raquels doorman Chris Lombard had left our firm because he said the club we worked in was too violent. He had gone to work at the Island nightclub in Ilford instead. I hadn't heard anything of Chris after that until Thursday, 5 December 1996, almost one year to the day since Tucker, Tate and Rolfe had been blown away in their Range Rover. I had stopped at a newsagent's outside Liverpool Street station in London to pick up a paper as I had to wait half an hour for a train to Essex. I glanced at the front page and then stared in horror. I could not believe what I saw or what I began to read. The headline read 'Murdered doing his job' and alongside was a picture of Chris.

The report said he had been shot dead and another man seriously injured after a hail of gunfire ripped through the club where they worked. Chris, only thirty at the time, was fatally wounded when seven shots were fired through the glass of a locked door at the club.

A group of young men had turned up a few minutes after the doors had closed to customers. They had demanded to be let in, but Chris had told them he was not allowed to do so because a condition on the club's licence prevented people entering after a certain time. The men became abusive, vowing to return. Shortly afterwards, as the door staff chatted in the foyer, shots rang out and Chris lay dead. The club, which I knew well, was just yards from the local police station, but this fact had not deterred the gang. Chris had been shot once in the head and twice in the chest with what police believed was an automatic pistol. The head doorman, Albert St Hilaire, aged 40, had been shot once in the back, the bullet lodging itself near his spinal cord. The third doorman escaped injury when a bullet grazed his neck.

Having regained the 'respect' they thought they had lost by not being allowed into the club, the gang fled into the night. Chris, a giant of a man, had a passion for basketball. He had coached a local school team and taken part in tournaments in America as a semi-professional player. He hated door work and always said he was only doing it to tide him over. Now some wannabe gangster had snuffed out his life because he had dared to refuse him entry to a nightclub. It was a terrible waste of a life.

As the year drew to a close, I looked back and realised I hadn't moved forward at all. Twelve months earlier, I had been wishing away 1995 and now I found myself counting the days to the end of 1996. I kept telling myself that once the Betts trial was over, I could get on with my life. However many times I told myself that things would get better, I still found it hard to believe that my life could ever return to any sort of normality. Debra was feeling the strain too. We had begun arguing, and when we weren't arguing we were not even talking. I couldn't blame Debra: the shit we were in was all my fault.

On Monday, 9 December 1996, the Betts trial finally opened at Norwich Crown Court. The first day was taken up with legal arguments, which I didn't have to concern myself with, but I was told to prepare myself to be called the following day or the day after. I spent that night at home like a caged animal. I couldn't sit down or think straight.

I paced the room, trying to talk myself in and out of my forthcoming ordeal. The trial at Southend Magistrates' Court had been the dress rehearsal for this trial, which would be scrutinised and reported on by all sections of the media. Now, if ever, was the time I was going to take some flack. The police phoned me a couple of times to see if I was OK, but I knew they were just checking that now the pressure was on I hadn't done a bunk. I was also treated to the sight of a patrolling police car, which drove up and down the lane outside my home. I lived at the end of a remote farm track, the sea to our right, a mile of woodland to our left – hardly mean streets, certainly not worthy of a regular police patrol.

When I was called into court, I remained in the witness box for the entire afternoon. Stories about Tucker and Tate threatening to shoot me, their executions and Mark Murray being responsible for supplying the pill that killed Leah rather than the man on trial kept those in the public gallery mesmerised. When it was all over the police escorted me to a waiting room. Alone at last, I felt a great sense of relief. I just wanted to get out of there. Nothing happened for ten or fifteen minutes, and then suddenly I was off in a rush between two detectives. I was taken outside and told to lie in the back of the van. A blanket was thrown over me.

When Leah's parents emerged from the court, the press surrounded them. At the same time, the van I was in slipped away into the evening traffic. I sat at home the following day, waiting for news of the trial. The final witnesses gave evidence on Friday, 13 December. The jury was told it wouldn't be sent out to deliberate until Monday because it was too late in the afternoon. That weekend dragged on like no weekend before or since.

On Monday, 16 December, the jury retired, but there was no further news all day. The judge arranged for the jury to spend the night in a hotel and they deliberated throughout the following day. Eventually, they told the judge they were unable to reach a verdict and they were discharged. I was absolutely devastated. I knew the prosecution wouldn't throw in the towel. I knew I would have to go through the whole thing again. I was going to spend 1997 wishing yet another year away.

On Monday, 24 February 1997, the second Leah Betts trial began at Norwich Crown Court. It was far more low-key on this occasion: the media had milked the story dry and the whole country was suffering from 'tales of Ecstasy' fatigue. I was called to give evidence on the second day of the trial. The questioning wasn't as detailed as before and I was only in the witness box for 20 minutes. To be honest, I didn't care how long I spent in there because I knew, whether there was a verdict or not, the prosecution would not seek a third trial. Whatever happened that day, my ordeal would be over. I could begin the new life I had been trying to start for two years. When the defence barrister asked me his last question and sat down, the judge asked the prosecutor if he wished to ask me any further questions. 'I don't, my Lord. Mr O'Mahoney will no longer be required.'

No longer fucking required! No longer fucking required – it felt like I had just been given a clean bill of health after being diagnosed with a terminal illness. I savoured those words. These people had entered my life like a runaway train, they had fucked up my head with worry and now they were saying, 'We've finished with you, goodbye.' At the outset, the police had talked about assistance with moving, even a new identity, but I had declined. I had made my decision, I had to live by it. I wasn't going to pretend it hadn't happened and I wasn't going to deny who I was for anybody. We all make mistakes.

When the police dropped me off they thanked me and wished me well. I had got to know them quite well on our trips to and from court, the trouble one of them had with his mortgage and their silent admiration for some of the more colourful, less-serious criminals. I could not thank them, though I did wish them well.

On Friday, 28 February, the trial ended and the jury retired to consider its verdict. But once more they could not agree. Mr Justice Wright formally found the defendant not guilty after the jury foreman said that there was no realistic chance of them reaching a majority verdict in the case after four hours of deliberation.

For me, the ordeal was over. But the legacy of misfortune that remained for former members of the Essex Boys firm was like a bad disease. As one firm member emerged from a crisis or was lost within it, another became infected.

In March 1997, I read in a local newspaper that ex-firm member Chris Wheatley had been jailed for seven years after admitting his part in a major drugs operation in Southend. Detectives had swooped on Chris after a lengthy undercover operation. They found more than 200 grams of cocaine, 2.63 grams of amphetamine, 357 Ecstasy pills and £950 in cash. The court heard that Chris had become addicted to drugs in 1995, he had been unable to work and his marriage had been ruined.

I know Chris took the treatment he had received from Tucker badly following Tate's release. They had been good friends until Tucker had got involved with Tate and kicked Chris into touch. From being Tucker's right-hand man to becoming the subject of his jokes and snide remarks hurt Chris deeply.

On New Year's Eve 1995, Chris and I had worked on the door at a private function and he had told me he was glad Tucker and Tate had been murdered. He was rambling on in a drugged up, confused, barely audible mumble. It was terrible to witness. I never saw Chris alive again. His drugged, vacant features are another of the many images my friends have left me with and that I have been trying to erase from my mind ever since. Shortly after Chris was released from his seven-year prison sentence, he died after collapsing outside a gymnasium. Another of our number dead, another family devastated. I reckon the only people who ever made serious money out of our firm were undertakers and florists.

Chapter 14

There are two very distinct types of protected witness. The first is the innocent bystander – for example the man who witnesses a murder in the street outside his home. If he agrees to give evidence, he can be settled in a new job, be paid a 'salary' equivalent to what he was earning and, in extreme cases, he may even be relocated overseas. The second type of protected witness enjoys no such privileges. He is a career criminal who has decided to inform on his former associates in order to avoid a lengthy term of imprisonment. The authorities never let this type of witness forget that he is a criminal. Rather than being housed in a hotel or a safe house, he is more likely to spend his time being moved between police stations and specialist prison units. He must also confess to every single crime he has ever committed or witnessed, or of which he has knowledge. He must plead guilty in court and accept whatever sentence is imposed upon him. Any ideas Nicholls may have had about becoming some sort of celebrity witness for the police were soon dashed when he arrived at HMP Woodhill in Milton Keynes to a unit known only as HMP Alpha.

The unit is a secure prison within the prison. The idea is not to prevent the inmates from escaping but to prevent those who they are about to give evidence against from breaking in. Nicholls was told that everything within the unit was kept secret, but as soon as he walked in the other inmates were saying, 'You're that geezer who's grassing up the blokes over the triple murder, aren't you?' They all then sat around Nicholls wanting to know the details of the case.

While he was on the unit, Nicholls became friendly with another protected witness named Geoffrey Couzens. Unbeknown to Nicholls, Couzens kept a prison diary in which he detailed all of the conversations he had with other inmates. In this diary, he wrote that he first met Darren Nicholls on 24 October 1996.

When a new person joins the Witness Protection Scheme, there is a natural interest by other members of the unit to find out who they are and the reason for their involvement in the scheme. Darren Nicholls was no exception, as he readily spoke to members of the unit about his involvement in the Rettendon Range Rover murders.

Darren was only on the Protected Witness Unit for a few days before he was returned to police custody. During this period, I recall that he was in general conversation with the inmates on the unit. He told them that while he had no prior knowledge of, or involvement in, the murders, he had taken two men in his car to the murder scene, four men arrived at the scene in the Range Rover and after the murders had been committed Darren took three men from the scene in his car. When he told his version of events, which was on an almost daily basis, he always laboured the point that he had no prior knowledge that the men were going to be shot. I formed the impression that he did know and he was lying. The impression was just my gut feeling based on the amount of times he kept denying his involvement over and over again.

As I mentioned, Darren left the Unit after a few days and I next met him after the Unit had been transferred to HMP Parkhurst in November 1996. Darren's story concerning the murders had changed dramatically. I recall overhearing Darren engaged in a conversation with the inmates on one occasion. He was talking about the murders and although I wasn't directly involved in the conversation, I was listening to him and heard what he said. On this occasion, he said that he had taken two men to the scene in his car and another three men had arrived in the Range Rover. He never said who had travelled in which vehicle, whether it was the gunman or the deceased. I noticed the number of people in each account did not tally up. Darren also said that he knew everybody's movements because they had traced their mobile phones to various transmitters or relay stations. I asked Darren if they could get an accurate triangulation fix on a mobile phone, but he just gave me a blank look. From that, I took it to mean that he didn't understand the technicalities of police methods or the word 'triangulation'. Darren did say that he was aware it would cause problems if his statement did not fit the mobile phone evidence.

On one occasion while Darren and I were in my cell, Darren asked my opinion on a matter associated with charges against him. He told me that he had been charged with involvement in the importation of cannabis but he wondered whether he should admit to involvement in Class A drugs. The logic was that if Darren admitted more serious offences, his credibility when he gave evidence would be higher in the eyes of the jury, but he would not be the subject of a more severe sentence by the judge. I told Darren that such an idea did not make sense to me. While it was necessary that he did admit all he had been involved in – otherwise the defence may be able to challenge his honesty when he gave evidence – there was no reason for him to admit things that he hadn't done.

He said that he wanted the new identity being offered and a fresh start, and that if that meant admitting to offences he hadn't committed and committing perjury, then he was willing to do so.

Beyond the prison walls, Nicholls's wife Sandra and their children were struggling with a world that had been turned upside down. As soon as Nicholls had agreed to give evidence against Whomes and Steele, his family had been taken from their home in the middle of the night. The children – young, confused and frightened – were told they had to leave because an old Second World War bomb had been found nearby. Isolated from family and friends in a police safe house, Sandra was terrified of saying anything to anybody in case it placed her and the children in danger. When neighbours asked innocent questions, such as 'Where do you come from?' or 'What do you do?', Sandra would just turn and walk away.

The Nicholls family was not the only one being torn apart by the events that had led to the demise of the Essex Boys firm. Although we appeared to be emerging from the doom and gloom in which the events of 1995 had immersed myself and my family, the underlying strain on us all proved to be too much.

Paul Betts had appeared on television, calling me a bastard and saying I was responsible for the death of his daughter Leah. He based his allegations on the fact I had admitted in court that I had turned a blind eye to the drug dealing that went on in Raquels. The publicity generated by his allegation resulted in older children telling my children at school that their father was a murderer. How can you tell your tearful son or daughter to ignore such nonsense? What can you possibly say when they ask if it's true? In an effort to stop this ridiculous witch-hunt, I wrote an open letter to Paul Betts, which was printed in the press. I urged him to confront me on live TV so we could debate who was really responsible for Leah's death, but, unsurprisingly, he declined.

It was becoming apparent to me that remaining with my children was causing them to be unfairly tarnished. Debra, a decent, honest woman, was also being subjected to an unjustified whispering campaign. My family were suffering for something none of us was directly responsible for. Paul Betts's accusations were causing the children so much upset, Debra suggested, and I agreed, that we should part for their sake. Debra and I had to look at the situation in a cold, clinical manner and do what was best for them and not what suited us. We sold our home in Mayland and Debra moved to a home near her mother. I returned to Basildon. True love is an extremely painful thing to acknowledge.

I did not arrive in the best of moods. I was in turmoil over my family and I was tired of being blamed for causing the death of a girl who had been foolish enough to take drugs. It wasn't as though Leah was experimenting for the first time; she had regularly taken Ecstasy and speed and had smoked cannabis. I felt Paul Betts's allegation was ridiculous; it was like somebody blaming a pub landlord for getting him or her convicted of drunk-driving. He should learn that we all have choices in life and we all have to take responsibility for our actions, however unsavoury they may be. It's not always somebody else's or society's fault. Likewise, his son, William, is soley responsible for his recent assault on two girls, aged thirteen and fourteen, which resulted in his name being added to the sex offenders register. Unsurprisingly, Mr Betts was not so vocal about his son's behaviour.

My decision to help the police put me out in no-man's-land; not only were the firm's victims' families condemning me, but my former associates and their sidekicks were also swearing bloody revenge on me for daring to assist the police. Whichever way I turned, Bernard O'Mahoney had done wrong. I grew sick of hearing about so-called gangsters in Basildon who were allegedly trying to kill me, and I was sick of being advised by police where I should or should not go to avoid my imaginary assassins. So many people appeared to have opinions about me, yet few knew me and none had ever had any dealings with me. If people didn't like me living in Basildon, it was a matter for them, not me. I had been driven out of one home; I was not going to be driven out of another.

I started drinking in my old haunts. Most people I met droned on and on about the murders of Tucker, Tate and Rolfe. Few in the town believed the men accused of the murders were guilty; in fact, many believed I had been instrumental in luring the trio to their deaths. Nobody said they had a problem with me personally and several had nothing but good memories of the trouble-free rave nights we had created at Raquels.

A few months after moving back to Basildon, I bumped into a girl named Emma Turner, whom I had first met at Raquels. Emma and I had always been good friends and we found we had a lot to catch up on, which resulted in us spending more and more time together. Not least was the fact that our close friendship had resulted in the Rettendon murder squad detectives giving Emma a hard time.

Back in April 1996, DC Scott from the Essex drugs squad had contacted me about 'Tucker's girlfriend', Emma Turner. An informant had said 'the head of the firm' was going out with Emma and the police had assumed the informant was referring to Tucker when in fact the informant was talking about the head doorman at Raquels, which was me. DC Shakespeare, who had been tasked to contact and interview Emma, turned up at her mother's home and left a message saying that if she continued to avoid him, she would be arrested. Fearing she was in some sort of trouble, Emma contacted me and I telephoned the police to explain the situation on her behalf. Eventually, DC Scott was able to confirm that there had been a mistake and Emma had had no involvement with Tucker whatsoever.

Emma and I began to go out together regularly. Eventually, I gave up the flat I had rented and moved in with her. Since the catalogue of court appearances connected to the Betts case had ended, I had been able to take on a full-time job driving a tipper lorry. Within a short period of time, I was given a managerial position and offered a post in Peterborough, Cambridgeshire. I didn't want to move away from my children because being able to see them every other day had lessened the trauma of being separated from them. Instead, I chose to drive to Peterborough every day, leaving the house at 4.30 a.m. and returning at 8 p.m. Being straight was proving to be a real strain and the rewards were hardly compensatory.

John Rollinson, or 'Gaffer' as he liked to call himself, the dealer who had bankrolled Mark Murray after the police raid at Club UK, had been telling people in Essex that he was looking for me. He was apparently unhappy that I had named Murray as a drug dealer at the Betts trial. Rollinson may have been well advised to keep his big mouth shut about the fact he had financed the batch of drugs that led to Leah's death, but he wasn't the brightest of people. He was the type who tried to make himself seem important by having views and opinions on villains others looked up to. *Gaffer* (Blake Publishing, 2003), a recent book published about Rollinson's life, describes him as 'one of the most dangerous men in the country'. It goes on to claim that Rollinson has made the villains' Hall of Fame after a 'lifetime of unmitigated violence, driven by a fearsome rage'. Only the gullible and naive take any notice of the likes of Rollinson and his ridiculous boasting.

It was a good friend of Rollinson who told me he had been badmouthing me, but I was not the slightest bit concerned. I had never done anything to Rollinson. If he had just cause to be upset with anybody, it should have been his tailor. I knew that he had no right to have a grievance with me because I hardly knew the mug. 'It's Gaffer trying to involve his name in a high-profile case,' I told his friend. 'You know what he's like. The boy's a fool, he just wants to feel important.'

Then one evening, when Emma and I were out having a drink over at the Festival Leisure Park in Basildon – a large entertainment complex comprising bars, nightclubs, a bowling alley, a cinema and fast food restaurants: some of the more witty locals refer to it as 'Bas Vegas' – a small, thin drug-ravaged man started shouting 'Fucking cunt!' at me. He threw his baseball cap on the floor and kept spitting each time he did so. 'Cunt, fucking cunt,' he shouted. I thought the man may have been mentally challenged or was suffering from some sort of embarrassing disorder, so I thought it best to ignore him.

Emma, not used to witnessing such alarming behaviour, clutched my arm and asked me who he was. It was only when the man started shouting about 'grassing Mark Murray up' that I took a closer look and realised it was the 'legendary' Gaffer. I hadn't seen him since I had worked at Raquels and he had lost a lot of weight. He looked gaunt and thin, no doubt the result of a low-life existence, popping pills and feeding a cocaine habit.

When you are out with your partner for a drink, you don't really relish the thought of rolling around on the floor with a drunk or a loud-mouthed druggie, so I apologised to Emma and told her we would have a drink at the other end of the bar, but if Gaffer continued to be abusive or offered violence, I would have to give him a clip around the ear.

Gaffer was not alone, so his actions were despicable. What sort of man starts on another man who is out with his partner having a drink? No doubt he is another gangster who follows the criminal code; so much for showing women respect. Throughout the evening, Gaffer kept glaring down the bar at me and tipping his hat like some second-rate performing clown.

'Come on,' I said to Emma, 'I've had enough of this, let's go.'

As I walked past Gaffer, the gutless coward squirted me in the eyes with ammonia. I was temporarily blinded, so Emma opened the door for me and I stepped outside. Gaffer had been telling everybody in Essex that he was going to 'do' me – now that I was temporarily blinded and standing in front of him, he had the best chance he was ever going to get to carry out his threat. My vision began to clear, so I made my way to the taxi rank outside the club. Gaffer and his friend followed us, which frightened Emma, so I turned and confronted them. I knew Gaffer was not capable of fighting, so I was expecting him to pull out a weapon. To Gaffer's friend's credit, he stepped back, making it obvious he wanted no part in any trouble.

As Gaffer advanced, I grabbed his head and shoved him backwards. I was not the slightest bit concerned about what he may try to do, or what he may try to do it with, because, unknown to him, I had a double-bladed 12-inch combat knife down the back of my trousers. If he got within striking distance of me with a weapon, I was more than prepared to bury the knife deep in his head.

When I had shoved Gaffer backwards, his cap had fallen off. As he approached me again, I could see in his eyes that he was unsure of himself. He pulled out a Jif lemon container and after lunging forward, squirted me once more in the eyes with ammonia. The red mist rose and, at that moment, I wanted to end his miserable and pointless life. I pulled out the knife and raised it. He saw it, screamed like a hysterical girl and ran back into the club calling for help.

'What the fuck am I doing?' I thought. 'How do I end up getting involved with these fools? I could end up serving a life sentence because some little low-life nobody has chosen to attack me.' A bouncer came out and told me the police had been called.

'You're on CCTV as well, Bernie,' he said. 'You had better make yourself scarce.'

Emma and I tried to get in a taxi but the driver refused to take us. The other taxis in the rank drove away empty. I could see Gaffer hiding in the club foyer behind the bouncers. It looked as though he was crying, so I knew he wouldn't be troubling us again that night.

We didn't live too far from the leisure park, so we decided to walk. We made our way across the car park to the main road, where two police cars pulled up. My mind was racing, I had a certain prison sentence tucked down the back of my trousers and I didn't fancy being locked up because of a loser like Gaffer. 'The knife, the knife, how the fuck can I explain away the knife?' I was thinking. I knew everybody had seen it and I knew the CCTV had recorded me brandishing it, so it was pointless denying its existence. There was only one thing for it, I thought: I was going to have to bluff my way out of it. I pulled out the knife and approached the police officers.

'It's OK officers,' I said, 'I've got the knife.'

'Drop the weapon, drop the weapon!' they shouted.

I laughed and told them it was OK. 'It's not my weapon,' I said. 'I took it off a lunatic.'

I threw the knife on the ground. One of the police officers forced my hands behind my back and slapped a pair of handcuffs on.

'You're under arrest for possessing an offensive weapon,' he said.

I asked the police to make sure Emma got home all right. They said they would. They then put me in the back of the car and took me to Basildon police station. By this time, my eyes were becoming increasingly painful. They were red and swollen from the ammonia and now I had the handcuffs on, I was unable to wipe or try to clean them.

At the police station, I mentioned again that I had been squirted with ammonia. I said I needed to wash my eyes out, but was told I was not allowed to do so until I had seen a doctor. An argument developed and the mood became pretty hostile. Eventually, they agreed to remove my cuffs. I was then bundled into a cell by the arresting officers and the door was slammed shut.

The following morning, I washed my eyes out with the tea that had been brought to me for breakfast. It helped, but they remained painful and my vision was impaired. Eventually, at 3 p.m., a detective came to my cell to take me to the interview room. I had a rough idea of what I was going to say, but I was unaware of how much evidence the police had on me, so decided I would wait to hear what the detective had to say before telling my side of the story.

The interviewing officer told me a member of staff at the club had called the police after a man had run inside screaming that I had brandished a knife outside the premises. He told me they had seized the CCTV footage and it clearly showed me lunging at this man with a large combat knife. I asked the officer if they had the video footage from inside the club. He said he hadn't because the video inside the club wasn't working. As soon as he said that, I knew I was home and dry. I told him that he only had half of the story.

'What do you mean?' he asked.

'That man attacked me inside the club, sprayed me with ammonia and pulled out a knife when we started to struggle,'

I replied. 'When he tried to stab me, I took the knife from him and, fearing for my safety, went outside. The man followed me and was asking me to give him back the knife. I didn't want to because I thought he was going to stab me, so I refused. When he came towards me, I pushed him away, but then he attacked me with a Jif lemon container full of ammonia. Having been temporarily blinded, I feared for my safety. I pulled out his knife, which I had secreted down the back of my trousers, and he ran away screaming. I had pulled out his knife purely to defend myself. When he ran back into the club, I did not run inside after him as the danger had passed.

'I stood outside for five or ten minutes. No taxis would take Emma and me home, so we walked across the car park, where I was arrested approximately fifteen minutes after the incident. If you ask the arresting officers, they will tell you I said, "It's OK, I've got the knife, I took it off a lunatic."'

'But that's not what other people are saying,' the investigating officer said. 'They're saying it's your knife.'

'Well, you had better get these people to make statements because it's not my knife, it belongs to the man who attacked me. He owns the knife.'

The detective said he had spoken to Gaffer and he did not want to make a statement. I knew Gaffer wouldn't give evidence against me, so my defence was safe. I told the detective that Gaffer didn't want to make a statement because he had the knife in the first place and he's the one who attacked me. The officer insisted he had other witnesses and therefore I would be charged.

'Fair enough,' I said, 'fucking charge me.'

The detective read the following charge to me: 'That without lawful authority or reasonable excuse, I had with me in a public place an offensive weapon, namely a knife.' He also alleged that I had used or threatened unlawful violence towards another and my conduct was such as would cause a person of reasonable firmness present at the scene to fear for his personal safety. When he told me I had caused a person of reasonable firmness present at the scene to fear for his personal safety, I started laughing.

'How can you call a person reasonable when they are trying to blind you with ammonia?'

The officer just looked at me and said, 'Those are the charges. Have you anything to say?' I did not reply. I was bailed to appear at Basildon Magistrates' Court and then released.

It's hard to explain how depressing an incident like this can be. You go out for a drink with your partner and you end up being locked up for the best part of 24 hours. After your release, you spend months agonising over whether or not you will receive a prison sentence. And for what? For some drug-peddling peasant, who took it upon himself to try to attack you in the presence of your girlfriend and for no reason blinded you with ammonia. His motive? You assisted the police, who then lock you up and charge you for resisting his attack. Your attacker, meanwhile, walks free. It is absolutely sickening. I can fully understand why some people end up serving life sentences for murdering this type of sub-human. The law tells you to turn the other cheek and walk away from it, but what is the point of walking away when these lowlifes will just stab you in the back, cut you, maim you or try to blind you? It is pointless walking away. I should have left him lying in the gutter where he belonged.

Once more, the never-ending trauma of going back and forth to court became part of my life. The uncertainty of my future and the pressure of preparing for yet another trial left me marking time in complete misery.

Chapter 15

In early 1997, Dr Robert Fox compiled a report on Sandra Nicholls as part of a bail application for her husband, Darren. He had spent his first Christmas away from his wife and children and he was beginning to show doubts about going through with assisting the police. Similarly, Sandra began talking about moving back to Essex and divorcing her husband since their marriage was all but over. As tensions mounted, Nicholls spent his time arguing with the police, saying that the only way to save his family was to allow him to live with them. At first, the police refused point-blank, but when Nicholls made it clear that he was prepared to withdraw his statements, they agreed to refer Sandra to Dr Robert Fox and place the decision in his hands.

Dr Fox reported that Sandra felt lonely and miserable without her husband and had neither been sleeping nor eating properly. He concluded that it would be best if the family was reunited as soon as possible.

On 24 February 1997, Darren Nicholls was granted bail on condition that he reside at the safe house with his family and adhere to strict guidelines. There was to be a curfew, which meant he could only leave his house between 8 a.m. and 8 p.m., he was not permitted to travel more than 25 miles from his front door and he was not allowed to seek any form of employment. Any breach of these conditions would result in Nicholls being returned to prison immediately.

At first, Nicholls and Sandra were happy to be back together. But soon Nicholls's behaviour caused a rift between the couple. Sandra said that because her husband was unable to work he was around the house 24 hours a day and was growing increasingly frustrated. Once a week the police would call to check on them and give them the equivalent amount of money they would receive if they were on the dole. As soon as the police left, Nicholls would take the money and go to the pub to get drunk.

'We never expected much,' said Sandra. 'It wasn't like we were expecting a foreign villa and a life of luxury, but they gave us nothing. Less than nothing.'

The police were absolutely terrified of being accused of bribing their main witness. If there was any hint of someone benefiting in some way after being made a supergrass, the defence would jump all over it and the case would collapse. What the police love best is being able to stand in front of a judge and say, 'Look, your Honour, we did absolutely nothing for this bloke and he still gave evidence. In fact, we made his life much worse than it was before and he still turned up. He must be telling the truth.' And that's just what they wanted to do with Nicholls.

Whatever Sandra thought and whatever the police wanted to do, Darren Nicholls, as usual, had other plans. In September that year, the trial opened in Court 2 at the Old Bailey in London. The first suspicions that the police may have arrested the wrong men came soon after Nicholls was called to give his evidence.

Through the auspices of the Police and Criminal Evidence Act (PACE) 1984, there are strict guidelines that prevent officers from discussing any evidence or aspect of a case with someone in custody except during formal recorded interviews. Officers are allowed to make 'welfare visits' to ensure the person in custody is being properly cared for. Ideally, the officers responsible for such visits should not be the same officers responsible for conducting the interviews with the person in custody. The two officers who had been interviewing Nicholls were DC Michael Brown and DC Christopher Winstone. As the evidence unfolded in court it emerged that during his first week in custody DC Winstone and DC Brown had made some 36 hours' worth of 'welfare visits' to Nicholls between them, including one that lasted 7 hours and 43 minutes.

Steele's barrister, Graham Parkins QC, explained to the jury exactly what the defence thought had happened. He alleged that Essex Police, desperate to convict Steele, had used the visits to give Nicholls a 'script' detailing what would later become his 'evidence'. The entire story Nicholls had been given to recite was in fact a fabrication and Nicholls was prepared to play along purely to save himself from more serious charges. Essex Police strenuously denied this allegation.

Mr Parkins accused DC Winstone of helping Nicholls, prompting him and suggesting things that he hadn't said in order to make his story sound more convincing. Mr Parkins was able to show that during one interview the tape was turned off for 20 minutes while Nicholls visited the toilet. When Nicholls returned, his solicitor confirmed that no discussions had taken place while the tape had been switched off. In fact, Nicholls's solicitor had been out of the room making telephone calls at the time and had no idea whatsoever what may or may not have been discussed.

Extracts of other recorded interviews were played. In one, Nicholls, being his usual bold and brazen self, almost casually described a sequence of events, then suddenly stopped and said, 'I've fucked the story up here again.'

'No, you're all right, mate,' a voice said. 'Go on.'

On another tape, Nicholls stopped talking when he failed to remember the name of a person. In the background, a faint yet audible voice was heard before Nicholls suddenly remembered the name he was trying to recall. In other interviews, defence experts stated that it sounded as if he was reading from a prepared script rather than speaking in his own words. What sounded like papers being shuffled or sifted through could also be heard. Mr Parkins invited the jury to read the statements that Nicholls had made first. None, he said, told the same story as the one Nicholls had now told the court. Mr Parkins also pointed out that Nicholls only started blaming Steele and Whomes for the killings after he himself had been told he would be charged with the murders.

While Nicholls had been giving evidence for the prosecution, he had appeared relaxed and confident. Under cross-examination by the defence, he was unsure and forgetful.

'Has anyone told you to keep it vague?' Mr Parkins asked him. 'I put it to you that the final version of what the jury has heard is not your own work. You have been prompted, helped and guided by other police officers.'

'That's not true.'

'Mr Nicholls, are you a truthful man by nature?'

'I don't think you could say I am.' After a long pause Nicholls added, 'But I'm telling the truth now.'

'But, Mr Nicholls, how does one know when you are lying and when you are not? You are both a blatant and persistent liar. An opportunist, I suggest, grasping at straws to save yourself. By 6 December, you knew Mr Steele very well and had the means to make up a plausible story about him and his colleagues.'

'Yes, if I wished to do so, but they did do the killings.'

'Are you falsely accusing these men when you know who was really responsible?'

'They did it.'

'Do you want to protect yourself and others who are not before this court?'

'No, they did it.'

'Were you involved in these murders yourself, with other men?'

'Look, I've told you, I picked them up from the murders they committed. I was badly affected by it.'

'Were you indeed? You told those officers you didn't really want anything to do with Mr Steele after the killings. You had been duped into ferrying the men to and from a triple shooting. If you are telling the truth, an awful, evil thing has been done to you.'

'Yes, that's right.'

'Mr Steele would hardly be on your Christmas card list.'

'No.'

'Can you explain, then, why you sent his family a card for Christmas 1995?' Nicholls stood rooted to the floor of the witness box, his head dropped. He didn't reply. Mr Parkins continued. 'You also gave this man you claim was a killer a case of canned beer and a bottle of wine.'

'Yes,' Nicholls mumbled, 'but only because he gave my children a present.'

'Ah, yes, a radio-controlled aeroplane in which you went flying at Mr Steele's house. Isn't it true that you then took your children to the house of this triple killer so they could watch the rabbits running in the garden?'

'Yes,' Nicholls whispered.

When Mick Steele was called to give his evidence he said that at 5.01 p.m. on 6 December 1995, the precise time Nicholls had claimed he was meeting him outside the motorbike shop at Marks Tey, he had absolute proof that he was elsewhere. Steele produced a credit card receipt he had signed himself that showed he had purchased petrol from a Texaco garage some eight miles and at least twenty minutes away from the bike shop. Additionally, the vehicle that Nicholls claimed Steele was driving when he met him ran on diesel. This was without doubt as strong as alibis get.

217

Steele said he and his partner, Jackie, then drove to Tesco and he waited in the car while Jackie went in and purchased two bottles of wine. After leaving the supermarket, they drove to the village of Bulphan, where they picked up a boat trailer from the house of Dennis Whomes, Jack's uncle. Steele told the jury that he and Jackie drove home, arriving at around 7.25 p.m. The murders of Tucker, Tate and Rolfe had, according to the prosecution, been committed by this time. Steele said that five minutes after arriving home his sister-in-law and her daughter arrived to view his property because they were considering buying it.

'Did you go to Rettendon on that night?' asked Mr Parkins.

'Nowhere near Rettendon,' Steele replied. 'We came straight home.'

When Jack Whomes was called to give evidence, he broke down in the witness box. Wiping away tears, he told the jury, 'I could not even kill a sparrow. Anyone who knows me, knows I am not capable of killing. To say I killed those men is ridiculous. I did not know Mr Tucker and I did not know Mr Rolfe. The last time I saw Pat Tate was when he was being transferred from a prison near Haverhill with my brother, Johnny. He was a friend.'

When it was suggested that Whomes was asked to do the shooting by Steele, Whomes raised his voice. 'I would not do it for anybody. I could not do it. Why would I want to do it? I deny it. I deny any suggestion that I had anything to do with drugs or murder. All the stuff about the duff drugs deal is rubbish. I would much rather put money into motors. I would never deal in drugs.'

Whomes told the jury that while he had been working as a bouncer, he had seen a girl high on drugs take her clothes off and dance naked. 'There was a girl like Leah Betts. She'd had some bad gear and was foaming at the mouth. That worried me sick and I called an ambulance for her. I asked undercover police to come in and search for drugs.'

Whomes leaned forward at this point and began sobbing loudly. 'I didn't do anything like that. What they are suggesting is ridiculous. You don't know what I'm going through, being locked up. They won't even let me cuddle my own son.'

Other witnesses testified to the poor condition of the Passat Nicholls claimed was used as the getaway car. It had no heater, a noisy exhaust and a clutch that was unusable. The idea that anybody would use it as a getaway vehicle for a triple murder was laughable. No tyre marks were found along the lane matching those of the Passat and no traces of oil were found despite the vehicle's poor condition. Forensic tests failed to find any blood, glass or gun residue inside the Passat; in fact, they failed to find any link whatsoever to tie it to the murder scene, even though Nicholls described Whomes as entering the vehicle dripping with blood, body tissue and brains following the shootings.

Although Whomes allegedly lay in wait for the Range Rover in the bushes by the gate, he managed to glide invisibly away leaving no forensic trace, an impressive feat for a man 6 ft 2 in. tall and weighing almost 19 stone.

Finally, there was only a single footprint found on the ground by the offside back door of the Range Rover where the assassin would have stood. Forensic scientists identified the print as coming from a size 8 or 9 Hi-Tec training shoe. Whomes's barrister, Mr David Lederman QC, pointed out that Jack Whomes wore a size 11 and, according to Nicholls's evidence, was wearing wellington boots when he carried out the murders. There was nothing whatsoever to suggest that Mick Steele or Jack Whomes had ever been down the lane where the murders were committed.

'If the jury look at the facts,' said Mr Lederman, 'Whomes could not possibly be responsible for the murders.'

After four long months, the trial ended. In his summing up, the Honourable Mr Justice Anthony Hidden told the jury that they should treat the evidence of Darren Nicholls with 'great caution, as it was in his own interest to become a prosecution witness', adding, 'knowing he will have to come back to court for sentence, he hopes to get less time to serve'.

The jury deliberated for four and a half days and on Tuesday, 20 January 1998, Mick Steele and Jack Whomes were found guilty of importing cannabis and of murdering Craig Rolfe, Tony Tucker and Pat Tate. Steele was cleared of possessing the shotgun Nicholls had hidden in his barn. Whomes and Steele looked at each other in disbelief before turning to look at the judge.

'There is no other sentence I can pass on you for these horrifying murders of which you have been convicted than that of life imprisonment,' Mr Justice Hidden told the pair. 'There is little that can be said usefully about either of you at this stage. You two were responsible, in my view, for taking away the lives of these three victims in a summary way. You lured them to a quiet farm track and executed them. They had crossed your path and you showed them no mercy. There is about these killings a hard and ruthless edge which can only horrify and stagger the non-criminal mind. You are extremely dangerous men and you have not the slightest compunction for resorting to extreme violence when you thought it was necessary.'

Mick Steele and Jack Whomes were both told that they would have to serve three life sentences and a minimum of 15 years in prison. But Home Secretary Jack Straw later reviewed this and demanded a minimum of 25 years. The distraught family of Jack Whomes stood outside the court trying to come to terms with the fact their son and brother might be behind bars for the rest of his life. Jack Whomes senior said his wife, Pam, was devastated by the verdict.

'How would any mother feel?' he said. 'She just cannot talk about it at the moment. The whole family is gutted.' Jack's brothers and sister were also present to hear the jury foreman announce they had found the thirty-six year old guilty of three cold-blooded killings.

Mrs Whomes had appeared at the Old Bailey on the first day of the long-running trial wearing a T-shirt bearing the slogan 'Jack Whomes is innocent'. She sat in court day after day to hear the evidence against her son but refused to believe he could be involved in anything so horrendous. Jack's wife, Gail, was left to break the news to their two children, JJ – Jack Junior – and Lucy, that their father would not be coming home.

Craig Rolfe's mother, Lorraine, told reporters that she had no hate for the killers of her youngest son. 'I do have a lot of anger,' she admitted, 'but I can honestly say I don't have any hate in me. I never have.' She heard the pathologist tell the Old Bailey about Rolfe's horrendous head wounds. They had been inflicted by a shotgun into his head at point-blank range. However, medical experts said Rolfe wouldn't have had time to know what was happening. 'It was vicious the way they died,' she said. 'Craig didn't deserve it, but when I heard how quick it was that did put my mind at rest.'

Mrs Rolfe remained on friendly terms with Whomes's mother throughout the trial. 'There was no point in falling out. I would bring her copies of the local newspaper because she didn't get to see what was being written about the trial,' she said. 'I was very close to Craig, he was the youngest, the baby of the family. I saw him near enough every day. As far as I knew, he was working for Tucker on the security side. I called him a gofer. Tucker supplied security men to the stars and that's what attracted Craig. He was on a high, living that lifestyle. But I don't blame Tucker for his death – Pat Tate was responsible. If he hadn't come on the scene, they would have been alive today.'

The news of the convictions came on the radio as I was driving home. I couldn't believe what I was hearing. I pulled over and tuned in to another station. Surely, I had misheard it. I couldn't believe that the jury had accepted what a man like Nicholls had said. The story he had told was just not right. This saga, I guessed, was far from over.

In September 1998, Nicholls found himself back in custody because he was required to give evidence in the case concerning Russell Tate and six others for drug smuggling. Despite Nicholls telling police that Whomes and Steele were heavily involved in this operation, they were never charged or required to attend court. Nicholls claimed he was not interested in giving evidence in Russell Tate's trial. He said he had only given evidence against Steele and Whomes because they had threatened to kill him, a claim he had not made previously. Nicholls said that everyone seemed to think that just because he had informed on his former friends, he was willing to grass the world up.

'The truth was,' he conceded in an interview, 'I hated what I had become and I wanted to get on with my life.' Nicholls appears to have forgotten that he had not only been informing on his associates all of his life but had also been involved in conspiring to frame innocent people on several occasions. Regardless of what Nicholls wanted, the conditions of the witness protection programme were that he cooperate fully with the authorities – and that included giving evidence against Russell Tate and his gang. Nicholls spent two days in the witness box detailing his and others' involvement in the importation of cannabis from Spain.

When Russell Tate was called to give his evidence, he stunned the packed courtroom by claiming he had only got involved in the smuggling venture because he knew all along Steele had murdered his brother and he wanted to bring him to justice. Tate said he believed that by befriending Nicholls and Steele he might eventually gather some evidence that would help police convict those responsible for murdering his brother. Only Nicholls was alleged to have imported drugs with Russell Tate; Steele was neither charged nor in court as a witness, so it was not a very plausible story and he was found guilty.

Mr Justice Jeffrey Rucker agreed and said Russell Tate had prepared 'an ingenious story as a way of explaining his involvement in the conspiracy, but it did not simply bear the scrutiny of common sense and day-to-day experience of life – it was wholly untrue. In listening to the evidence, I do not for one moment believe that Tate had ever suspected Steele of murdering his brother.'

Russell Tate was sentenced to five years' imprisonment and Craig Androliakos, who had been stopped driving the car Nicholls had hired, received two years.

On Friday, 13 November 1998, Darren Nicholls appeared at Woolwich Crown Court to be sentenced for the importation of cannabis. Mr Justice Hidden said, 'I have no doubt that without the evidence provided by this man, a terrible crime would never have been solved and two killers would still be walking the streets. In return, Mr Nicholls will undoubtedly have to spend the rest of his life in fear. I have no hesitation in awarding him full credit for the assistance he provided both police and Customs in this matter.' Mr Justice Hidden then sentenced Nicholls to 15 months' imprisonment, but he walked free because the length of time he had spent in custody prior to the Rettendon trial more than covered the sentence.

You will find no trace of Darren Nicholls now. His birth certificate and marriage licence have been deleted. His National Insurance number has been withdrawn, his passport details destroyed. All his bank and building society accounts have been closed down, along with all his old store cards and hire-purchase loans. His driver details have been erased from the computer at Swansea and he no longer appears on the electoral roll. Even his criminal record is no more. Every way of tracking him down has been blocked.

Nicholls may have vanished, but he was never going to stop boasting and bragging about himself and his exploits. For once, Mick Steele and Jack Whomes were going to be pleased that Nicholls could not stop talking.

Chapter 16

When I arrived at Basildon Magistrates' Court to face the charges relating to the incident with Gaffer, I was horrified to see a group of demonstrators gathered outside the main entrance holding placards with my photograph on them. I had no idea what their intentions were but when they saw me they immediately began to chant, 'Essex Police cover-up, Essex police cover-up.'

I recognised one of the demonstrators as John Whomes, Jack's younger brother. I had seen him on television several times protesting his brother's innocence. 'They only let you walk because you helped them, O'Mahoney,' John shouted.

The idea that the police had not investigated me fully concerning the Rettendon murders was a view many held in Essex. People thought that I had been deliberately 'overlooked' by the police because I had assisted them with the media-sensitive Leah Betts case. The truth, of course, was the total opposite. The police had not overlooked me at all. I was considered a suspect, I was investigated and eventually eliminated from the inquiry, although you have to say the police investigation into the murders wasn't worthy of much, if any, praise.

I could see that John and those with him were irate, so I thought it best to ignore them rather than risk a confrontation. I walked into the court and John followed me. Not wanting to be in John's company, I went and sat in the public gallery of Court 2, where my case was going to be heard.

When the usher called my name, I went and stood in the dock and John sat immediately behind me in the public gallery. The prosecution asked me to confirm my name and address but before I could reply John stood up and began shouting about Essex Police ignoring evidence that could implicate me in the Rettendon murders. I didn't know where to look or what to say. John, after all, was only trying to draw attention to his brother's plight. I had to admire him: he couldn't care less about the magistrate's objections, he was going to have his say regardless.

Once John had been ushered out of the court under threat of arrest and imprisonment for contempt, my case was adjourned and I walked outside. John and the other demonstrators immediately confronted me.

'Give me a break, John,' I pleaded. 'I know your brother and Mick Steele didn't iron out those three, but I didn't do it either.'

I had an appointment with my solicitor, so I gave John my mobile phone number and asked him to call me later that afternoon. 'If I can help you, John, I promise you I will. Whoever did murder those three did the world a favour, but, trust me, it wasn't me.'

Later that day, John telephoned me and we arranged to meet at a pub in Marks Tey the following night. There was, to say the least, a degree of mistrust between us. I was a former member of the firm whose leaders John's brother Jack had been convicted of murdering. For all John knew, he was being lured into a trap so their deaths could be avenged.

I arrived at the pub with Emma because I wanted to demonstrate to John I had no intention of doing anything untoward. John was not at the pub when Emma and I arrived, but he turned up shortly afterwards with a friend. We all shook hands and ordered a drink. The pub was extremely busy and therefore not an ideal setting to discuss a triple murder, so Emma and I invited John and his friend to our home. They said they would follow me in their car, which, oddly enough, was a blue Range Rover identical to the one in which Tucker, Tate and Rolfe had been murdered. As we reached the outskirts of Basildon, my mobile phone rang. It was John. 'You're having a fucking laugh, aren't you, Bernie? Are you sure about this?'

I laughed. I had already guessed John wouldn't be feeling too confident about driving through the areas Tucker and the firm had once controlled. 'Trust me, John, our house is only around the corner.'

'I don't trust anyone, especially you,' he replied.

When we arrived, John and I sat down together and talked into the early hours of the morning about the murders and the events that led up to them. It soon became obvious to me that, despite his noble intentions regarding his brother's case, John was going to have problems learning the truth about the murders because he didn't know any of the characters involved in the murky Essex underworld, a maze of deceit, mistrust and extreme danger. If John did manage to locate any of them, it was highly unlikely they would acknowledge him, never mind answer questions that may implicate the real executioners. Unlike John, I knew all of the main players: I knew what they were involved in and I knew how to contact them. My safety among them was no longer assured, but I told John that I would do all I could to help him, his brother and Mick Steele. But before I could help anyone, I had to help myself.

I had written to the Crown Prosecution Service after the first two court hearings concerning the knife incident with Gaffer asking them to drop the charges because there was little or no evidence to disprove my version of events and only a little to support theirs. Eventually, after a lot of haggling and mind-numbing games, the charges were dropped. To say I was relieved is an understatement. I was overjoyed because I wanted to get on with my life free from any sort of trouble.

Deep down, both Emma and I knew it would be impossible living in Basildon, where so much had gone on in the past. I had expanded the haulage business I managed in Cambridgeshire considerably and it was now taking up more and more of my time. My working day was growing longer and this was affecting my relationship with Emma. Her mother, Terry, had also recently been killed in a tragic accident, which police initially thought was murder.

Emma and I had gone to Paris together for a weekend to celebrate her 21st birthday. It was the first time we had travelled abroad together and we had a fantastic time. We arrived home late on the Sunday night and talked about visiting Emma's mum the following day, which was Emma's birthday. When I left home for work early the next morning, I noticed the street where Emma's mum lived was cordoned off with police tape. I rang Emma to tell her and a few hours later she rang me to say her mum had been killed. Terry's partner had telephoned for an ambulance after finding her at the bottom of the stairs with head injuries. Because of the nature of those injuries and his unusual behaviour, he was arrested for her murder but later released without charge. I cannot imagine how Emma felt losing her mum, especially on such an important birthday. The incident brought us closer together, but Emma felt isolated and lonely when I wasn't there for her.

The answer was staring me in the face: we both had to leave Essex if we wanted our relationship to work. Emma needed fresh surroundings to help her block out the circumstances of her mum's death and I needed fresh surroundings to move on from the dreadful events of 1995.

In the summer of 1999, Emma and I moved to a place called Stanground in Peterborough and soon settled in.

It's hard to describe how I felt. It was as if the troubles of the world had been lifted from my shoulders. For the first time in years, I felt happy and free. The sensible thing to do would have been to forget all about the events in Essex, but I have never been described as sensible and I had warmed to John Whomes as soon as I'd met him. Additionally, I firmly believed his brother and Mick Steele were innocent. I couldn't just turn my back on them. I knew there were many villains in Essex who had theories and possible information concerning the murders. I also knew the penalties for grassing or implicating other villains were extremely harsh. Therefore, some, if not all, of these villains would be too afraid to talk openly in case the wrong people got to hear about it. But I was convinced some would talk if given a safe medium to do so.

After considering the problem, John and I decided to set up a website on the Internet. Martin Moore, a friend and computer genius from Devon, agreed to design and run the site on our behalf. To generate interest in it, all of the evidence from the case, including crime-scene photos, were uploaded, as were all of the numerous media reports about the case. Putting the crime scene photos on the site was not a decision we reached easily. To protect the victims' loved ones from seeing them accidentally, we had three warnings they had to click on before they could be viewed. I thought the photos were a powerful deterrent for any would-be villain who thinks being a gangster is glamorous. I saw it as no different to those photographs of Leah Betts lying in a coma in hospital with tubes attached to her that were splashed across newspapers to highlight the dangers of taking drugs.

John Whomes didn't see things my way – nor did Essex Police, who had taken the photos and retained the copyright on them. They threatened to sue me if the images were not removed. I did comply but only after John Whomes asked. He thought it was a step too far in highlighting the case. I still think it was right to show them because numerous young men did contact the website saying they were not aware of the horrors of 'living that life'. One claimed he had since given up crime because the images haunted him. On TV and in films victims who are shot fall over clutching a small patch of blood on their clothing. The reality is far more gruesome. There is nothing glamorous whatsoever about murder.

We were soon inundated with emails and messages from people claiming they had information about the shootings. Initially, theories rather than facts about the crime came flooding in. Kenneth Noye, ex-members of the Kray firm and the notorious north London Adams family were blamed, as was I. Tucker and Tate's threats to shoot me were common knowledge amongst the criminal fraternity in Basildon. For many, it gave me a motive to carry out the killings. I had also toyed with the idea of parting with Tucker prior to Leah's death. Wanting 'rid of him', albeit in a business sense, had added to people's suspicions about me.

In early November 1995, when relations between Tucker, Tate and me had begun to sour, I had been offered what was described as a 'swansong' by a villain from Southend. A 'swansong', he explained, was a final job that would earn me enough money to disappear from Essex for good. I was on bail for possessing a gun at the time, so it was certain that I would lose my doorman's licence when convicted. Once I had lost that I would lose my job and so would be without any income, the man explained. 'You'll need money to support your family, Bernie,' he said. 'And this is an easy way of getting it.' The words 'disappear from Essex for good' set off alarm bells in my head. It sounded more like a death threat than a genuine offer to assist me.

I had already thought about how I might earn a living after the court case for possessing the gun and had approached a man I knew named Lawrence. I had asked him to front a door-staff agency for me if I did lose my door licence. I would recruit door staff, employ them to work the doors and travel from venue to venue checking everything was trouble-free without officially 'working' on the door myself. Lawrence would say it was his company and I worked for him but not as a member of the door staff.

Lawrence agreed it was a good idea and together we decided that I would end my partnership with Tucker and control Raquels and other venues from 'behind the scenes'. Lawrence was so keen to go into business with me he even looked into the possibility of setting up an offshore company so we could avoid future tax payments. But Lawrence soon became concerned about any merger with me when I revealed I had been offered the swansong. This grand finale, I was told, was shooting dead a man in Cornwall.

The intended victim had fled Essex after running into debt with drug dealers. Those who had a grievance with him had located him and now they wanted me to carry out their dirty work. The death of Leah Betts shortly after I had been approached to do the job took any decision out of my hands because as soon as she had collapsed every aspect of my life fell under police scrutiny. I do not think I could have done it, in any event; I certainly wouldn't have been prepared to do it with Essex Police breathing down my neck.

I never did find out who tried to implicate me in the plot, but Essex Police were certainly made aware of my potential involvement. When they questioned me about it, they rather surprisingly also offered me a 'swansong', albeit less lucrative. Their deal involved me pretending to go through with the plot to shoot the man, then they would arrest the conspirators and put me on the witness protection programme. I declined.

Not long after the Rettendon murder trial, a journalist gave John Whomes a very detailed document that included names, addresses, dates and venues in relation to the Cornish murder plot and my possible involvement in the Rettendon murders. I have to say it was pretty convincing because it was factually true, but the facts had been woven together to produce a totally misleading picture. It was this document that initially made John think that I was guilty of luring Tucker, Tate and Rolfe to their deaths. No doubt those in Essex wishing to see the back of me had a hand in producing it.

In July 1998, Steele and Whomes were refused leave to appeal against their life sentences. The pair had hoped to have their convictions quashed but a High Court judge ruled that Whomes and Steele would not even be allowed the chance to present their case before the Court of Appeal in London. News of the rejection shocked all of those involved in the campaign to free the two men. Jack Whomes's mother had been delighted when her son decided to appeal. She said that Jack had the full backing of his legal team, who had maintained his innocence throughout the murder trial.

John could not see how the appeal judge had the time to read the paperwork supporting the appeal in full. 'The way I look at it is that the papers had to be ready by 2 July, which only left 3 July for the judge to study them,' he commented to the press at the time. 'The paperwork was about four feet high and he would had to have read everything all in one day. That's absolutely impossible. My brother has been wrongly convicted: there was no murder weapon, no money and no drugs found. Even the papers proving the men's time of death were lost.

'Jack is very shaken up, my parents are devastated and the rest of the family are extremely unhappy about the decision to refuse permission to appeal.'

In order to highlight what John and his family saw as a

gross injustice, John and his friend, Peter Ager, attempted to hang a 350-foot banner from Orwell Bridge in Ipswich proclaiming, 'Jack Whomes is innocent.'

Their attempt to protest, however, went horribly wrong. They had used Peter's 21-foot speedboat to check the bridge could be climbed, but it was when they returned to the marina that their problems began. Peter had been reversing his Land Rover Discovery and a trailer down the slipway when its wheels fell over the end, dragging the £12,000 vehicle with it. Water rapidly entered the vehicle and was rising over Peter's lap before he managed to scramble to safety out of the passenger window. After calling the coastguard and the vehicle recovery services, the Land Rover was finally rescued. It was to be the first of many stunts and protests John mounted in support of his brother and Steele. Fortunately, future protests were far more successful.

In January 1999, Steele and Whomes were once more refused leave to appeal. John vowed that his brother and Steele would now take their case to the European Court of Human Rights. Unknown to John at that time, Darren Nicholls, the man who had secured his brother's conviction, was unwittingly helping to bring about the appeal hearing everybody wanted.

In October 1998, Granada Television announced it was going to make a film 'inspired by the Rettendon murders' called *Essex Boys*. 'We have not cast the film yet, but it will be stars of film rather than television,' a Granada spokesperson said. 'The budget is not finalised, but the film will probably cost several million pounds. We hope we will be shooting some scenes at Rettendon and the rest will be done in other parts of the county. The film, which will take about two months to make, will be all about organised crime, will be purely fictional and will be shown in cinemas throughout the country.'

A few weeks after the announcement concerning the film, Darren Nicholls appeared in the media, talking about his involvement in the Rettendon trial. 'Of all the supergrasses in the system, I am the tops,' he boasted. 'I'm considered a major witness. The police really do feel that everyone wants me dead. There is a bounty on my head. I'm not sure how much it is – some say it's £250,000, others say £500,000 – but who's going to collect it? Who do you collect it from?

'At the trial, I tried not to look at Whomes and Steele. They scared me because of what I was doing to them. Obviously, they hate me, and I don't think I will ever be rid of them. Mick's quite old and hopefully he'll die in prison and Jack, hopefully, when he gets out will be older and wiser and will just get on with his life rather than try to have his revenge.

'If their sentences are quashed, I'm particularly worried about what will happen. No one likes the truth, especially the families of the people who did it. It's something they've got to come to terms with, not me.'

Happy to talk about his bravery in giving evidence for the prosecution, Nicholls failed to mention the fact that he now hoped to line his pockets by appearing in a television documentary. These facts only came to light a few days later after a newspaper article revealed that Essex Police were locked in discussions with programme makers in an effort to make last-minute changes to a documentary about Nicholls. Senior officers were said to be unhappy about certain parts of a BBC Inside Story programme that was due to be aired. Police were said to be anxious that parts of the documentary might lead to Nicholls's identification, so they were asking for his face to be blurred out. The article also revealed that Nicholls's story would soon be told in a book.

The programme was due to be shown at 10.15 p.m. on 3 February 1999 but at 9 p.m. Essex Police reportedly served an injunction on the BBC, preventing the documentary from being broadcast. Granting the injunction, Mr Justice Poole said, 'The programme should not reveal any physical characteristics of the plaintiff, or reveal details of his family or those living with him, or in any way identify his whereabouts.'

In reply, a BBC spokeswoman said, 'Having spoken at length to our solicitors, we are quite confident that we will be able to reverse this decision.' She said the BBC would seek to ensure the judge saw the film the following morning. 'The injunction was because of the images and some of what was going to be screened,' she added.

John Whomes rang me as soon as he heard the news. We both wondered what on earth Nicholls could have said that would make Essex Police seek an injunction to prevent the programme from being broadcast. We concluded that he might have given a different version of events relating to the murders. If true, this could have been regarded as fresh evidence, and Whomes and Steele could seek a fresh appeal.

On 17 February 1999, the BBC announced that it was in fact Darren Nicholls who had obtained the injunction preventing the programme from being shown and not Essex Police. They went on to say that they had since managed to have the injunction lifted.

Unfortunately for the BBC, Nicholls was granted leave to appeal, so the injunction remained in place until that appeal could be heard. In order to save public money and time, Nicholls and the BBC eventually negotiated a settlement. The programme could be shown if the BBC agreed to use actors to play the supergrass and his wife. It was finally broadcast in August 1999.

During the programme, Nicholls said he had considered telling the police he had lied in order to escape the constant fear of being tracked down. He had even considered suicide to escape being traced and punished for 'grassing' on his mates. 'I thought, if I told police I was lying, would [Mick Steele and Jack Whomes] like me again?'

'Micky Steele was like a father to me,' Nicholls reasoned, 'and I found it really difficult to betray him. When I agreed to take part in the documentary, I thought it was going to be about the witness protection programme and I wanted to show people that you aren't set up in luxury with millions. It's more like a handshake and directions to the dole office. If they had told me the programme was going to brand me a liar, I obviously wouldn't have got involved.'

John Whomes was overjoyed at the content of the documentary. 'We are feeling extremely hopeful after seeing the programme,' he told reporters. 'The members of the jury have now seen the real Nicholls. In court, he came across as a little boy who claimed he had been forced into being a getaway driver. On television, the actors portrayed the real man: a cocky liar. They also heard how Nicholls had to convince his own wife he was telling the truth. We intend to carry on campaigning until we finally get my brother out of there. The programme has really helped us with that fight.'

Sadly, there were others who also wished to continue fighting – not the case, but me. A former associate of the Kray brothers and Tucker and Tate telephoned John Whomes and offered to assist him with his enquiries. The man, named 'Frank K', warned John to be careful if he should ever meet 'that slag O'Mahoney'. When John asked why, he was simply told 'O'Mahoney's involved.' Quite what I was supposed to be 'involved' in, I shall never know because Frank refused to elaborate when pressed by John.

Frank did claim that in the weeks leading up to their deaths Tucker, Tate and Rolfe had acquired a mobile electric-driven crematorium from him. 'We had meetings,' Frank told John. 'They were going to murder O'Mahoney and ensure there would be no trace of him left for the police to find.'

The basic concept of an electric crematorium is to heat the coil to 500 degrees and insert the body for burning. It takes nearly thirty minutes for the chamber to reach the required heat and another two hours for cremation. 'Really?' said John sarcastically. 'That's amazing.' John telephoned me as soon as he had finished talking to Frank and told me what had been said. A mobile crematorium sounded like pub or drug-induced talk to me: anybody who talked so openly about murder and disposing of bodies to a stranger was, at best, a fool.

As well as fools with aspirations contacting us, there were people who had important information to offer. Geoffrey Couzens, the man who had spent time with Nicholls in the witness protection programme, first contacted me via the website. He said he was not prepared to talk on the telephone or via email – all he would do was talk face to face. I immediately agreed to meet him at a time and place of his choice.

A few days later, I set off early for a coastal town in the north-west of England. I left early because I had a four- or five-hour drive ahead of me before our rendezvous at what he said 'may' be a dockside bar. Couzens had given me a pay-as-you-go mobile phone number that he said wouldn't be worth keeping because he changed it every few months to avoid being traced. I rang him as I was leaving to ensure the meeting was still on. Despite being somewhat apprehensive and nervous, he assured me that he would meet me as agreed. Apart from mentioning a dockside bar, no specific location had been arranged for our meeting. Instead, I was told to come off the motorway at a certain junction and ring him.

When I exited at the junction later that day, I pulled over and telephoned Couzens. He said he was still willing to meet me but, he said, there was a condition. 'Forget any dockside bar, I want you to drive in towards the city centre. You will pass a very distinctive building and then you will see a large park on your left. Stop on the main road outside a row of shops and then walk to a bench in the middle of the park near a pond. Wait there until you hear from me.'

I didn't fancy sitting on a bench looking at ducks on a pond for hours, but I guessed Couzens was watching me from somewhere to ensure I was alone, so I sat there for what seemed like an age. Eventually, a slightly built man appeared from the rear of a gardener's shed and began walking towards me. I looked at him, but his face gave nothing away: he just stared ahead, above and beyond me. When he reached the bench, he sat down and, without looking at me, simply said, 'Bernie, right?'

'Yes, mate, how are you doing?' I replied. 'There really is no need for all of this James Bond shit, you know.'

Couzens laughed, got up and started to walk towards my car, so I followed him. He stood by the locked passenger door and said, 'When we get in, I'll give you directions.'

The only time Couzens spoke was when he asked me to turn left or right. Eventually, he asked me to pull up outside a pub, which was located down a residential street. Couzens told me that he had been a supergrass in a drug trial involving members of a very powerful north London family.

'I was the guy making Ecstasy for them,' he said. 'When the factory got raided, I was left without any assistance and the police asked me to implicate the main men involved in return for a reduced sentence, so I did.'

Couzens said that he had been in protective custody with Darren Nicholls and Nicholls had told him the police had asked him to lie at the trial and make sure his evidence matched mobile phone evidence in the case, and that Nicholls had read part of his evidence during interviews from pre-agreed scripts. I was really excited by Couzens's story, but I had to tell him to stop divulging any more information to me.

'If this is all true,' I said, 'I would prefer it if you went to see a solicitor and made a full statement about what Nicholls told you. I don't want anybody saying I may have advised or "coached" you.'

'No problem,' he replied. 'I will do it because I know Nicholls lied and two innocent men are languishing in prison because of it. I can't stand by and do nothing, knowing what I know.'

I didn't want to give Couzens time to reconsider, so I suggested he make a statement immediately. Couzens said that he was going to go away, prepare a statement, then return to me. 'We can go to a solicitor's then,' he said, 'and get it witnessed.'

Couzens pointed to the pub, told me to get myself a drink and remain in there until he returned. As he walked away, I had a terrible feeling that he was not going to return. To be honest, I wouldn't have blamed him: making a statement could have resulted in him having to appear in court, and being back in the public eye would undoubtedly put his life in danger. Two hours later, when I was just about to give up and go home, Couzens walked into the pub.

'I've typed out all I know in this statement,' he said, as he waved three or four A4 pieces of paper across his chest.

I didn't bother finishing my drink. We got in my car and drove around the city looking for a solicitor's office. Eventually, we found one. Polly Gledhill was clearly taken aback by Couzens's revelation that he was a supergrass on the witness protection programme. 'I must say, Mr Couzens,' she said, 'I have never had a genuine supergrass in here before. Things are a little tame in these parts.'

Polly asked who I was, and I told her that I was just a friend. An hour later, we were all shaking hands and saying our goodbyes. Once outside, Couzens asked me if I wanted to take the statement to the Whomes family but I said it would be better if he posted it and I played no part whatsoever. Couzens took their address from me, shook my hand and disappeared into a crowd of shoppers milling around the high street.

Driving home, I was excited and happy for Steele and Whomes. This, I knew, would be important evidence that may help them secure an appeal.

Chapter 17

In April 2000, Pat Tate's old friend and business associate Kenneth Noye was convicted of murdering 21-year-old Stephen Cameron, a man with Essex connections who had visited Raquels on more than one occasion. Danielle Cable, Cameron's fiancée, who witnessed the attack, said Noye had thrown the first unprovoked punch after cutting up their Rascal van on a motorway slip road. When she had screamed and begged other motorists for help, Noye had produced a knife and plunged it twice up to the hilt into Cameron's chest. As he lay dying at her feet, Cameron had managed to say, 'He stabbed me, Dan. Get his number.'

Noye drove off in his Land Rover Discovery at such speed that other motorists had to swerve to avoid him. The vehicle, which he had registered in a false name at a friend's address, was crushed within hours at a local scrapyard. When the case came to court, Noye, who had boasted of the party he would hold when he was cleared, told the jury in response to the question of why he had disposed of the car, 'I don't want no one to know where I live. I don't want no one to know what cars I have. I don't want no one to know nothing.'

The day after the stabbing, wearing a flat cap and carrying a briefcase full of cash, Noye flew by private helicopter to a golf course in France. He then travelled by private jet from Paris to Spain, where he hid on the south coast until

Danielle Cable was flown out with police officers from Kent and asked if she could identify Noye, who was in a restaurant. When she pointed him out, Noye was arrested by Spanish police. He fiercely fought extradition proceedings, but was eventually returned to England to stand trial. The police have since suggested that had Noye returned to Britain immediately after his arrest and challenged Cable's identification before a magistrate, the case could have been thrown out. Kent Police strengthened their evidence during the nine months in which he tried to remain in Spain by finding other witnesses who were able to identify him at the murder scene.

After his return to Britain, he was placed on an identification parade, where one motorist picked him out. Noye had claimed to Spanish police that he was not at the scene but later changed his story to say that Cameron had sworn, kicked and punched him as he walked towards the van. Noye told the jury that he feared Cameron would land a lucky punch, take the knife he had produced to warn him off and use it on him.

After Noye had been sentenced to life imprisonment, detectives announced they wanted to interview him about the murder of John Marshall, whom Tate had entrusted with the syndicate's drug money. Marshall had been shot in the head and chest the day before Stephen Cameron had been stabbed to death. His body had been found hidden under bales of straw in the back of his Range Rover fewer than ten miles away from the scene of Cameron's murder. Police said they were interested in Noye's relationship with Marshall, who was suspected of supplying him with false number plates for several vehicles, including the Discovery Noye had been driving when he murdered Cameron.

Despite establishing the link betwen Marshall, Noye and Tate, the police could not prove that Marshall was holding the syndicate's drug money for Tate and that a proportion of it was money that Noye had lent to Tate when I was with him at the meeting at a pub near Brands Hatch. To this day, John Marshall's murder remains unsolved. His family have always strenuously denied his involvement in any drug-related criminal activities.

The release of the film *Essex Boys* in July 2000 gave the campaign to free Steele and Whomes a breath of much-needed fresh air. The Whomes family, and my partner Emma and I, were all invited to attend the premiere, which was being held at the Odeon cinema in Southend-on-Sea. We decided we would all go together because it would give us an opportunity to talk to the media about the case and hopefully attract interest.

We were not disappointed. Sean Bean, Alex Kingston, Jude Law, Bill Murray and others who appeared in the film attended the premiere, ensuring that not only newspaper reporters but also various TV channels and radio stations were there in force. Jack's mother Pam, his brother John and I all gave TV, radio and newspaper interviews. We were more than pleased with the publicity we managed to give Jack and Steele's plight.

After watching what I considered to be an at best poor film, we were all invited to a private party that was being held by the film company. John and I had been asked to have our photographs taken with Sean Bean and others who starred in the film, and as we were doing so a woman appeared and started shouting at the top of her voice.

'You're a fucking bastard, O'Mahoney! You're fucking scum. You blamed my dead brother for killing those bastards! I hate you.'

Before I had a chance to ask the lady to calm down and stop casting doubt on my parentage, she started kicking and punching me. I genuinely had no idea who the woman was, but she certainly knew me and disliked me intensely.

It wasn't the first time I've had that effect on a woman. The door staff grabbed hold of her and asked her to calm down, but she became more distressed.

'You're a bastard, O'Mahoney,' she kept shouting. 'You fitted my dead brother up.'

Eventually, the door staff led the woman away and she was ejected.

In the early stages of the investigation into the Rettendon murders, police had arrested a man named Billy Jasper, an East End villain with all the right connections and a crack cocaine habit. Billy had told the police that he was having a drink in a bar called Moreton's when his friend, Jesse Gail, came in. Jesse invited Billy to a nearby Mexican restaurant, where a man named Dean joined them.

The conversation turned to Tucker and Tate and a drug deal that was going to happen in the near future. Billy claimed Dean asked, 'Why can't we rob them?' and that Jesse had replied, 'We can't rob them because there will be comebacks.' Dean is then alleged to have said, 'We will take them out of the game, then.' Turning to Billy, Dean asked, 'Do you want to earn five big ones [£5,000] to do a bit of driving?'

Billy told police he later drove Dean to a meeting with Tucker, Tate and Rolfe and that Dean had shot them. Gail, he said, had met himself and Dean earlier in the evening and supplied Dean with the firearm used to carry out the shootings. The police investigated Jasper's claims, but they found little or no evidence to support anything he had told them. To this day, Billy Jasper stands by his version of events. Jesse Gail was killed some time later in a bizarre car accident. Dean, the alleged gunman, understandably denies any involvement.

I was later told that the woman who had attacked me was Jesse Gail's sister. It was Billy Jasper, not I, who had claimed that Gail and the other man had been involved in the murders of Tucker, Tate and Rolfe – I had merely repeated what Jasper had told police in my book *Essex Boys*.

Around the same time as the film was released, the Criminal Cases Review Commission (CCRC) announced that it was going to look into the Rettendon murder case. Mick Steele's partner, Jackie Street, told a local newspaper that this had come about because Geoffrey Couzens, a former protected witness who had been kept in custody at HMP Woodhill at the same time as Nicholls, had now come forward and made a statement claiming Nicholls had told him that the evidence he was to give in court was a pack of lies. 'We are feeling very confident and believe this will prove what we have said all along – that Mick and Jack are innocent,' Jackie said.

She accepted that nothing was going to happen overnight and that the CCRC would not start full-time work on the case for three or four months. But it had been acknowledged there was significant new evidence to put before the appeal courts.

'Mick has never wavered – and has always refused to take part in programmes in prison which would make his situation easier and reduce his status as high risk,' Jackie added. 'He will not do that because it would mean admitting his guilt. He is innocent and will prove it. We feel that the tide is finally turning and we are 100 per cent confident that the truth will now come out.'

The search for the truth was not limited to those who had been imprisoned. Darren Nicholls's former police handler, DC Bird, had been suspended from duty following his arrest. DC Bird was charged with conspiracy to supply cannabis although the charges were later withdrawn. After four years on full pay, which was a salary of £26,000 a year, and an annual housing allowance of £4,000, Essex Police announced that a disciplinary hearing would take place at their headquarters in Chelmsford.

Steele's and Whomes's legal teams applied to Essex Police to permit a solicitor from their office to attend the hearing because they felt important information regarding Nicholls and his evidence may be divulged. This application was refused and they were told that the hearing would take place behind closed doors.

When John Whomes heard the news, he was incensed. He called it a cover-up and decided that he would protest in a way that would make not only the police but also the whole country listen. At approximately 9 a.m. on 22 May 2000, John and another man chained themselves to a gantry above the M25 at Thurrock in Essex and displayed banners declaring his brother's innocence and complaining that a disciplinary hearing involving two Essex Police officers had begun in private. The police closed the motorway because they were concerned drivers would be distracted by the protest that was being held above all three lanes. Diversions were set up around the M25, resulting in rush-hour chaos.

As the police tried to talk John and the other man down, John spoke to the media on his mobile phone. 'I'm doing it because two police officers at Chelmsford Police headquarters face disciplinary hearings which involve a supergrass who gave evidence in my brother's case. I want a legal representative at that hearing so we know exactly what this supergrass has been up to. I want the Home Secretary Jack Straw to know I'm up here and I want him to refer my brother's case back to the Court of Appeal. Jack is innocent of those murders, 100 per cent innocent.'

At 1.20 p.m., a trained police negotiator climbed the gantry and asked John to come down because he had made his point.

'I'm not coming down until Jack Straw knows I'm up here and why I'm up here,' John replied.

'The whole fucking country knows you're up here and

why,' the policeman said. 'You're on every TV station and every radio programme.'

Confident he had made his point, John agreed to come down, but he told police they would have to free him and the other man first because they had chained themselves to the gantry and thrown away the key. When John and the other man reached the ground they were arrested and taken to Grays police station, where they were questioned about causing danger to traffic. They were bailed pending 'further enquiries', but no charges were ever brought against them.

A year after John's protest, Essex Police announced, much to the disappointment of Steele and Whomes, 'DC Bird has tendered his resignation from the force. Having regard to his duties under the Police Act to maintain an efficient and effective police force and in exercise of his discretion, the chief constable has accepted the resignation. The disciplinary proceedings against DC Bird will therefore automatically conclude. A settlement between the parties has been reached.'

'You will see that an officer has resigned. A clause of confidentiality was signed,' said Anthony Peel, chairman of Essex Police Authority. 'I cannot make any further comment.'

Nobody therefore knows the details of DC Bird's settlement with Essex Police when he resigned and nobody will ever be able to find out just how much or how little he knows about the validity of Darren Nicholls's evidence.

Those re-investigating the case on behalf of the CCRC didn't take long to discover that Darren Nicholls's evidence was far from convincing. Nicholls had given police elaborate details of phone calls and meetings between himself, the alleged killers and the victims. A key piece of evidence in the trial centred on two mobile phone calls made by Whomes to Nicholls just before 7 p.m. on 6 December 1995 – just minutes after he had allegedly shot dead the three victims.

The first call cut off after a few seconds and the next, Nicholls claimed, was Whomes telling him to 'come and get me' from Workhouse Lane, where the shootings had taken place. The two calls were picked up on two different transmitters, meaning Whomes must have been using his mobile phone in an area where they overlapped. Workhouse Lane was in the centre of that area.

But Whomes denied that he was down the lane. He said that he was at the Wheatsheaf pub in Rettendon to pick up Nicholls's broken down VW Passat. During John Whomes's visits to prison, his brother Jack had repeatedly told him to test the mobile phone. Similarly, Whomes's solicitor repeatedly requested to have access to the phone, but every request was denied by Essex Police. It took two years for the defence team to get hold of Whomes's mobile phone for tests to prove his story. Telephone specialist David Bristowe, who had supplied mobile phone evidence that helped convict former Essex man Stuart Campbell for the murder of his niece, Danielle Jones, and who had also been a prosecution witness at the Soham murder trial of Ian Huntley, was appointed to carry out the tests.

It is important to understand that in certain places, a mobile call can connect to any one of three or four different servers. Whomes's call connected to what is known as the Hockley transmitter. David Bristowe made 20 test calls from the Wheatsheaf car park (where Whomes said he was) and 40 calls from Workhouse Lane (which was Nicholls's story). His results show that of the 20 calls he made from the Wheatsheaf, more than a third were picked up by the Hockley transmitter. Of the 40 calls from the murder scene on Workhouse Lane, not one connected with the Hockley transmitter. The calls were made with Whomes's own phone at the same time of year as the murders and the same time of day. It seems as though when Jack Whomes said he was in the Wheatsheaf car park and not at the murder scene, he was telling the truth.

According to Nicholls, Tate, Tucker and Rolfe died at approximately 7 p.m. However the CCRC discovered that several factors pointed to a much later time of death. The following morning when it was discovered, the Range Rover was untouched by snow or ice, despite standing out on a freezing night. Two local witnesses thought they heard shots between 10 p.m. and midnight, while a third who walked his dog along the murder lane at 7.30 p.m. was adamant that the Range Rover was not there.

On the night of the murders between 8.30 p.m. and 8.45 p.m., a man was driving his white van towards the Rettendon roundabout. Pulling up alongside him was a dark-blue Range Rover, carrying four men. The van driver immediately recognised the hulking figure in the back seat was Pat Tate – one of the most well-known men in that part of Essex.

According to Nicholls, he had already been dead for more than 90 minutes. The van driver also saw a second passenger. The man cut a striking figure: tall and thin, wearing what looked like a black trench coat, with shoulder-length blond hair. The Range Rover accelerated up Rettendon Hill, but a moment later the white van was forced to swerve violently to avoid being hit after the Ranger Rover U-turned and headed towards the murder scene.

There was a secondary point of interest in the van driver's story. Nicholls had told police that as he drove Whomes and Steele away from the murder scene, his shock caused him to almost crash into a white van. In fact, it was the blue Range Rover that had had the near-miss, again with a white van, in the same location Nicholls described. Pure coincidence? Or had Nicholls witnessed the first near-crash and used it to embroider his own story?

As the CCRC delved deeper and deeper into Nicholls's

story, the evidence against Whomes and Steele began to get weaker. As the case against Whomes and Steele started to crumble, the CCRC announced it had asked Hertfordshire Police to launch a special re-investigation into the way the original case had been handled by Essex Police. Detective Superintendent Steve Read, one of the force's most senior investigating officers, was to lead the inquiry. The move followed past reviews of the case by both Norfolk Police and the Metropolitan Police, who were asked by Essex Police to double-check that procedure had been followed.

'It is something we do not do very often, but we will if there are significant issues to be investigated,' a CCRC spokesman said. 'We have got certain expertise, but we do sometimes appoint an officer or force to carry out an inquiry for us. In this case, that has been done.'

Everybody involved in the campaign to free Steele and Whomes was delighted with the news, but the jubilation was short-lived, as shocking news from HMP Whitemoor came through: somebody in prison had attempted to murder Jack Whomes.

Jack had been taking a shower when another inmate had accused him of breaking wind. 'Dirty bastard,' the man had snarled.

Jack denied he had done any such thing but added, 'Surely everyone is entitled to break wind, mate, especially after eating the slop they serve us in here.' The man stormed off without replying and returned moments later, brandishing a large kitchen knife.

Jack, who had his back to the man, continued showering, unaware of the impending danger. When he became aware of the man, it was too late. He suffered three stab wounds to the abdomen in quick succession. Fearing for his life, Jack grabbed the man and pulled him to the floor while trying to disarm him. As the two struggled, prison officers alerted by the commotion ran into the room and overpowered the knife man. Jack knew he had been lucky to escape with his life. Pam Whomes later told the media that she was worried her son would be 'carried out of prison in a box' rather than walk free.

'My son's done remarkably well, but when he was stabbed, it terrified him, he really couldn't get over it,' she said. 'It's affected him mentally, too. He has spent the last eight years worrying and fighting to prove his innocence and now this happens. We want the CCRC to hurry up with their investigation so my boy can come home. We are all worried sick about him.'

In order to maintain public interest in the case, Martin Moore would collect any newspaper cuttings, photographs or documents relevant to the Rettendon case and upload them to the website he had created for others to view. While surfing the Internet for new material one day, Martin came across a document detailing the full Court of Appeal judgment concerning Nicholls and the injunction he had imposed on the BBC in order to prevent the screening of the Inside Story programme.

At first glance, it appeared to be a pretty boring document full of legal jargon, but as Martin began to read it, he realised that it held the key to unravelling the web of lies Nicholls had told since his arrest. Throughout Nicholls's cross-examination during the trial, he had been repeatedly asked what had motivated him to commit a crime and then inform on his fellow criminals.

'Money was important in your life, was it not?' Mr Lederman, QC for Jack Whomes, asked Nicholls.

'It's important in everyone's life,' Nicholls replied.

'More important in some people's lives than other people's, I suggest.'

'I suppose for people who have got money, yes, it's less important.'

'You were obsessed with money, were you not?'

'No. I liked earning money.'

Mr Lederman then went on to describe some of the ways in which Nicholls had 'liked' earning his money: the plot to rob drug couriers taking £150,000 abroad and the £400 reward he had been given when he set up two innocent men for the drugs he had dumped in the gravel pit lake; the plan to manufacture amphetamines and dish them out like sweets to the people of Braintree.

Despite the fact that Nicholls was being exposed as a man who would do practically anything for money, he was adamant that he had not benefited financially from giving evidence against Whomes and Steele. Mr Lederman reminded Nicholls that he had once told DC Bird that he would not supply him with information unless he was paid 'up front'.

'Money first, before you inform. That is your philosophy, is it not?' Mr Lederman asked.

Nicholls stared straight back at Mr Lederman and with a smirk on his face replied, 'Yes.'

Mr Lederman then asked Nicholls, 'In connection with money, if the price is right, you'll do it?'

Once again, Nicholls smirked. 'Yes,' he replied.

As Nicholls gave his evidence, John Whomes later told me that he couldn't help but feel he wasn't quite telling the whole truth about money he had received for assisting the police. 'He squirmed and couldn't look the barrister in the eye,' John had said. 'I just had a feeling there was more he was holding back.'

At Steele and Whomes's trial, Nicholls had without doubt rather dubious credentials as a witness of truth, so Justice Hidden had warned the jury to treat Nicholls's evidence with caution before they retired to consider their verdict. 'So much of the case hinges on the evidence of one person, it is important that you look at that person and see his evidence from every angle,' he said. 'It is important that you look at the character of the person giving that evidence. Darren Nicholls is a convicted criminal and has served a term of imprisonment. He is a person who was himself engaged in the serious criminality involved in importing drugs of abuse into this country. You will bear in mind that in giving evidence to the prosecution he may well have an interest of his own to serve in seeking to obtain some lesser sentence than would otherwise be the case.

'He was involved in the criminal activities about which you have heard. Further, when he was told by Superintendent Barrington the importance of telling the truth in everything he said from then on, he nonetheless in his third interview did not tell the complete truth and attempted to reduce or minimise the extent of his activity in the overall drug importation matters of criminality.

'You may consider, and I would advise you to do so, that because of these matters you should look at the evidence of Darren Nicholls with great caution before acting on it.'

What the defence, judge and jury did not know was that Darren Nicholls was profiting financially from giving evidence on behalf of the police, and had been for some time. The BBC injunction document revealed that within weeks of being arrested Nicholls had telephoned a journalist named Tony Thompson at *Time Out* magazine. Nicholls asked Thompson if he would write a book about his life and the Rettendon murders because he was going to be the principal prosecution witness at the trial. Thompson knew at once that such a high-profile case would not only make a lucrative book, but also there were possibilities for any such book to be made into an even more lucrative film.

Nicholls had been granted bail after Whomes and Steele had been charged with murder, but a condition of that bail was that he remain in police custody for his own protection. However, his police handlers would take him out on an almost daily basis to shops, fast-food restaurants, theme parks, pubs and anywhere else that took Nicholls's fancy. Because he was technically a free man, the police gave him access to telephones and he was rarely locked in his cell, which was fitted out with all the creature comforts of home. (This allowed Nicholls to have the freedom he needed to contact Thompson without the police becoming aware of what he was up to.)

Fewer than eight weeks after being arrested for murder and importing drugs, Nicholls was able to instruct Thompson to contact his agent, Caroline Dawnay, about the book they had agreed to write together.

On Thursday, 1 August 1996, Nicholls was being held at Colchester police station, but somehow he was able to attend a meeting with Thompson and Dawnay almost 40 miles away at Two Brydges Place, an exclusive members' club in the West End of London. The custody record at Colchester police station for that day was left blank, which was a breach of police rules and regulations. Every officer who had any responsibility for Nicholls throughout his time in police custody denies they took him to London that day.

At the end of the meeting, Dawnay was happy that Nicholls had sufficient material for a book and that they had a reasonable chance of finding a publisher. On 8 August 1996, she drew up a terms of business letter for Nicholls that authorised her company, Peters Fraser & Dunlop – PFD – to act as his agent. On 17 August, Nicholls signed a collaboration agreement between himself and Tony Thompson. This contract set out who owned the copyright to the book and how the proceeds would be divided. Nicholls was to receive 50 per cent of the first £10,000 received and then 75 per cent of any subsequent payments.

Two days later, the publishing company Little, Brown sent a contract to Nicholls's agent offering to publish his story. Nicholls signed the contract shortly afterwards.

Between them, Nicholls and Thompson received £20,000 as an advance payment for their book.

Thompson then began visiting Nicholls in police custody so that they could work on the manuscript together. This was achieved without the police having any knowledge that Thompson was a journalist.

In *Bloggs 19*, the book they eventually wrote together, Thompson claims that his initial meeting with Nicholls took place at a McDonald's in Romford and that Nicholls was accompanied by his minders, who had tailed Thompson's car. Both Thompson and Nicholls have since agreed that this was made up and the idea for this version of the meeting came from a gangster book called *Wise Guy*.

When defence barristers had trawled through Nicholls's statements, it became evident that he had encountered similar difficulty in getting right the story that had led to Whomes and Steele being charged. During his police interviews, Nicholls had changed the account he was giving after visits to his cell during 'rest breaks' from DC Winstone and DC Brown, the same two detectives he was being interviewed by: a practice totally against police procedure. On Nicholls's custody record, these encounters were recorded as 'welfare visits', even though Nicholls already had an appointed welfare officer, Detective Sergeant Crayling.

The custody record shows that on one occasion Nicholls spent 25 minutes with DS Crayling, then shortly afterwards he had spent an hour and a half with DC Brown. It reveals that there were numerous other occasions when Nicholls had received excessive visits concerning his welfare. For instance, DS Crayling is recorded as visiting Nicholls for 55 minutes and then DC Winstone spent 1 hour and 55 minutes with him. On another occasion, DS Crayling visited Nicholls for 35 minutes. This was followed by a visit from DC Winstone for 2 hours and 20 minutes.

When cross-examined at trial, Winstone and Brown said

they could not recall what was discussed. Nicholls denied the case was discussed and told the jury the officers had only visited him to 'cheer him up'. Indeed there is no evidence of any impropriety in these visits. Winstone and Brown did admit that they provided Nicholls with a writing desk, pens and paper so that he could 'make notes' about anything he may have remembered about his evidence.

The defence suggested that these visits had a far more sinister purpose. It was suggested that they were to remind Nicholls of a 'version of events' that would fit in with the mobile phone and other circumstantial evidence. Only Nicholls, Winstone and Brown know what was discussed, but it cannot be argued that Nicholls kept getting the story wrong and after each break would miraculously remember details and correct his mistakes.

During one interview, Nicholls had told police that on the day of the murders he had received a message on his answering machine to telephone Steele. When he returned Steele's call, Nicholls said he was asked by Steele to meet him at a motorbike shop called Ron Parkinson's at Marks Tey near Colchester. Nicholls said he remembered the meeting because while he was waiting for Steele he had purchased a new battery for his van. DC Winstone and DC Brown quite rightly thought this was an important piece of evidence because they could now visit the shop and check the sales for that day – if there was a record of a battery being sold, then it would support Nicholls's story. A few days later, Winstone and Brown had to explain to Nicholls that they had visited the motorbike shop and there was no record of him or anybody else purchasing a battery that day. In the next interview, Nicholls said that he had thought about the battery and he now remembered that he had in fact purchased a bulb for his motorcycle but had fitted it to the Land Rover that he was driving because the interior light had gone and it used the same type of bulb as his motorcycle. Unwittingly, Nicholls had not only changed his story about the battery which had been proven to be untrue, he had changed his story from travelling to meet Steele in his van to now travelling to meet Steele in his Land Rover.

After further welfare visits, Nicholls told DC Brown, 'I have had a thought about what car I was driving that night. Do you want me to tell you what I thought I was driving?'

'Yeah, yeah,' DC Brown replied.

Nicholls then blurted out: 'I was driving a Golf convertible.'

You would think that if you had been duped into taking a hit man to murder three people, as Nicholls claims he was, the events of that evening would be etched into your mind for all time. Unless you happen to be Darren Nicholls, that is, because he had difficulty remembering the simplest of details.

Nicholls told police that after the battery/bulb incident, he sat outside the motorbike shop in Steele's vehicle, waiting for Whomes. 'Well, anyway, when I'm talking to Mick in his Hi Lux, Jack has come along,' he said. 'He hasn't stopped or got out or nothing.' He told police, Mick then said for them to leave.

In a later interview, Nicholls changed his story and told police, 'Jack arrived, he pulled up beside us and he did come to the window of Steele's Hi Lux and had some conversation.'

Nicholls's errors were quite descriptive and therefore unlikely to be momentary losses of concentration, or created by confusion. He told police that Whomes had tried to fix false number plates while waiting in Brentwood Country Park prior to driving to the Halfway House pub where Tucker, Tate and Rolfe were allegedly going to meet Steele. Nicholls altered this account later to say that after Tucker, Tate and Rolfe had arrived at the

Halfway House to meet Steele, Jack, who was allegedly watching from the other side of the car park, had said, 'Right, off you go!'

'I pulled out of the Halfway House,' Nicholls said, 'and then Jack said, "Pull over here." I asked why and he said, "I want to change the number plates on the car." And I said, "Why, what's the matter?" He had some sticky tape on the number plates, but they wouldn't stick. It was wet.' Nicholls claimed that they drove to Rettendon, through the village along the A130, dropped down the hill and after about 100 yards he had dropped Whomes off on the left-hand side of the road. Whomes is then alleged to have got out of the car and walked away carrying a bag. In a later interview, Nicholls described driving through Rettendon village, down the hill and Whomes telling him to pull into a lane on the right-hand side of the road.

'I remember him saying, "When you come back, you reverse down here, so you're facing the right way to drive straight out,"' Nicholls said. He also said that after Whomes got back into the car after allegedly committing the murders, he noticed Whomes was wearing surgical gloves that had 'specks of blood all over them'. Nicholls later stated that he first noticed Whomes had surgical gloves on when he dropped him off at Steele's car after they had driven away from the murder scene. 'He took his overalls off and his wellington boots. I don't know if they had gloves on. I think I noticed Jack had on surgicals, I think he had surgicals on because I didn't get to look in the car because I was driving it. But I think Jack had blood over him like a fairish amount, you know what I mean.'

When asked which version of events was correct, Nicholls told police, 'Jack was sitting in the middle between the seats behind us and he had rubber gloves on. I do remember the rubber gloves. They had like specks of blood on. I'm sure it was specks of blood. Mick then started handing him bits of the gun covered in blood.' Every time Nicholls suffered a loss of memory and then managed to remember events, the case against Whomes and Steele just happened to get stronger and stronger for the police.

While Nicholls was busy sorting out his version of events, Tony Thompson was busy trying to sort out lucrative deals for himself and Nicholls by selling his story. Thompson approached Jeff Pope, who was the head of factual drama at London Weekend Television (LWT) with a suggestion for a film about Nicholls's life and his experiences on the witness protection programme. As a result, LWT commissioned a 'video diary' type of film featuring Nicholls to be screened on Channel 4.

On 22 May 1997, Nicholls, Thompson and LWT entered into an agreement in relation to the project. This 'option' agreement was basically a method of ensuring that Thompson and Nicholls did not go elsewhere with the programme idea. It bound them to LWT for a period of six months in return for a fee of £2,500. A further contract between the same parties was signed at the same time. In this it was agreed that Thompson would act as an associate producer. His services would include, inter alia, the recording of 30 hours of (video diary) footage of Nicholls before, during and after the murder trial.

Thompson and Nicholls were also contracted to provide details, access and introductions to third parties who had information relating to the trial. The contract stated that Thompson and Nicholls would receive contributors' fees – £5,000 and £15,000 respectively.

In order to film the video diary, Thompson smuggled a video recorder into Harlow police station. Wigs, false beards and a ski mask were also given to Nicholls so that he could prevent his true image being broadcast later on TV. Extensive video-diary filming was carried out by Nicholls and all the paraphernalia was kept in his cell. The police deny knowing it was there. The video tapes have since been 'lost', so nobody will ever know what Nicholls actually said during these recordings.

In October 1998, LWT entered into a new agreement with Thompson relating to the making of the film. However, later that month a new commissioning editor at Channel 4 decided that he did not wish to proceed with the film as then planned, so LWT approached the editor of the BBC Inside Story series, who commissioned a film about Nicholls in the form of a full-scale documentary rather than a video diary. It was against this programme that Nicholls later sought an injunction to prevent it from being broadcast.

In total, Thompson was paid in excess of £40,000 for the various deals he secured using Nicholls's story. It's unclear what Nicholls earned because he and Thompson cannot agree on what he received. Thompson thinks it was £14,500, but Nicholls claims it was two cash payments of around £4,000. Both agree that Nicholls received no money in respect of revenue from the sales of the book *Bloggs 19*.

In order to check the validity of Nicholls and Thompson's story, Hertfordshire Police on behalf of the CCRC interviewed everybody they could locate who had been in contact with Nicholls during his time as a protected witness. This included prison officers, fellow inmates in the protected witness unit, his police handlers and those in the media with whom he and Thompson had dealt.

Few had anything good to say about Nicholls, and some questioned his credibility as a witness. A prison officer from HMP Woodhill, known only as officer 'A', told police, 'I would describe [Darren] as a big, fat cry baby, who was always asking to see me about different things.' An officer known only as 'M' said, 'Nicholls was a reasonable man but moaned a lot.' This officer also stated that Nicholls was not particularly well liked by other prisoners in the unit and tended to keep himself to himself.

Officer 'V' told police, 'Nicholls was a whinger, and we were always phoning his police handlers on his behalf because of his demands to see them.'

Nicholls clearly lied to a prison officer identified only as 'X', who said that Darren had told him that he had only been questioned by the police about routine matters and he had not told them anything whatsoever about the Range Rover killings. 'Nicholls said that despite the fact he hadn't told the police anything, the killers believed he had spoken to the police and that they would get their revenge somehow. Darren said he didn't know what to do now.'

Inmates who had been in custody with Nicholls at HMP Woodhill who were interviewed by Hertfordshire Police portrayed him in an equally unflattering light. Supergrass Mike Hodgson said, 'I remember Darren telling me that the police had told the "baddies" that he was an informant. Darren said that he had no choice but to go along with the police. I remember Darren telling me that it was the police who had concocted the story about his involvement in the Range Rover killings.'

Supergrass Ian Wimsey, also known as Damien or Damon, said, 'I would describe Darren as a bit of a bragger. When I explained that I was going through some difficulties with my police handlers, Darren suggested that I could make some money out of my story. I remember Darren at some stage talking about figures of £25,000 for a newspaper story and more for a television documentary. He told me that a reporter he knew was working for *Time Out* magazine.

'A couple of weeks later, I had a visit from my girlfriend and son. Darren had a simultaneous visit from a black man. During the visit, he kept looking towards me. At some point during the visit, I met Darren in the toilet, where he explained that the man was the journalist he knew. I was introduced to the man by Darren and he gave his name as Tony Thompson. I believe I saw Thompson between three and six more times at the prison after that.'

At the conclusion of their investigation, Hertfordshire Police submitted their findings to the CCRC, who immediately referred the case back to the Court of Appeal. Everyone connected with the campaign to free Whomes and Steele was ecstatic. They felt that if the jury at the original trial had known Darren Nicholls had been making money writing books and agreeing to lucrative TV deals prior to giving evidence, they might well have taken a very different view of his testimony. All they had to do now was convince the appeal judges of that fact and Whomes and Steele would be going home.

Chapter 18

It's 7.20 a.m. on 18 January 2006. The taxi horn has just sounded outside my home. Bleary eyed, I open my door to a cold, dark, miserable morning. The bleak conditions reflect how I am feeling. It's my wife Emma's 28th birthday today. I should be happy. We were married just eighteen months and three days ago at Peterborough Cathedral. Emma and I had agreed that we would start a family this month; she was convinced that we would only ever produce daughters. 'Having you to look after is enough,' she would joke. 'I don't want another disruptive male child to care for.'

Emma had even chosen a name for our firstborn: Emily, a nickname I often called my beautiful wife. Sadly, our dreams of family bliss are no more. Emma died just four months after our wedding. In December 2004, we had both fallen ill with flu. We were not bedridden or unable to leave our home; we had contracted the same strain of flu many people suffer from each winter. While watching TV one evening, Emma started telling me over and over again that she loved me. Not being the romantic type, my initial thought was that she wanted to start our family earlier than planned, but there was a sense of fear in her voice, panic almost. I telephoned a doctor but realising my wife's condition was rapidly deteriorating, I dialled 999 and summoned an ambulance. Moments later, Emma clutched her chest, gasped what was to be her final breath and lay motionless in my arms. I gave Emma the kiss of life, but my efforts were in vain. By the time the ambulance arrived, the girl I loved was gone. A pathologist told me later that the flu virus had attacked Emma's heart. This had caused it to slow down and eventually stop.

The weeks that followed are a painful blur. So many good people tried to console and assist me. I'm not sure if I could have made it through my darkest hours without them. Pam and John Whomes had over the years become good friends with Emma and me. They did all they possibly could to help me following Emma's death and they were there to help me through the dreadful day of her funeral.

Jack Whomes, enduring his own personal nightmare in Whitemoor prison, wrote to me as soon as he heard of Emma's death. Enclosed within Jack's letter to me was a second letter addressed to Emma. At first I thought it rather odd that somebody would write to a deceased person, but when I read it I wept. Jack was thanking my wife for all the support she had given to him and his family and regretting the fact he had never been able to thank her in person as a free man. He asked me to let her family and friends read the letter, so they could understand just how much she meant to those she had tried to help.

That's why I am heading to London this dark miserable morning. Jack and Mick Steele's appeal is being heard in the High Court. I should visit Emma's grave because it's her birthday, but I know in my heart where she would want me to be today. Emma had accompanied me to my first meeting with John Whomes at a pub in Marks Tey nearly a decade ago. Now that the campaign that was launched that night was reaching a conclusion, Emma would want me to be in court to show our support for Pam, John and Jack. 'They were there when you needed them,' Emma would say, 'you have to be there for them now that they need your support.'

Helping and supporting other people is important in life, but in the past I have put so much time and effort into doing so, I have ended up making those I love suffer. As the train I am now sitting on hurtles towards London, I am thinking how in the late 1980s, I campaigned to raise money for a young boy named James Fallon who needed specialist medical equipment. I became so involved with his plight, I quit my job and rarely saw my own children. Sadly, James died before he could be given the equipment he needed. I think about how I was foolish enough to campaign to free Lisa and Michelle Taylor, two sisters who had been convicted of murder but whom I believed were innocent. This blind loyalty to two complete strangers eventually caused my then partner Debra and me to separate, albeit temporarily. When the Taylor sisters were released following an appeal, I discovered that they were in fact guilty of the murder and so spent a further three years in and out of court fighting for the right to publish the fact. Again, my family suffered because of the amount of time and money I wasted trying to prove that Bernard O'Mahoney was right.

Hopefully today, Mick and Jack will be free to restart their lives because in many ways their release will be freeing me too. I have had enough of campaigning and talking about dead Essex villains. Once this case is over I want to visit the lane where Tucker, Tate and Rolfe met their deaths. I need to recall all that has been rotten in my life, remember those that suffered at the hands of the Essex Boys firm, try to make sense of it all and then walk away for good. Easier said than done, I guess.

After leaving the train, I am still thinking about my bloody past when I approach the Appeal Court. I don't notice the groups of TV, radio and newspaper journalists gathered near the entrance, but as soon as they see me I am surrounded. Microphones and cameras are shoved in my face and a stream of questions is directed at me. 'Do

you believe Mick Steele and Jack Whomes are innocent?'
'If they didn't commit the murders, who do you think did?'
I answer as best as I can while still walking.

Moments later, I enter the confines of the court. Because
filming and recording is prohibited in court buildings,
the media scrum has to remain outside. When I meet the
Whomes family, they tell me that they have been allowed
to enter court via a back door to avoid the press attention.
I have to laugh: John has been staging various protests for
years in the hope of attracting media interest in his brother's
plight; today, he is doing his best to avoid them because he
doesn't want to run the risk of saying or doing anything
that may be misinterpreted and create bad publicity for his
brother.

The wooden benches of courtroom number six, where the
case is going to be heard, soon fill up with family members,
journalists and members of the public who have over the
years become fascinated with the Essex Boys murder case.
At 10.30 a.m. precisely, the three appeal judges, Lord
Justice Maurice Kay, Mr Justice Openshaw and Sir Charles
Mantell, enter the court and take their seats. Then Mick
Steele and Jack Whomes enter the dock flanked by four
prison officers. A decade in prison has taken its toll on both
men: Jack has lost a lot of weight and Mick looks much
older, tired even.

Over the next five days, the court listened intently to
the full extent of Darren Nicholls's conniving and deceit.
Everyone was convinced that the appeal could not possibly
fail. Waiting for the judgment to be read out proclaiming
their innocence appears to be a mere formality rather than
a tense and agonising wait for the unknown.

At precisely 10.36 on the final day of the hearing,
the judges enter the court. Moments later, Mick Steele
and Jack Whomes take up their places in the dock now
surrounded by six prison officers. I am suddenly filled

with an overwhelming sense of doom. The fact six officers instead of just four are now guarding Mick and Jack make me think things are not going to go their way. Police officers take up positions around and in the court, indicating they are expecting some sort of disorder. Mr Munday for the prosecution is laughing and joking with officers from Essex Police. My confidence is drained completely as the moment we have waited for is about to arrive.

When the hearing gets under way, Lord Justice Kay turns towards Whomes and Steele and says, 'None of the grounds of appeal in relation to any appellant persuades us that any of the convictions is unsafe. This is an important case and we have been careful to consider it not only as a series of separate grounds of appeal but also on a holistic basis. We detect no element of unsafety and, accordingly, all appeals against conviction are dismissed.'

Steele shakes his head as the devastating news hits home. Jack sits stoney-faced, staring straight ahead. His mother Pam begins to cry and is comforted by John.

Lord Justice Kay then outlines the reasons for dismissing the appeal. 'The case for the appellants is that the police officers, and particularly Detective Constables Brown and Winstone, deliberately withheld information about contacts with the media. We do not consider that this conclusion could properly be reached; indeed, we are sure that this did not happen. Undoubtedly, one or more police officers must have known of the visit to central London on 1 August 1996. What is not established is whether any particular police officer knew or had reason to know of the potential significance of that occasion.

'We are prepared to assume, without finding, that one or more police officers (but not Detective Constables Brown and Winstone) knew in 1996 that Nicholls was liaising with the media with a view to making arrangements which would lead to financial reward. However, that assumption does not enable or entitle us to proceed to a conclusion that that or those police officer or officers were acting in bad faith by not taking steps to ensure that their knowledge was shared with the defence.

'It is common ground that not every failure to disclose automatically gives rise to an unfair trial. As we are not persuaded that any police officer has been shown to have acted in bad faith, and in the light of the conclusion we have reached about the safety of the convictions when considered in the light of what is now known about Nicholls's media contacts, we do not consider that the trial can properly be characterised as unfair.'

I cannot quite believe what I have just heard. Winstone and Brown were clearly not found guilty of any wrongdoing, but it has been accepted that somebody had taken Nicholls from his police cell in Colchester to a meeting with the media in central London prior to the trial and this has been deemed as not significant enough to inform the defence.

Steele's counsel Baroness Kennedy QC gets quickly to her feet and says, 'The court's judgment has come as something of a surprise to the defence.' An application will be made later for permission to appeal to the House of Lords. 'This judgment may be seen as licensing police misconduct and that would be a source of public concern.'

Lord Justice Kay replies that the defence has 28 days to lodge their appeal. The case, for now, is closed.

Steele stands up and faces the Essex Police officers. 'This is the most corrupt judgment I have ever heard in all my life,' he shouts. 'You are a corrupt lot. You won't always have the bench there to protect you. We will be back.' Seconds later, he and Jack are led away.

I make my way outside to ensure Pam is OK. Friends and family are comforting her and I think it rude to intrude, so I go in search of John.

As soon as I step outside the court building, the media

descend upon me. 'How have the Whomes family reacted to the news?' a journalist asks.

'The World Cup is being played this summer – don't be surprised if you see John Whomes on your screens running across the pitch with a banner proclaiming his brother's innocence,' I reply. 'This isn't the first time these people have fallen in this fight; they have got up to fight on before and I have no doubt they will get up and fight again.'

As I finish talking, John Whomes appears and addresses the media. 'Our legal team in there have said they are staggered about what's happened. This case has not finished. It's absolutely devastating. I will not let them beat us. We've had ten years fighting and, if need be, we will fight on for another ten years.'

Steele's solicitor, Chris Bowen, adds, 'While I live and breathe and represent Michael Steele, I will fight to ensure that he does not die in prison for offences he did not commit. Mr Steele himself will never admit these offences because he did not commit them. He has always protested his innocence and will continue to do so.

'Our legal team is preparing to challenge the ruling in the House of Lords and we may have to fight it in the European courts. Europe may provide a crucial key to unlock the door to freedom. The campaign for Mr Steele and Mr Whomes will continue to grow – a new front is about to open.'

With all the talk of fighting going through my mind, I walk away from the court and make my way to Temple Underground station, which is crowded with stampeding commuters jostling for seats on crowded Tube trains. I don't fancy joining in the mêlée just yet, so I sit in the station café and order a cup of tea and a sandwich. I decide I'll read the newspapers for an hour before heading home.

A short, stocky man aged about 60 years old is sitting at the table next to mine. 'Did I see you in that appeal hearing today?' he asks.

'I was at an appeal hearing today,' I reply, 'but I'm afraid I don't remember seeing you there.'

'What do you think of Essex Police, then?' the man asks.

I laugh and tell him it is probably best that I do not say.

'I'm Les Balkwell,' the man says, as he leans over and extends his hand. 'My 33-year-old son Lee was murdered and Tony Tucker's mate covered it up. That's why I went to the appeal. I want Essex Police to acknowledge the fact that my son and two other lads were murdered, but so far they have refused to do so.'

For the next two hours, I sit and listen as Les tells me the most extraordinary story relating to former members of the Essex Boys firm, their associates, Essex Police and the murders of three young men.

Lee Balkwell lived with his partner and their five-month-old son in Elm Park, Essex. On 18 July 2002 at 1.30 a.m. he was found dead in the mechanism of a concrete mixing machine in the yard where he worked. Initially everybody thought that it had been a tragic accident, but rumours began to circulate, which compelled his father Les to investigate the incident further. His findings to date are extremely alarming. So alarming, in fact, his local MP, James Brokenshire, has publicly demanded that Essex Police re-investigate not only Lee's death but also the deaths of others. While carrying out his investigation, Les has discovered evidence linking those allegedly involved in his son's death to those of at least two others. A 30-year-old man named Bradley Kendall was shot dead in his Brentwood home in December 2002. Despite the gunman writing a full confession, admitting the shooting, he did not face any charges in relation to Bradley's death. A third man, who also had links with the Essex Boys firm, was shot dead on 28 February 2001. Dean Boshell was discovered lying spreadeagled in allotments on Manchester Drive,

Leigh-on-Sea, with a single shotgun wound to the back of his head.

The members of the Essex criminal fraternity that had forever lurked in the background of the Rettendon murder case keep cropping up as Les tells me his story. I know several of the people he mentions and I know they are more than capable of committing the acts he believes they have carried out. I feel for Les and can feel myself being drawn into yet another campaign for justice. I want to help this desperate man learn the truth about the circumstances of his son's death and the events that led up to the other young men's deaths. Unfortunately I have to explain to Les I cannot help him. I owe it to myself and my children.

After hearing all the talk about continuing to fight, I realise that unlike the Whomes family and Chris Bowen, I have lost my will to fight another day for anybody. I have done all I can for Mick and Jack. From today, I need to focus on re-building my life. I am sure that Pam, John and Chris will never give up their struggle until Jack and Mick are finally released. I am equally certain that somebody reading this will assist Les Balkwell in his campaign. What remains of my life, I have to live for myself and those that I love. There have been too many wasted days already.